INTRODUCTION TO THE ANALYSIS
OF THE
DATA ENCRYPTION STANDARD (DES)

Wayne G. Barker

ISBN: 0-89412-169-3 (soft cover)
ISBN: 0-89412-170-7 (library bound)

AEGEAN PARK PRESS
P.O. Box 2837
Laguna Hills, California 92654
(714)586-8811

Manufactured in the United States of America

Dedicated

to the memory of

J. Rives Childs

TABLE OF CONTENTS

FOREWORD

This book will find itself of interest to two categories of persons — those interested in the implementation of the DES and those interested in the analysis of the DES. Those interested in the implementation of the DES will surely find the writer's simplified DES algorithm of great interest. In every way it duplicates the original DES algorithm as published in the National Bureau of Standards' Publication 46. Moreover, it is very likely that the writer's simplified DES algorithm will enable the software implementation of the DES to be accomplished more rapidly than it is at the present time using the original algorithm. For those interested in the analysis of the DES, by using the writer's simplified DES algorithm such analysis can be accomplished in an easily presentable manner. It should be quickly pointed out, however, that this book does not provide a quick and easy solution to the DES.

The writer has found no so-called "trap-door" solution to the DES. But he he must hasten to say that from a pragmatic viewpoint a solution to the DES does exist. This solution has been pointed out by a number of writers, so the writer takes no credit for it. This solution is simply that which can be termed the "brute force" attack; that is, keys are tested, one after the other, until a solution is reached. Here the writer would like to think that even in this solution, his simplified DES algorithm would be of great value in "speeding up" the trial-and-error testing of keys.

It goes without saying that the writer has spent a number of months putting this book together. Without the assistance of particularly two individuals, who provided material to verify the validity of the simplified DES algorithm, the writer might not have been able to complete this book. As these two highly respected individuals, both noted cryptanalysts in their own right, are involved with the government, the writer deems it better not to give their names, but they know who they are and he greatly thanks them.

The DES provides an analytical problem that the writer would not like to see again. It is a problem that is filled with frustrations. On numerous occasions the writer felt he was on the brink of a genuine solution, only to find with subsequent more close study that he had overlooked a line of bits here or a line of bits there.

If any unforeseen errors occur in the text, the writer hastens to take responsibility for them. Particularly he has tried to make sure that the digits which comprise the simplified DES algorithm are correct and that they reflect the actions of the original DES algorithm.

Comments of readers of course are always welcome.

Wayne G. Barker

Chapter I

A FIRST LOOK AT THE DES

The writer wants to begin by emphasizing that this book does not provide any heretofore undiscovered special or unique solution for the Data Encryption Standard or DES as it is perhaps more commonly termed. Still, in the eyes of the writer this book is not without its merits. This book provides what the writer believes to be a new approach to understanding the cryptography of the DES as well as the potential cryptanalysis of the DES.

One major contribution of this book is the provision of a simplified version of the DES algorithm when compared to the DES algorithm which was presented to the public in early 1977 in the National Bureau of Standards' Publication 46. This latter publication, known simply as FIPS 46, is provided in Appendix A.

This simplified version of the DES, which in a sense forms the foundation of this book, enables us to do several things. First, we can analyze the cryptography of the DES more easily, certainly more easily than trying to follow the cryptography of the DES as found in FIPS 46. Second, and perhaps the most important value of this book's version of the DES algorithm, at least from the viewpoint of practicability, is that it provides an efficient and possibly a more rapid method of implementing the DES, particularly from the viewpoint of software implementation.

STREAM CIPHER SYSTEMS VS. BLOCK CIPHER SYSTEMS

Algorithms used for the encipherment and decipherment of computer data (messages) can in general be divided into two types. One type produces stream cipher systems, termed stream ciphers, and one type produces block cipher systems, termed block ciphers. In stream cipher systems, with a stream of successive keybits being generated by a keystream generator, the units of plaintext, usually single letters, are enciphered one following another. On the other hand, in block cipher systems, a fixed number of given plaintext bits, termed plabits, are enciphered as a collective block of bits. As blocks of plabits are enciphered, blocks of cibits result. Similarly, in the decipherment process, blocks of plabits are deciphered as collective blocks, so that blocks of plabits result.

In terms of classical cryptographic terminology, stream cipher systems in a sense might be considered as monographic systems and block cipher systems as polygraphic systems. Stream cipher systems might also be termed monobit systems and block cipher systems as polybit systems.

The Data Encryption Standard or DES provides a good example of a block cipher system. Its plaintext bits are enciphered in blocks of 64 plabits; and the resulting ciphertext likewise appears in blocks of 64 cibits. With an ASCII character containing eight bits, we might also say that the DES algorithm enciphers the plaintext in blocks of eight ASCII characters.

THE DES KEY

Let us now look at the enciphering process of the DES where blocks of 64 plabits are successively turned into blocks of 64 cibits. As each block (of plabits) is enciphered, a key is involved. On the surface the key for each block of encipherment (or decipherment) contains 64 keybits. But in reality only 56 of these bits are effective, so that the effective key for one block of encipherment (or decipherment) contains only 56 keybits.

In this book we are not going to discuss the management of the DES keys as they are used from one block to another. The same key may be used for the encipherment (or decipherment) of every block or the key may change in some fashion. Instead, this book will focus on the cryptography or what happens during the encipherment of a single block (of plabits).

As noted above, although the DES key appears to contain 64 keybits, as eight of the keybits are not used during the enciphering (or deciphering) process, the effective number of keybits is 56. Therefore, with respect to the ciphering process of a single block of bits, the number of possible keys is 2^{56}. Since 2^{56} is equal to 72,057,594,037,928,036, this becomes the number of trials that the cryptanalyst might have to make if he were to attack the DES by trying every possible key until he found the one that would open the door to solution.

VIEWING THE DES ALGORITHM BY NUMBER OF BITS

Let us look at the DES algorithm in terms of the number of bits in the key, plaintext, and ciphertext. The DES enciphering equation in terms of number of bits can be viewed as follows:

KEY (56 keybits) + PLAINTEXT (64 plabits) = CIPHERTEXT (64 cibits)

And the deciphering equation in terms of number of bits can be viewed as follows:

KEY (56 keybits) + CIPHERTEXT (64 cibits) = PLAINTEXT (64 plabits)

A COUPLET

A couplet is a pair of known 64 bit sequences, where one is a block of 64 plabits and the other is the block of 64 cibits resulting from the DES encipherment of the first. The term couplet represents what FIPS 46 refers to as "known input and output" — where the input is 64 bits of plaintext and the output is 64 bits of ciphertext. In classical terms we might say that a couplet represents a crib, plaintext known to be present in the ciphertext — plus of course the given or known ciphertext.

The analyses of given couplets having common keys form the foundation of this book.

ITERATIONS OR ROUNDS

One traditional method of increasing the cryptographic security of a cipher system is to repeat the same encipherment process more than once. A common belief is that if plaintext is initially enciphered and then again enciphered in the same manner, the resulting ciphertext will be more secure than that of only a single encipherment. This is often true. For example, a double transposition cipher can be expected to be more secure than a single transposition cipher. But there are exceptions. A monoalphabetic-ally enciphered plaintext subsequently again enciphered monoalphabetically is no more secure than a single monoalphabetically enciphered plaintext. In fact, regardless of the number of successive monoalphabetical encipher-ments, the result will still be only monoalphabetically enciphered text. But as a general rule, in the case of most cipher systems, the more repet-itive encipherments that take place, the more secure will be the resulting ciphertext.

Turning to the Data Encryption Standard or DES, its enciphering process is repeated 16 times, each time with a different key, these keys being derived from the 56 effective bits of the initial 64-bit key. The initial 64-bit key can be termed the master or external key of the DES ciphering process and the different keys used for each iteration can be termed sub-keys. Later we shall discuss in more detail the initial DES key and its relationship to the sub-keys used in each iteration.

OUR GENERAL APPROACH IN ANALYZING THE DES

In analyzing the DES we shall begin by examining the DES ciphering process where only a single iteration or round has taken place. As might be expected, the solution of the DES where only a single iteration has taken place is largely trivial. By solution we mean that given one or a number of couplets, all the result of the same initial key, we can recover that key. In the case of a one-iteration DES problem, given several couplets, recovery of the bits which comprise the first sub-key is almost automatic. Although trivial, the examination or analysis of a single-iteration problem still provides an important vehicle to learn and understand the unique features of the DES ciphering process, especially when we look at the DES ciphering process in terms of the simplified version of the DES algorithm found in this book.

After analyzing and understanding the ciphering process of the single-iteration DES cipher, we will proceed to the analysis and understanding of the two-iteration DES problem. Here we will again find that the two-iter-ation DES problem — like the single-iteration problem — is also largely trivial. But on the plus side, our understanding of the DES ciphering process will have expanded and we will be in a better position to approach the solution of the three-iteration DES problem.

When we reach the three-iteration and four iteration DES problems, we will find that although analyzing the problems are not difficult, the sol-utions become more difficult. In fact, after four or five iterations, the problem facing the cryptanalyst in many respects is very comparable to the ultimate problem facing the cryptanalyst after 16 iterations.

Since the intent of this book is to essentially provide an introduction to the cryptanalysis of the DES, and because, frankly, the solution of the

Data Encryption Standard (DES) is not easily describable in analytical terms without the use of exhaustable trial and error tests or "brute force" techniques, we are not going to go beyond the four—iteration DES problem. While this does not provide a firm step—by—step approach to the solution of the 16—iteration DES problem, in the final chapter, after the reader has a fairly complete understanding of the cryptography of the DES, the writer will give his candid opinion regarding the practical solution of the Data Encryption Standard (DES).

THE DES INITIAL KEY AND SUB—KEYS

The initially entered DES key for each block of encipherment (or decipherment) contains 64 bits.   But of these 64 bits, only 56 are actually involved in the DES ciphering process. Eight bits, every eighth bit of the initially entered DES key, have no effect on the subsequent DES ciphering process. Let us now look at how the effective 56 keybits are used in the 16 iterations which the encipherment (or decipherment) of one block of 64 plabits (or cibits).

The initial DES key can also be termed the _master_ or _external_ key of the DES ciphering process. Its 64 bits are often expressed in hexidecimal or hex form. For example, the hexidecimal key 07A7137045DA2A16 represents the bits 0000011110100111000100110111000001000101110110100010101000010110. As pointed out above, of these 64 keybits, only 56 are actually effective, the other eight bits having no effect on the DES ciphering process.

In order to analyze and at the same time to more easily understand the ciphering process of the DES, the positions of the effective bits in the master or external key are numbered. In this manner we can follow a particular keybit throughout the ciphering process. On a computer output or run the master or external key will look as follows:

```
64-BIT 'DES' MASTER OR EXTERNAL KEY --

2113355-1025554-0214434-1123334-0012343-2021453-0202435-0110454-
1031975-1176107-2423401-7632789-7452553-0858846-6836043-9495226-
-----------------------------------------------------------------
0000011110100111000100110111000001000101110110100010101000010110

   KEY IN HEXADECIMAL FORM = 07A7137045DA2A16
```

It is seen that the first bit of the key is identified as 21, the second as 10, the third as 13, etc. Since every eighth bit is ineffective there is no need to give these bits any identifying numbers.

It will be noted that the bits of the initial key are not numbered in numerical order, i.e., from 01 to 56. Actually, they might well have been numbered in straight numerical order. But the reason for the seemingly random numbering system, which incidentally contains the numbers 01 through 28 and 30 through 57, is for the convenience of viewing the keybits which comprise KEY 1, the sub-key for the first iteration, in numerical order. More specifically, we find that the sub-key for the first iteration, termed KEY 1, contains 48 keybits, 01 through 24 and 30 through 53, all taken from the initial, master or external key; and these keybits in KEY 1 will be in their natural numerical order, 01 through 24 and 30 through 53.

Very simply, if the keybits in the initial key were to be put in their natural numerical order, 01 through 56, the keybits in KEY 1 would be in mixed order. We have selected to put the keybits of KEY 1 in numerical order instead. Moreover, because an important restriction concerns the the keybits selected for the sub-keys, the 56 bits comprising the initial key are divided into two groups, 01 through 28 and 30 through 57.

The restriction concerning the keybits selected for the sub-keys is the following — the first 24 bits of each sub-key will always be from the key-bits designated 01 through 28, and the second 24 bits of each sub-key will always be from the keybits designated 30 through 57. The first 24 bits of each sub-key are shown in Appendix C and the second 24 bits of each sub-key are shown in Appendix D.

Other than realizing that this restriction concerning the keybits which are selected for the sub-keys has arisen because of the DES algorithm, why the restriction exists is unknown. While this restriction cannot help the degree of security afforded by the DES, whether or not the restriction reduces the security afforded by the DES is frankly not clear. But in any case, the restriction provides the would-be cryptanalyst with perhaps a potential "wedge" towards solution.

Chapter I
QUESTIONS

True or False.

1. This book provides a newly discovered special or unique solution for the Data Encryption Standard (DES).

2. This book provides what the writer believes to be a new approach to understanding the cryptography of the DES as well as the potential cryptanalysis of the DES.

3. A major contribution of this book is the provision of a much simplified version of the DES algorithm than that presented to the public in 1977 in FIPS 46.

4. With a simplified version of the DES algorithm we can now analyze the cryptography of the DES fairly easy and from a practical viewpoint the simplified version of the DES algorithm provides an efficient and possibly more rapid method of implementing the DES.

5. Algorithms used for the encipherment and decipherment of computer data (messages) can in general be divided into three types.

6. In block cipher systems a fixed number of plabits are enciphered as a collective block.

7. The Data Encryption Standard or DES provides a good example of a stream cipher system.

8. In the enciphering process of the DES plaintext bits are enciphered in blocks of 56 plabits and the resulting ciphertext likewise appears in blocks of 56 cibits.

9. Although the DES key appears to contain 64 keybits, actually the number of effective keybits is 56.

10. With respect to the DES ciphering process of a single block of bits, the number of potentially possible keys is 2^{64}.

11. A couplet is a pair of known 56 bit sequences, one a block of 56 known plabits and the other a block of 56 known cibits, the latter resulting from the DES encipherment of the first.

12. The analyses of given couplets having common keys form the foundation of this book.

13. The enciphering process of the DES is repeated 16 times, each time with a different key, these 16 keys being derived from the 56 effective bits of the initial 64-bit key.

14. The positions of all bits in the master or external key are numbered.

15. Every sixth bit of the master or external key is ineffective.

16. The numbering system of the bits in the master or external key contains 56 bits, the numbers 01 through 28 and 30 through 37.

17. Although the numbered bits in the master or external key appear to be random, the bits of the sub-key for the first iteration, termed KEY 1, are in numerical order, 01 through 24 and 30 through 53.

18. There are 56 bits in each of the sub-keys.

19. The 56 bits comprising the master or external key are divided into two groups, 01 through 28 and 30 through 57.

20. The first 24 bits of each sub-key will always be from the key-bits that are designated 01 through 28, and the second 24 bits of each sub-key will always be from the key-bits that are designated 30 through 57.

Chapter II

A FURTHER LOOK AT THE DES

Before analyzing and examining in the next chapter the cryptography of a single-iteration DES problem, let us continue our look at the DES from a general viewpoint. At the same time, let us follow this up with a more closely defined object of our DES analysis.

S-BOXES

In a broad manner of speaking the S-boxes are the heart of the security found in the DES iterations. As each iteration occurs, sequences of bits which come from the previous iteration are added to the sequence of bits which comprise the sub-key for that iteration. The resulting bits then form the bits which enter the S-boxes. And the bits that exit the S-boxes are therefore enciphered bits.

Let us pause here to define what we mean by "adding" bits. Throughout the cryptography of the DES, sequences are added to or combined with other sequences. By adding the bit sequences we mean combining their relative single bits by addition modulo 2. When adding two bits, if their sum is even, as 0 + 0 or 1 + 1, then their combined value is 0; but if their sum is odd, as 0 + 1 or 1 + 0, then their combined value is 1. Expressed in another way, if the bits being added are the same, the result of their addition is 0; but if the bits being added are different, the result of their addition is 1.

An example of adding or combining two sequences is the following:

```
0011 - 1110 - 1101 - 1000 - 1000 - 0101 - 1001 - 0001
1010 - 0000 - 1100 - 0101 - 0110 - 1100 - 0001 - 0010
1001 - 1110 - 0001 - 1101 - 1110 - 1001 - 1000 - 0011
```

The analyst is interested in the relationship between all three of the sequences, the two sequences which are added together and the sequence that results. He knows that given the sequence that results plus one of the original sequences he can obtain the missing sequence by using the same addition modulo 2 logic. In other words, given any two of the sequences, the third can easily be obtained.

Let us return now to the discussion of the S-boxes, described earlier as the heart of the security found in the DES iterations.

The S-boxes are eight in number. They are designated respectively as S-1, S-2, S-3, S-4, S-5, S-6, S-7, and S-8. The boxes provide a form of substitution. A total of 48 bits enter the S-boxes, six bits entering each box. From the S-boxes exit 32 bits, now enciphered, four bits from each box. Put another way, six bits enter each of the eight S-boxes and four enciphered bits exit each box.

Consider the following example where a sequence of 48 bits, 01100010110-01100111100100001111111111100101010111, enter the eight S-boxes and exit as a sequence of 32 bits, 10101001000000000110110100110100:

01-1000 10-1100 11-0011 11-0010 00-0111 11-1111 10-0101 01-0111 ENTER

    1010 - 1001 - 0000 - 0000 - 0110 - 1101 - 0011 - 0100 EXIT

The dashes between the digits (bits) are provided to make the encipherment process of the S-boxes more understandable. The first six bits, 01-1000, are enciphered using the S-1 box, the second six bits, 10-1100, are enciphered using the S-2 box, etc.

Consider the first six bits, 01-1000, which are enciphered by the S-1 box. The first two bits are termed the index bits and the last four bits the operating bits. The dash, therefore, serves to separate the index bits from the operating bits.

The contents of the S-1 box are as follows:

	0000	0001	0010	0011	0100	0101	0110	0111
00	1110	0100	1101	0001	0010	1111	1011	1000
01	0000	1111	0111	0100	1110	0010	1101	0001
10	0100	0001	1110	1000	1101	0110	0010	1011
11	1111	1100	1000	0010	0100	1001	0001	0111

	1000	1001	1010	1011	1100	1101	1110	1111
00	0011	1010	0110	1100	0101	1001	0000	0111
01	1010	0110	1100	1011	1001	0101	0011	1000
10	1111	1100	1001	0111	0011	1010	0101	0000
11	0101	1011	0011	1110	1010	0000	0110	1101

Looking at the contents of the S-1 box it can be seen that when the bits 01-1000 enter the box, the bits that exit are 1010. That is, with respect to the S-1 box when the index bits are 01, the operating bits 1000 exit the box as 1010.

In the example shown the reader can confirm the correctness of the bits which exit the remaining seven S-boxes by looking at the contents of all S-boxes provided in Appendix E.

It might be appropriate here to point out that the contents of the eight S-boxes which are found in Appendix E are in what we term to be the direct mode. In this mode, given the index bits and the operating bits, we can directly find the exit bits. Conversely, the contents of the S-boxes might be in what we term the reverse mode. In this mode, given the index bits and the exit bits, we can directly find the original operating bits. The contents of the S-boxes in the reverse mode are primarily of interest to the cryptanalyst, and later we will be using the contents of the S-boxes in the reverse mode when we analyze various DES problems. The contents of the S-boxes in the reverse mode can be found in Appendix F.

THE BRUTE-FORCE ATTACK

The expression brute-force attack essentially means an exhaustive trial and error means of reaching some cryptanalytic goal. The expression often means in its simplest form the act of attacking a cryptographic system, not by a step-by-step analysis of the system, but rather by trying every "key" until a solution is reached. But this is a rather simplistic definition and the writer feels that he should provide, especially in light of the present book, a better and perhaps a more appropriate definition of the expression "brute-force" attack.

A brute-force attack is a trial and error means of reaching a particular cryptanalytic goal. The goal may or may not be the final solution of a cryptanalytic problem. The goal, for example, may be a preliminary step towards the final solution. The number of "trials" also may be an extremely large number of trials or the number may only be a limited number of trials. In short, by brute-force attack we mean simply a cryptanalytic procedural attack whereby we test (often by using computer techniques) various hypotheses — with a correct hypothesis evident in some fashion by the results attained by the testing procedure.

In the case of modern, computer-type cipher systems, systems based on the manipulation of bits rather than on letters, as in the case of the classical cryptographic systems, we can say that the brute-force attack as a weapon in the hands of the cryptanalyst is indispensible.

This might also be a good place to briefly discuss how the efficiency of the brute-force is measured. Can we say that the number of trials involved in the brute-force attack provides a measure of the effectiveness of the brute-force attack? Is a brute-force of fewer trials more effective than a brute-force of a larger number of trials? While the number of trial and error tests involved in a brute-force attack probably does have a bearing on the efficiency or effectiveness of the attack, of much greater importance is the <u>time</u> it takes to accomplish the attack. Very simply, the cryptanalyst is really only interested in how long it takes to complete the brute-force attack, not how many trials are involved in the attack. In fact, a major task of today's cryptanalyst when he attacks a modern, computer-type cipher system is to reduce the time necessary to execute a brute-force attack. In the case of the Data Encryption Standard (DES) this is especially true.

Reducing the time necessary to execute the brute-force attack can be done by various means. An obvious means is to use stronger or more powerful computers which will speed-up the time necessary to accomplish a trial. Here we are talking about computers which can execute algorithms in milliseconds instead of seconds.

A more important means of reducing the time necessary to accomplish a brute-force attack is by using new, massive, parallel computers. These modern computers, instead of containing a single processor, contain hundreds, and even thousands of processors. With this great multiplicity of processors, a large number of trials can be executed at the same time. For example, today we see available computers with as many as 2^{16} or 65,536 processors. With a computer of this size the task of executing 2^{56} trials, as in the case of the brute-force against the DES, in terms of time the problem is reduced to that of executing 2^{40} trials.

While the parallel computer is a great weapon to reduce the time necessary to accomplish a brute-force attack, time can also be reduced by other means. The cryptanalyst can often change or modify the algorithm in some fashion so that the number of program lines of instruction are reduced, thereby hopefully reducing the time necessary to complete a trial. In the case of the DES, for example, the analyst might modify the algorithm so that when testing the validity of a key, given a couplet, instead of going through 16 iterations, he might reduce the number of iterations to eight and still verify the key. This reduction of iterations, incidentally, will be discussed in more depth in the final chapter.

Another means of reducing the time necessary to accomplish a brute-force attack may involve a restructuring a part of or the entire ciphering algorithm upon which the brute-force attack depends. Regardless of how complicated a ciphering algorithm might appear or how seemingly intimidating a ciphering algorithm might be, there may be a means of simplifying the ciphering algorithm, making it less intimidating and easy to understand, as well of course easy to use. The end result often will be an increase in the speed of the ciphering operation which equates to a reduction in the time necessary to accomplish a brute-force attack. A good example of how a ciphering algorithm can be restructured is the simplified version of the DES found in this book.

VALIDATING THE CORRECTNESS OF THE SIMPLIFIED DES ALGORITHM

In Chapter I, page 1, it was stated that a major contribution of this book is the provision of a simplified version of the DES algorithm than that which was presented to the public in January 1977 in the National Bureau of Standards' Publication FIPS 46. Advantages of the simplified DES algorithm were also discussed at the same time.

The question arises regarding the validity of the simplified version of the DES algorithm. To answer this question the writer has turned to the National Bureau of Standards' Special Publication 500-20, Revised September 1980. This publication is furnished in Appendix B.

In Publication 500-20 are many couplets together with their keys. The writer has used many of these couplets with their keys, particularly those found on page 33 of Publication 500-20, to verify the correctness of the simplified DES algorithm. Still, it must be admitted that there is a small possibility, hopefully remote, that an error exists in the simplified DES algorithm. If an error does exist, the writer accepts responsibility — although the error or errors can surely be corrected and the principles put forth in the book of course remain very valid.

A computer program, written in BASIC, of the simplified version of the DES algorithm is provided in Appendix G. This program was used to test the validity of the simplified DES algorithm. An example of such a test is furnished in Appendix H. This example provides the reader with the encipherment of a 64-bit block of plabits, through 16 iterations, ending with the final output of a 64-bit block of cibits. The particular couplet and key used in this example are from those found on page 33 of Publication 500-20.

THE TERM SOLUTION DEFINED

We can define in the case of a block cipher system the term solution most simply as the ability to recover the key of a given couplet. At the same time, especially from a practical viewpoint, we can define the term solution from a more liberal viewpoint. For example, given a number of couplets, even a dozen or more, all the result of a common key, the ability to recover the key would still constitute a solution. Even if certain conditions have to be met or have to be just right, recovery of the key would still constitute a solution. In other words, any recovery of the key, regardless of how it is recovered, constitutes a solution. In fact, a solution does not even have to be effected by cryptanalysis, but this opens up a whole new area of study. For now, we can define solution as the recovery of the key in any manner.

OBJECTIVE OF THIS BOOK

The objective of this book essentially is to give the reader a clear understanding of the Data Encryption Standard (DES) so that he will be able to not only continue his own analysis of the DES, but he will be able to approach the solution of other block cipher systems with a feeling of confidence and feeling that somehow a solution can be effected.

Chapter II
QUESTIONS

Fill in the Blanks.

1. In a broad manner of speaking the _____ are the heart of the security found in the DES iterations.

2. When adding two bits by addition modulo 2, the combined value of 1 + 1 is _____.

3. When adding two sequences of bits by addition modulo 2, the bits 0101 + 1100 become _____.

4. With respect to adding two sequences by addition modulo 2 to obtain a third sequence, we can say that given any _____ of the sequences, we can easily obtain the third.

5. With respect to the S—boxes found in the DES there are _____ in number.

6. A total of _____ bits enter the S-boxes, six bits entering each box.

7. From the S-boxes exit 32 bits, now enciphered, _____ bits from each box.

8. Put another way, _____ bits enter each of the S-boxes and _____ bits exit each box.

9. Consider the bits 01-1000 which are enciphered by the S-1 box. The first two bits are termed the _____ bits and the last four bits the _____ bits.

10. The contents of the S-boxes are shown in two modes, the direct mode and the _____ mode.

11. The contents of the S-boxes in the _____ mode are primarily of interest to the cryptanalyst.

12. The expression _____ attack essentially means an exhaustive trial and error means of reaching some cryptanalytic goal.

13. A major task of today's cryptanalyst when he attacks a computer-type cipher system is to reduce the time required for a _____ attack.

14. With new, massive, _____ computers, a large number of trials can be executed at the same time.

15. An increase in the speed of the ciphering operation will equate to a reduction in the time necessary to accomplish a _____ attack.

16. In the case of a block cipher system the term solution can be defined as the ability to recover a _____ when given a couplet.

17. Any recovery of the _____, regardless of how it is recovered, constitutes a solution.

18. Publication 500-20 contains many couplets together with their _____.

19. Another means of reducing the _____ necessary to accomplish a brute-force attack may involve a restructuring a part of or the entire ciphering algorithm upon which the brute-force attack depends.

20. As each iteration occurs, sequences of bits coming from the previous iteration are added modulo 2 to the sequence of bits which comprise the sub-key for that iteration. The resulting bits then form the bits which enter the _____.

Chapter III

THE SINGLE-ITERATION PROBLEM

We are going to first describe the single-iteration DES encipherment. Thereafter, we are going to analyze a single-iteration DES problem. It is important to note that this single-iteration encipherment, like all the subsequent DES encipherments found in this book, uses a simplified version of the Data Encryption Standard (DES). Do not be concerned, therefore, if the enciphering scheme described does not match that described in FIPS 46. Realize, of course, that the results of using the simplified version are exactly the same as using the algorithm described in FIPS 46. The reader will quickly find that the "spinning wheels", as the writer likes to think of them, and the redundancies found in the algorithm of FIPS 46 are largely eliminated in the simplified version.

After describing the single-iteration DES encipherment, we shall turn to the analysis of a single-iteration problem. Given several couplets with a common key, our objective will be to recover the key. This DES problem, although somewhat trivial, will give the reader a good understanding of the DES ciphering scheme and will set the stage for more difficult problems that follow in later chapters.

DESCRIPTION OF THE SINGLE-ITERATION ENCIPHERMENT

On the next page the reader will find the step-by-step encipherment of a 64-bit block of plabits — in hexadecimal form, 3BDD119049372802 — using the hexadecimal key, 07A7137045DA2A16. After the single iteration the resulting ciphertext in hexadecimal form is 2FC914C00C672847.

Following the steps of the encipherment is not difficult. Each line of the encipherment is numbered and following the encipherment is an explanation of the lines keyed to the numbers.

The manner in which the bits in the encipherment scheme are identified will soon become clear and the reader will quickly find that the seemingly complex and distracting steps in the algorithm described in FIPS 46 have become fairly simple and easy to understand when viewed from the viewpoint of the simplified version of the DES used in this book.

A SINGLE-ITERATION ENCIPHERMENT

64-BIT 'DES' MASTER OR EXTERNAL KEY --

```
2113355-1025554-0214434-1123334-0012343-2021453-0202435-0110454-
1031975-1176107-2423401-7632789-7452553-0858846-6836043-9495226-
------------------------------------------------------------------
```

(1) → `0000011110100111000100110111000001000101110110100010101000010110`

KEY IN HEXADECIMAL FORM = 07A7137045DA2A16

64-BIT BLOCK OF PLABITS -- (BITS WHICH FORM M-0 AND M-1)

```
14140425263603031415251426033625252514032525253603140411414030315
79029157801335462480791391572424136846668023546602795780356813 2491
------------------------------------------------------------------
```

(2) → `0011101111011101000100011001000001001001001101110010100000000010`

PLABITS IN HEXADECIMAL FORM = 3BDD119049372802

```
------------------------------------------------------------------------------

        3333      3334      4444      4444      4555      5555      5556      6666
        3456      7890      1234      5678      9012      3456      7890      1234
        ----      ----      ----      ----      ----      ----      ----      ----
```
(3) → `0011  -  1100  -  0110  -  0000  -  0100  -  1011  -  1001  -  0110   M-0`

```
        0000      0000      0111      1111      1112      2222      2222      2333
        1234      5678      9012      3456      7890      1234      5678      9012
        ----      ----      ----      ----      ----      ----      ----      ----
```
(4) → `0010  -  0001  -  1100  -  0110  -  0010  -  0010  -  1001  -  1100   M-1`

```
· · · · · · · · · · · · · · · · · · · · · · · · · · · · · · · · · · · · · · · · · · · · · · · · · · · · · · · · · · · · ·

       22-1022   20-2121   10-0122   20-0131   13-0021   11-3200   02-1130   01-2102
       59-6701   11-9287   75-1536   62-5810   02-2844   49-2739   92-9306   66-2145
       -- ----   -- ----   -- ----   -- ----   -- ----   -- ----   -- ----   -- ----
```
(5) → `11-0000   00-1010   00-0110   00-0001   10-0101   11-0011   10-1010   00-0001   M-1 EXP`

```
       00-0000   00-0111   11-1111   12-2222   33-3333   33-3344   44-4444   44-5555
       12-3456   78-9012   34-5678   90-1234   01-2345   67-8901   23-4567   89-0123
       -- ----   -- ----   -- ----   -- ----   -- ----   -- ----   -- ----   -- ----
```
(6) → `00-1110   01-0010   00-0101   01-0010   00-1000   10-0011   01-0111   10-1011   KEY 1`

(7) → `11-1110   01-1000   00-0011   01-0011   10-1101   01-0000   11-1101   10-1010   ENTER`

(8) → `  0110  -  1100  -  1110  -  0101  -  0011  -  1010  -  0010  -  1010   EXIT`

(9) → `+ 0011  -  1100  -  0110  -  0000  -  0100  -  1011  -  1001  -  0110   M-0`

```
        3333      3334      4444      4444      4555      5555      5556      6666
        3456      7890      1234      5678      9012      3456      7890      1234
        ----      ----      ----      ----      ----      ----      ----      ----
```
(10) → `= 0101  -  0000  -  1000  -  0101  -  0111  -  0001  -  1011  -  1100   M-2`

```
------------------------------------------------------------------------------
```

RESULTING 64-BIT BLOCK OF CIBITS -- (FORMED FROM M-1 AND M-2)

```
14140425263603031415251426033625252514032525253603140411403031415
79029157801335462480791391572424136846668023546602795780352413 6891
------------------------------------------------------------------
```

(11) → `0010111111001001000101001100000000000011000110011100101000010001 11`

CIBITS IN HEXADECIMAL FORM = 2FC914C00C672847

The following is an explanation of the step-by-step encipherment of a 64-bit block of plabits through a single iteration as shown on the previous page:

(1) The positions of each keybit have been numbered. The first keybit is given the number 21 and hereafter that bit can be referred to as keybit 21. The second keybit is keybit 10, etc. The numbered bits run from 01 through 28 and from 30 through 57. There is no keybit 29. Every eighth bit of the master or external key has no effect on the DES ciphering process. Therefore, the length of the key which the analyst will seek to recover contains 56 bits.

(2) Like the keybits, the plabits have been numbered. The plabits divide themselves into two groups, those that form M-0 [3] and those that form M-1 [4]. The positions of the plabits are numbered so that the bits of M-0 run from 33 through 64 and the bits of M-1 run from 01 through 32.

(3) 32 bits of the 64-bit block of plabits [2] form M-0. The bits of M-0 are divided into groups of four to conform with the ciphering effects of the eight S-boxes which are effective between steps (7) and (8).

(4) 32 bits of the 64-bit block of plabits [2] form M-1. Like the bits of M-0, the bits of M-1 are divided into groups of four to conform with the ciphering effects of the eight S-boxes.

(5) The 32 bits of M-1 are expanded to form eight groups of six bits each.

(6) The keybits for the first iteration, or round 1, are selected from the master or external key. These selected 48 keybits comprise KEY 1. Note particularly that the selected keybits for the first four S-boxes run from 01 through 24 and the selected keybits for the second four S-boxes run from 30 through 53.

(7) The keybits [6] are added modulo 2 to the bits of M-1 EXP, the expanded bits of M-1 [5] to form the bits that <u>enter</u> the S-boxes.

(8) 32 bits <u>exit</u> the S-boxes, the first four bits exit S-1, the second four bits exit S-2, etc.

(9) These 32 bits are M-0 of (3).

(10) These bits, termed M-2, are formed by the addition modulo 2 of the bits that <u>exit</u> the S-boxes [8] and the bits of M-0 [9].

(11) The 64-bit block of cibits resulting from this single-iteration encipherment is formed by the bits from M-1 [4] and M-2 [10].

ANALYZING A SINGLE-ITERATION DES PROBLEM

Let us now turn to the analysis of a single-iteration DES problem. With several given couplets having a common key, our task will be to recover the common key.

Consider the following three couplets which have a common key:

Couplet No. 1 - Plaintext: 305532286D6F295A
                 Ciphertext: 645567283C6E6D1E

Couplet No. 2 - Plaintext: 1AEAC39A61F0A464
                 Ciphertext: 0FBB82CA20F4F430

Couplet No. 3 - Plaintext: 869EFD7F9F265A09
                 Ciphertext: C2CEBD3ACF731A4C

The encipherment processes of the above three couplets are provided on the next three pages. Since we know the plaintext and the ciphertext of each couplet -- after all that is the definition of a couplet -- we know immediately certain of the designated sequences within the encipherment processes. For example, we know from the plaintext, the sequences M-0 and M-1. Likewise, from the ciphertext we know the sequences M-1 and M-2. In addition, the sequences which <u>exit</u> the S-boxes are also known, since they are the sum modulo 2 of M-0 and M-2.

The known sequences of bits in the encipherment processes are indicated by being shaded. Thus, in the encipherment processes the only unknown sequences or lines of bits are those comprising the master or external key, those comprising KEY 1 — the sub-key for the first iteration — and the bits which <u>enter</u> the S-boxes. These latter bits are the sum modulo 2 of M-1 EXPanded and KEY 1.

Let us now see how we can recover the bits of KEY 1.

64-BIT 'DES' MASTER OR EXTERNAL KEY --

2113355-1025554-0214434-1123334-0012343-2021453-0202435-0110454-
1031975-1176107-2423401-7632789-7452553-0858846-6836043-9495226-
----

   KEY IN **HEXADECIMAL** FORM =

64-BIT BLOCK OF PLABITS -- (BITS WHICH FORM M-0 AND M-1)

1414042526360303141525142603362525251403252525360314041414030315
7902915780133546248079139157242413684668023546027957803568132491

0011000001010101001100100010100001101101011011110010100101011010

PLABITS IN **HEXADECIMAL** FORM = 305532286D6F295A

3333	3334	4444	4444	4555	5555	5556	6666	
3456	7890	1234	5678	9012	3456	7890	1234	
----	----	----	----	----	----	----	----	
1011 -	0100 -	0100 -	1101 -	0101 -	1001 -	0001 -	0110	M-0

0000	0000	0111	1111	1112	2222	2222	2333	
1234	5678	9012	3456	7890	1234	5678	9012	
----	----	----	----	----	----	----	----	
0100 -	1001 -	0110 -	0110 -	0110 -	0011 -	0100 -	0101	M-1

. . . .

22-1022	20-2121	10-0122	20-0131	13-0021	11-3200	02-1130	01-2102	
59-6701	11-9287	75-1536	62-5810	02-2844	49-2739	92-9306	68-2145	
-- ----	-- ----	-- ----	-- ----	-- ----	-- ----	-- ----	-- ----	
00-0000	00-0000	01-0111	11-1101	11-1111	11-1000	00-1010	00-0100	M-1 EXP

00-0000	00-0111	11-1111	12-2222	33-3333	33-3344	44-4444	44-5555	
12-3456	78-9012	34-5678	90-1234	01-2345	67-8901	23-4567	89-0123	
-- ----	-- ----	-- ----	-- ----	-- ----	-- ----	-- ----	-- ----	

                                                               KEY 1

                                                                ENTER

0100 -	0111 -	1111 -	0001 -	1100 -	1000 -	0110 -	0100	EXIT
+ 1011 -	0100 -	0100 -	1101 -	0101 -	1001 -	0001 -	0110	M-0

3333	3334	4444	4444	4555	5555	5556	6666	
3456	7890	1234	5678	9012	3456	7890	1234	
----	----	----	----	----	----	----	----	
= 1111 -	0011 -	1011 -	1100 -	1001 -	0001 -	0111 -	0010	M-2

RESULTING 64-BIT BLOCK OF CIBITS -- (FORMED FROM M-1 AND M-2)

1414042526360303141525142603362525251403252525360314041403031415
7902915780133546248079139157242413684668023546027957803524136891

0110010001010101011001110010100001111000110110011011010001111 0

   CIBITS IN **HEXADECIMAL** FORM = 645567283C6E6D1E

64-BIT 'DES' MASTER OR EXTERNAL KEY --

2113355-1025554-0214434-1123334-0012343-2021453-0202435-0110454-
1031975-1176107-2423401-7632789-7452553-0858846-6836043-9495226-
----

   KEY IN HEXADECIMAL FORM =

64-BIT BLOCK OF PLABITS -- (BITS WHICH FORM M-0 AND M-1)

1414042526360303141525142603362525251403252525360314041414030315
7902915780133546248079139157242413684668023546027957803568132491

0000110101110101011000011100110100110000111110000101001000110010 0

PLABITS IN HEXADECIMAL FORM = 1AEAC39A61F0A464

3333	3334	4444	4444	4555	5555	5556	6666	
3456	7890	1234	5678	9012	3456	7890	1234	
----	----	----	----	----	----	----	----	
0100 -	1101 -	0111 -	0001 -	0001 -	1010 -	0001 -	0000	M-0

0000	0000	0111	1111	1112	2222	2222	2333	
1234	5678	9012	3456	7890	1234	5678	9012	
----	----	----	----	----	----	----	----	
1011 -	0010 -	1011 -	0010 -	0001 -	0110 -	1101 -	1011	M-1

. . . .

22-1022	20-2121	10-0122	20-0131	13-0021	11-3200	02-1130	01-2102	
59-6701	11-9287	75-1536	62-5810	02-2844	49-2739	92-9306	66-2145	
-- ----	-- ----	-- ----	-- ----	-- ----	-- ----	-- ----	-- ----	
11-0110	01-1110	00-1111	10-0010	01-0000	00-1011	11-0000	00-1111	M-1 EXP

00-0000	00-0111	11-1111	12-2222	33-3333	33-3344	44-4444	44-5555	
12-3456	78-9012	34-5678	90-1234	01-2345	67-8901	23-4567	89-0123	
-- ----	-- ----	-- ----	-- ----	-- ----	-- ----	-- ----	-- ----	

   KEY 1

   ENTER

| 1101 - | 1110 - | 1111 - | 0011 - | 0000 - | 1001 - | 1001 - | 1010 | EXIT |

| + 0100 - | 1101 - | 0111 - | 0001 - | 0001 - | 1010 - | 0001 - | 0000 | M-0 |

3333	3334	4444	4444	4555	5555	5556	6666	
3456	7890	1234	5678	9012	3456	7890	1234	
----	----	----	----	----	----	----	----	
= 1001 -	0011 -	1000 -	0010 -	0001 -	0011 -	1000 -	1010	M-2

RESULTING 64-BIT BLOCK OF CIBITS -- (FORMED FROM M-1 AND M-2)

1414042526360303141525142603362525251403252525360314041403031415
7902915780133546248079139157242413684668023546027957803524136891

0000111110111011100000101100101000100000111101001111010000110000

CIBITS IN HEXADECIMAL FORM = 0FBB82CA20F4F430

64-BIT 'DES' MASTER OR EXTERNAL KEY --

2113355-1025554-0214434-1123334-0012343-2021453-0202435-0110454-
1031975-1176107-2423401-7632789-7452553-0858846-6836043-9495226-
----

KEY IN **HEXADECIMAL FORM** =

64-BIT BLOCK OF PLABITS -- (BITS WHICH FORM M-0 AND M-1)

1414042526360303141525142603336252525140325252536031404141403 0315
7902915780133546248079139157242413684668023546027957803568132491

1000011010011101011111101011111111001111100100110010110100000 1001

PLABITS IN HEXADECIMAL FORM = 869EFD7F9F265A09

```
      3333     3334     4444     4444     4555     5555     5556     6666
      3456     7890     1234     5678     9012     3456     7890     1234
      ----     ----     ----     ----     ----     ----     ----     ----
      0010  -  1110  -  1011  -  0110  -  0110  -  0101  -  0110  -  1011   M-0

      0000     0000     0111     1111     1112     2222     2222     2333
      1234     5678     9012     3456     7890     1234     5678     9012
      ----     ----     ----     ----     ----     ----     ----     ----
      0111  -  1101  -  0001  -  1100  -  1100  -  1110  -  1011  -  0101   M-1
```

. . . .

```
  22-1022  20-2121  10-0122  20-0131  13-0021  11-3200  02-1130  01-2102
  59-6701  11-9287  75-1536  62-5810  02-2844  49-2739  92-9306  66-2145
  -- ----  -- ----  -- ----  -- ----  -- ----  -- ----  -- ----  -- ----
  10-0001  10-0111  11-0010  01-1100  01-1101  10-1110  01-0111  10-1011   M-1 EXP

  00-0000  00-0111  11-1111  12-2222  33-3333  33-3344  44-4444  44-5555
  12-3456  78-9012  34-5678  90-1234  01-2345  67-8901  23-4567  89-0123
  -- ----  -- ----  -- ----  -- ----  -- ----  -- ----  -- ----  -- ----
```

KEY 1

ENTER

```
    0100  -  0010  -  1001  -  0001  -  1011  -  1111  -  0101  -  1111   EXIT

+   0010  -  1110  -  1011  -  0110  -  0110  -  0101  -  0110  -  1011   M-0

    3333     3334     4444     4444     4555     5555     5556     6666
    3456     7890     1234     5678     9012     3456     7890     1234
    ----     ----     ----     ----     ----     ----     ----     ----
=   0110  -  1100  -  0010  -  0111  -  1101  -  1010  -  0011  -  0100   M-2
```

RESULTING 64-BIT BLOCK OF CIBITS -- (FORMED FROM M-1 AND M-2)

1414042526360303141525142603336252525140325252536031404140303 1415
7902915780133546248079139157242413684668023546027957803524136891

1100001011001110101110100111010110011110111001100011010010011 00

CIBITS IN **HEXADECIMAL FORM** = C2CEBD3ACF731A4C

Recovery of the keybits of KEY 1 is accomplished one S-box at a time. With respect to the first S-box, S-1, consider the available data from the three couplets:

Couplet No. 1	Couplet No. 2	Couplet No. 3	
22-1022	22-1022	22-1022	
59-6701	59-6701	59-6701	
-- ----	-- ----	-- ----	
00-0000	11-0110	10-0001	M-1 EXP
00-0000	00-0000	00-0000	
12-3456	12-3456	12-3456	
-- ----	-- ----	-- ----	
			KEY 1
			ENTER
0100	1101	0100	EXIT

By examining the contents of the S-boxes in their <u>reverse mode</u>, which are provided in Appendix F, the possible six-bits that enter the S-box to yield a given four-bit value can be found. With respect to the S-1 box, therefore, the above exit values in each case can only arise from four six-bit values:

00-0001	00-0010	00-0001
01-0011	01-0110	01-0011
10-0000	10-0100	10-0000
11-<u>0100</u>	11-<u>1111</u>	11-<u>0100</u>
0100	1101	0100

By adding modulo 2 to these four possible six-bit values the six bits of the M-1 EXPanded line, the four possible six-bit values of KEY 1 for each of the couplets can be found:

00-0001	11-0100	*10-0000
01-0011	*10-0000	11-0010
*10-0000	01-0010	00-0001
11-<u>0100</u>	00-<u>1001</u>	01-<u>0101</u>
0100	1101	0100

The six-bit key common to the three couplets is 10-0000, indicated by asterisks. Using the contents of the S-1 box, we have therefore succeeded in recovering six keybits. In the same manner we can attack the remaining seven S-boxes.

It is now evident that the single-iteration DES problem offers only trivial difficulty. Moreover, in the case of the single-iteration DES problem, we now know that we need more than one couplet in order to firmly identify the keybits contained in KEY 1; and we now know also that we can only recover the values of 48 keybits, the keybits comprising KEY 1.

With the reader now understanding and probably feeling comfortable in analyzing the single-iteration DES problem, we can turn our attention in the next chapter to the two-iteration DES problem.

EXERCISE

The following two couplets have a common key:

Plaintext — DD7F121CA5015619

Ciphertext — 9D3F534CA145571D

Plaintext — 2E8653104F3834EA

Ciphertext — 7AD703055F6D35AF

From these couplets the following parallel lines are obtained:

```
22-1022   20-2121   10-0122   20-0131   13-0021   11-3200   02-1130   01-2102
59-6701   11-9287   75-1536   62-5810   02-2844   49-2739   92-9306   66-2145
-- ----   -- ----   -- ----   -- ----   -- ----   -- ----   -- ----   -- ----
00-0001   10-0001   10-0001   11-0010   01-1000   00-1011   10-0100   00-0110   M-1 EXP

00-0000   00-0111   11-1111   12-2222   33-3333   33-3344   44-4444   44-5555
12-3456   78-9012   34-5678   90-1234   01-2345   67-8901   23-4567   89-0123
-- ----   -- ----   -- ----   -- ----   -- ----   -- ----   -- ----   -- ----
                                                                              KEY 1

                                                                              ENTER

   0100  -  1000  -  0011  -  1100  -  1001  -  0001  -  0001  -  1000    EXIT
```

```
22-1022   20-2121   10-0122   20-0131   13-0021   11-3200   02-1130   01-2102
59-6701   11-9287   75-1536   62-5810   02-2844   49-2739   92-9306   66-2145
-- ----   -- ----   -- ----   -- ----   -- ----   -- ----   -- ----   -- ----
10-1000   01-0010   00-1110   01-0001   10-1011   11-0001   10-1001   11-0111   M-1 EXP

00-0000   00-0111   11-1111   12-2222   33-3333   33-3344   44-4444   44-5555
12-3456   78-9012   34-5678   90-1234   01-2345   67-8901   23-4567   89-0123
-- ----   -- ----   -- ----   -- ----   -- ----   -- ----   -- ----   -- ----
                                                                              KEY 1

                                                                              ENTER

   0101  -  1000  -  1101  -  1001  -  1111  -  0111  -  0101  -  0111    EXIT
```

Recover the 48 keybits comprising KEY 1.

Chapter IV

THE TWO-ITERATION PROBLEM

As might be expected the two-iteration DES problem is only slightly more difficult than the single-iteration problem. We can begin by looking at the enciphering scheme.

DESCRIPTION OF THE TWO-ITERATION ENCIPHERMENT

If the reader understands the cryptography and step-by-step description of the single-iteration DES encipherment shown on page 18, he will no difficulty in understanding the two-iteration encipherment that follows:

```
64-BIT 'DES' MASTER OR EXTERNAL KEY --

2113355-1025554-0214434-1123334-0012343-2021453-0202435-0110454-
1031975-1176107-2423401-7632789-7452553-0858846-6836043-9495226-
------------------------------------------------------------------
0000011110100111000100110111000001000101110110100010101000010110

    KEY IN HEXADECIMAL FORM = 07A7137045DA2A16


64-BIT BLOCK OF PLABITS -- (BITS WHICH FORM M-0 AND M-1)

1414042526360303141525142603362525251403252525360314041414030315
7902915780133546248079139157242413684668023546027957803568132491
------------------------------------------------------------------
0011101111011101000100011001000001001001001101110010100000000010

PLABITS IN HEXADECIMAL FORM = 3BDD119049372802
```

```
------------------------------------------------------------------------------

    3333      3334      4444      4444      4555      5555      5556      6666
    3456      7890      1234      5678      9012      3456      7890      1234
    ----      ----      ----      ----      ----      ----      ----      ----
    0011   -  1100   -  0110   -  0000   -  0100   -  1011   -  1001   -  0110   M-0

    0000      0000      0111      1111      1112      2222      2222      2333
    1234      5678      9012      3456      7890      1234      5678      9012
    ----      ----      ----      ----      ----      ----      ----      ----
    0010   -  0001   -  1100   -  0110   -  0010   -  0010   -  1001   -  1100   M-1

    ..............................................................................

    22-1022   20-2121   10-0122   20-0131   13-0021   11-3200   02-1130   01-2102
    59-6701   11-9287   75-1536   62-5810   02-2844   49-2739   92-9306   66-2145
    -- ----   -- ----   -- ----   -- ----   -- ----   -- ----   -- ----   -- ----
    11-0000   00-1010   00-0110   00-0001   10-0101   11-0011   10-1010   00-0001   M-1 EXP

    00-0000   00-0111   11-1111   12-2222   33-3333   33-3344   44-4444   44-5555
    12-3456   78-9012   34-5678   90-1234   01-2345   67-8901   23-4567   89-0123
    -- ----   -- ----   -- ----   -- ----   -- ----   -- ----   -- ----   -- ----
    00-1110   01-0010   00-0101   01-0010   00-1000   10-0011   01-0111   10-1011   KEY 1

    11-1110   01-1000   00-0011   01-0011   10-1101   01-0000   11-1101   10-1010   ENTER
```

```
  0110  -  1100  -  1110  -  0101  -  0011  -  1010  -  0010  -  1010   EXIT

+ 0011  -  1100  -  0110  -  0000  -  0100  -  1011  -  1001  -  0110   M-0

  0000     0000     0111     1111     1112     2222     2222     2333
  1234     5678     9012     3456     7890     1234     5678     9012
  ----     ----     ----     ----     ----     ----     ----     ----
= 0101  -  0000  -  1000  -  0101  -  0111  -  0001  -  1011  -  1100   M-2

.........................................................................

22-1022  20-2121  10-0122  20-0131  13-0021  11-3200  02-1130  01-2102
59-6701  11-9287  75-1536  62-5810  02-2844  49-2739  92-9306  66-2145
-- ----  -- ----  -- ----  -- ----  -- ----  -- ----  -- ----  -- ----
11-1010  00-1010  00-0000  01-0100  00-1011  11-0101  10-1010  01-0011  M-2 EXP

11-2122  10-0122  02-2202  00-1010  54-4453  34-3344  45-5355  34-5333
01-5660  74-6917  58-3422  37-4921  06-3947  34-0287  06-1835  51-7946
-- ----  -- ----  -- ----  -- ----  -- ----  -- ----  -- ----  -- ----
01-0101  01-0001  10-1000  10-0000  11-1000  00-0111  10-0011  01-1001  KEY 2

10-1111  01-1011  10-1000  11-0100  11-0011  11-0010  00-1001  00-1010  ENTER

  0000  -  1010  -  1011  -  1010  -  0111  -  0010  -  1100  -  0011   EXIT

+ 0010  -  0001  -  1100  -  0110  -  0010  -  0010  -  1001  -  1100   M-1

  3333     3334     4444     4444     4555     5555     5556     6666
  3456     7890     1234     5678     9012     3456     7890     1234
  ----     ----     ----     ----     ----     ----     ----     ----
= 0010  -  1011  -  0111  -  1100  -  0101  -  0000  -  0101  -  1111   M-3
```

RESULTING 64-BIT BLOCK OF CIBITS -- (FORMED FROM M-2 AND M-3)

```
14140425263603031415251426033625252514032525253603140414030314 15
79029157801335462480791391572424136846680235460279578035241368 91
----------------------------------------------------------------
0001101011010110011110011101010000011100110010110100010110001010
```

CIBITS IN HEXADECIMAL FORM = 1AD679D41CCB458A

The two-iteration ciphering process uses two sub-keys, KEY 1 and KEY 2, with the bits for these sub-keys coming from the master or external key. Here an important point must be mentioned. Keybits 01 through 28 are used in all sub-keys exclusively for the first four S-boxes, while keybits 30 through 57 are used in all sub-keys exclusively for the last four S-boxes. On the surface this appears to be a potential weakness in the algorithm of the DES, but taking advantage of this potential weakness when analyzing the DES is not quite so easy. Even knowing the values of 28 keybits, either 01 through 28 or 30 through 57, of which there are 2^{28} possibilities, does not provide necessarily an easy path towards solution.

Let us turn now to the analysis of a two-iteration DES problem.

ANALYZING A TWO-ITERATION PROBLEM

Consider the following two couplets which have a common key:

Couplet No. 1 –   Plaintext: A3006208C908042F

Ciphertext: 57C47B17F1C3CABC

Couplet No. 2 –   Plaintext: DEF4810BBFC58176

Ciphertext: 01AC34A736282835

Knowing these two couplets having a common key, our task is to recover the key. Our immediate step is to lay-out the two couplets, with the known lines of bits indicated by shading.

COUPLET NO. 1

64-BIT 'DES' MASTER OR EXTERNAL KEY --

```
2113355-1025554-0214434-1123334-0012343-2021453-0202435-0110454-
1031975-1176107-2423401-7632789-7452553-0858846-6836043-9495226-
----------------------------------------------------------------
```

KEY IN **HEXADECIMAL FORM** =

64-BIT BLOCK OF PLABITS -- (BITS WHICH FORM M-0 AND M-1)

```
1414042526360303141525142603362525251403252525360314041414030315
7902915780133546248079139157242413684668023546027957803568132491
----------------------------------------------------------------
1010001100000000011000100000100011001001000010000000010000101111
```

PLABITS IN **HEXADECIMAL FORM** = A3006208C908042F

3333 3456	3334 7890	4444 1234	4444 5678	4555 9012	5555 3456	5556 7890	6666 1234	
----	----	----	----	----	----	----	----	
0100 -	0101 -	0001 -	0000 -	0010 -	1000 -	1000 -	0000	M-0
0000 1234	0000 5678	0111 9012	1111 3456	1112 7890	2222 1234	2222 5678	2333 9012	
----	----	----	----	----	----	----	----	
1100 -	0000 -	0110 -	0100 -	1110 -	1001 -	1000 -	0001	M-1

. . . .

22-1022 59-6701	20-2121 11-9287	10-0122 75-1536	20-0131 62-5810	13-0021 02-2844	11-3200 49-2739	02-1130 92-9306	01-2102 66-2145	
-- ----	-- ----	-- ----	-- ----	-- ----	-- ----	-- ----	-- ----	
10-0001	11-0001	10-1000	01-0101	11-1011	11-1000	00-1000	00-0101	M-1 EXP
00-0000 12-3456	00-0111 78-9012	11-1111 34-5678	12-2222 90-1234	33-3333 01-2345	33-3344 67-8901	44-4444 23-4567	44-5555 89-0123	
-- ----	-- ----	-- ----	-- ----	-- ----	-- ----	-- ----	-- ----	

KEY 1

ENTER

| 1000 - | 0110 - | 0011 - | 1001 - | 0111 - | 0100 - | 0111 - | 0100 | EXIT |

– 29 –

```
 + 0100  -  0101  -  0001  -  0000  -  0010  -  1000  -  1000  -  0000   M-0

   0000      0000      0111      1111      1112      2222      2222      2333
   1234      5678      9012      3456      7890      1234      5678      9012
   ----      ----      ----      ----      ----      ----      ----      ----
 = 1100  -  0011  -  0010  -  1001  -  0101  -  1100  -  1111  -  0100   M-2

..............................................................................

 22-1022   20-2121   10-0122   20-0131   13-0021   11-3200   02-1130   01-2102
 59-6701   11-9287   75-1536   62-5810   02-2844   49-2739   92-9306   66-2145
 -- ----   -- ----   -- ----   -- ----   -- ----   -- ----   -- ----   -- ----
 10-1111   11-0010   00-1001   11-0100   00-1100   00-0100   01-0110   01-1101   M-2 EXP

 11-2122   10-0122   02-2202   00-1010   54-4453   34-3344   45-5355   34-5333
 01-5660   74-6917   58-3422   37-4921   06-3947   34-0287   06-1835   51-7946
 -- ----   -- ----   -- ----   -- ----   -- ----   -- ----   -- ----   -- ----

                                                                          KEY 2

                                                                          ENTER

   0010  -  1110  -  1001  -  0100  -  0011  -  0101  -  0101  -  0100   EXIT

 + 1100  -  0000  -  0110  -  0100  -  1110  -  1001  -  1000  -  0001   M-1

   3333      3334      4444      4444      4555      5555      5556      6666
   3456      7890      1234      5678      9012      3456      7890      1234
   ----      ----      ----      ----      ----      ----      ----      ----
 = 1110  -  1110  -  1111  -  0000  -  1101  -  1100  -  1101  -  0101   M-3
```

RESULTING 64-BIT BLOCK OF CIBITS -- (FORMED FROM M-2 AND M-3)

```
1414042526360303141525142603362525251403252525360314041403031415
7902915780133546248079139157242413684668023546027957803524136891
----------------------------------------------------------------
0101011111000100011110110001011111110001110000111100101010111100
```

CIBITS IN HEXADECIMAL FORM = 57C47B17F1C3CABC

COUPLET NO. 2

64-BIT 'DES' MASTER OR EXTERNAL KEY --

```
2113355-1025554-0214434-1123334-0012343-2021453-0202435-0110454-
1031975-1176107-2423401-7632789-7452553-0858846-6836043-9495226-
----------------------------------------------------------------
```

    KEY IN HEXADECIMAL FORM =

64-BIT BLOCK OF PLABITS -- (BITS WHICH FORM M-0 AND M-1)

```
1414042526360303141525142603362525251403252525360314041414030315
7902915780133546248079139157242413684668023546027957803568132491
----------------------------------------------------------------
1101111011110100100000010000101110111111110001011000000101110110
```

PLABITS IN HEXADECIMAL FORM = DEF4810BBFC58176

```
      3333       3334       4444       4444       4555       5555       5556       6666
      3456       7890       1234       5678       9012       3456       7890       1234
      ----       ----       ----       ----       ----       ----       ----       ----
      1110  -    0100  -    1110  -    1101  -    1001  -    0101  -    0101  -    0110  M-0

      0000       0000       0111       1111       1112       2222       2222       2333
      1234       5678       9012       3456       7890       1234       5678       9012
      ----       ----       ----       ----       ----       ----       ----       ----
      1000  -    0110  -    1001  -    0100  -    1011  -    1100  -    1101  -    0011  M-1
.......................................................................................

   22-1022    20-2121    10-0122    20-0131    13-0021    11-3200    02-1130    01-2102
   59-6701    11-9287    75-1536    62-5810    02-2844    49-2739    92-9306    66-2145
   -- ----    -- ----    -- ----    -- ----    -- ----    -- ----    -- ----    -- ----
   10-0111    11-0111    10-1001    10-0010    01-0001    11-1001    11-1001    10-1001  M-1 EXP

   00-0000    00-0111    11-1111    12-2222    33-3333    33-3344    44-4444    44-5555
   12-3456    78-9012    34-5678    90-1234    01-2345    67-8901    23-4567    89-0123
   -- ----    -- ----    -- ----    -- ----    -- ----    -- ----    -- ----    -- ----
                                                                                        KEY 1

                                                                                        ENTER

      0100  -    1001  -    1110  -    1111  -    1101  -    0010  -    0000  -    1100  EXIT

    + 1110  -    0100  -    1110  -    1101  -    1001  -    0101  -    0101  -    0110  M-0

      0000       0000       0111       1111       1112       2222       2222       2333
      1234       5678       9012       3456       7890       1234       5678       9012
      ----       ----       ----       ----       ----       ----       ----       ----
    = 1010  -    1101  -    0000  -    0010  -    0100  -    0111  -    0101  -    1010  M-2
.......................................................................................

   22-1022    20-2121    10-0122    20-0131    13-0021    11-3200    02-1130    01-2102
   59-6701    11-9287    75-1536    62-5810    02-2844    49-2739    92-9306    66-2145
   -- ----    -- ----    -- ----    -- ----    -- ----    -- ----    -- ----    -- ----
   01-0000    01-1010    01-1111    10-1110    00-0110    00-0010    01-0001    10-1000  M-2 EXP

   11-2122    10-0122    02-2202    00-1010    54-4453    34-3344    45-5355    34-5333
   01-5660    74-6917    58-3422    37-4921    06-3947    34-0287    06-1835    51-7946
   -- ----    -- ----    -- ----    -- ----    -- ----    -- ----    -- ----    -- ----
                                                                                        KEY 2

                                                                                        ENTER

      0110  -    0110  -    1001  -    0000  -    1101  -    1000  -    0011  -    0010  EXIT

    + 1000  -    0110  -    1001  -    0100  -    1011  -    1100  -    1101  -    0011  M-1

      3333       3334       4444       4444       4555       5555       5556       6666
      3456       7890       1234       5678       9012       3456       7890       1234
      ----       ----       ----       ----       ----       ----       ----       ----
    = 1110  -    0000  -    0000  -    0100  -    0110  -    0100  -    1110  -    0001  M-3
```

RESULTING 64-BIT BLOCK OF CIBITS -- (FORMED FROM M-2 AND M-3)

```
1414042526360303141525142603362525251403252525360314041403031415
7902915780133546248079139157242413684668023546027957803524136891
----------------------------------------------------------------
0000000110101100001101001010011100110110001010000010100000110101
```

CIBITS IN HEXADECIMAL FORM = 01AC34A736282835

Since the cryptanalyst knows all four of the generated M sequences in the two-iteration DES problem, recovery of the keybits generally parallels the problem faced in the single-iteration DES problem.

Keybits of either KEY 1 or KEY 2 can be recovered by playing couplets against each other "one S-box at a time". Consider the attack against the S-1 box of KEY 1:

Couplet No. 1	Couplet No. 2	
22-1022	22-1022	
59-6701	59-6701	
-- ----	-- ----	
10-0001	10-0111	M-1 EXP
00-0000	00-0000	
12-3456	12-3456	
-- ----	-- ----	
		KEY 1
		ENTER
1000	0100	EXIT

By looking at the contents of the S-1 box in their <u>reverse mode</u>, which are provided in Appendix F, we can find the four possible six-bit values that might have entered the S-1 box:

00-0111	00-0001
01-1111	01-0011
10-0011	10-0000
11-0010	11-0100
1000	0100

By adding modulo-2 the six bits found in the M-1 EXPanded line, the four possible six-bit values of KEY 1 can be found for each of the couplets:

* 10-0110	* 10-0110
11-1110	11-0100
00-0010	00-0111
** 01-0011	** 01-0011

Here we find two possible keys, 10-0110 and 01-0011, either of which is possible as the key for the S-1 box in KEY 1. By using the same procedure with another S-box, particularly an S-box in KEY 2, where some of the same keybits, 01 through 06, might have been used, we can attempt to identify which of the two keys, 10-0110 or 01-0011, is correct. For example, let us go through the same procedure with the S-2 box in KEY 2:

Couplet No. 1	Couplet No. 2	
20-2121	20-2121	
11-9287	11-9287	
-- ----	-- ----	
11-0010	01-1010	M-2 EXP
10-0122	10-0122	
74-6917	74-6917	
-- ----	-- ----	
		KEY 2
		ENTER
1110	0110	EXIT

This time we look at the contents of the S-2 box in their reverse mode. We find the four possible six-bit values that might have entered the same box:

00-0011	00-0100
01-0111	01-1100
10-0001	10-1011
11-1110	11-1001
1110	0110

We add modulo 2 the six bits found in the M-2 EXPanded line to the above values:

* 11-0001	01-1110
10-0101	00-0110
01-0011	* 11-0001
00-1100	10-0011

Here there is no conflict. The keybits identified above are 11-0001. Moreover, since we now know that the keybits 04 and 06 are respectively 1 and 0, it is evident that in the previous S-1 box of KEY 1 that the correct key is 10-0110 — where keybits 04 and 06 are likewise 1 and 0.

By this time it is clearly evident that the two-iteration DES problem

really offers no particular analytical difficulty. Having several couplets
with a common key is enough to make solution almost trivial. Before leaving the two-iteration DES problem, however, let us discuss one other method
of attack. This involves an attack against only a single couplet.

AN ATTACK AGAINST A SINGLE TWO-ITERATION DES COUPLET

Consider the following couplet:

Plaintext: 7FEA2840187C34D5

Ciphertext: BCFF68883B0A2E2A

From this couplet our task is to recover the 56 bits which comprise the
master or external key.

Our attack is divided into two parts. In the first part we will attempt
to recover the keybits used in the first four S-boxes, keybits 01 through
28. In the second part we will attempt to recover the keybits used in the
last four S-boxes, keybits 30 through 57. Since the two parts are accomplished in the same manner, we will describe here only the attempt to recover the keybits 01 through 28.

As usual, we can begin by making an "outline" of the problem, shading
those lines of bits which are known:

64-BIT 'DES' MASTER OR EXTERNAL KEY --

2113355-1025554-0214434-1123334-0012343-2021453-0202435-0110454-
1031975-1176107-2423401-7632789-7452553-0858846-6836043-9495226-
----

   KEY IN HEXADECIMAL FORM =

64-BIT BLOCK OF PLABITS -- (BITS WHICH FORM M-0 AND M-1)

1414042526360303141525142603362525251403252525360314041414030315
7902915780133546248079139157242413684668023546027957803568132491

0111111111101010001010000100000000011000011111000011010011010101

PLABITS IN HEXADECIMAL FORM = 7FEA2840187C34D5

| 3333 | 3334 | 4444 | 4444 | 4555 | 5555 | 5556 | 6666 |
3456	7890	1234	5678	9012	3456	7890	1234
1100 -	0001 -	1100 -	0011 -	1011 -	0011 -	1101 -	1000 M-0

```
   0000     0000     0111     1111     1112     2222     2222     2333
   1234     5678     9012     3456     7890     1234     5678     9012
   ----     ----     ----     ----     ----     ----     ----     ----
   0011  -  0000  -  1100  -  0111  -  0100  -  0011  -  1011  -  0010   M-1
```

....

```
22-1022  20-2121  10-0122  20-0131  13-0021  11-3200  02-1130  01-2102
59-6701  11-9287  75-1536  62-5810  02-2844  49-2739  92-9306  66-2145
-- ----  -- ----  -- ----  -- ----  -- ----  -- ----  -- ----  -- ----
10-1000  00-0010  00-0110  00-0111  10-0011  10-0111  10-0000  01-0011   M-1 EXP

00-0000  00-0111  11-1111  12-2222  33-3333  33-3344  44-4444  44-5555
12-3456  78-9012  34-5678  90-1234  01-2345  67-8901  23-4567  89-0123
-- ----  -- ----  -- ----  -- ----  -- ----  -- ----  -- ----  -- ----
                                                              KEY 1

                                                              ENTER
```

```
   0011  -  0100  -  0000  -  1101  -  0101  -  0010  -  1010  -  0111   EXIT
 + 1100  -  0001  -  1100  -  0011  -  1011  -  0011  -  1101  -  1000   M-0
   0000     0000     0111     1111     1112     2222     2222     2333
   1234     5678     9012     3456     7890     1234     5678     9012
   ----     ----     ----     ----     ----     ----     ----     ----
 = 1111  -  0101  -  1100  -  1110  -  1110  -  0001  -  0111  -  1111   M-2
```

....

```
22-1022  20-2121  10-0122  20-0131  13-0021  11-3200  02-1130  01-2102
59-6701  11-9287  75-1536  62-5810  02-2844  49-2739  92-9306  66-2145
-- ----  -- ----  -- ----  -- ----  -- ----  -- ----  -- ----  -- ----
01-0000  01-1011  10-1101  11-0111  11-1111  11-1111  10-1111  10-0010   M-2 EXP

11-2122  10-0122  02-2202  00-1010  54-4453  34-3344  45-5355  34-5333
01-5660  74-6917  58-3422  37-4921  06-3947  34-0287  06-1835  51-7946
-- ----  -- ----  -- ----  -- ----  -- ----  -- ----  -- ----  -- ----
                                                              KEY 2

                                                              ENTER
```

```
   0000  -  0101  -  0001  -  0111  -  0100  -  0011  -  1110  -  0000   EXIT
 + 0011  -  0000  -  1100  -  0111  -  0100  -  0011  -  1011  -  0010   M-1
   3333     3334     4444     4444     4555     5555     5556     6666
   3456     7890     1234     5678     9012     3456     7890     1234
   ----     ----     ----     ----     ----     ----     ----     ----
 = 0011  -  0101  -  1101  -  0000  -  0000  -  0000  -  0101  -  0010   M-3
```

RESULTING 64-BIT BLOCK OF CIBITS -- (FORMED FROM M-2 AND M-3)

```
1414042526360303141525142603362525251403252525360314041403031415
7902915780133546248079139157242413684668023546027957803524136891
----------------------------------------------------------------
1011110011111111011010001000100000111011000010100010111000101010
```

CIBITS IN **HEXADECIMAL** FORM = BCFF68883B0A2E2A

The foundation for our attack against the single two-iteration couplet are the following lines, taken from the "outline" of the problem:

```
22-1022   20-2121   10-0122   20-0131   13-0021   11-3200   02-1130   01-2102
59-6701   11-9287   75-1536   62-5810   02-2844   49-2739   92-9306   66-2145
--  ----   --  ----   --  ----   --  ----   --  ----   --  ----   --  ----   --  ----
10-1000   00-0010   00-0110   00-0111   10-0011   10-0111   10-0000   01-0011   M-1 EXP

00-0000   00-0111   11-1111   12-2222   33-3333   33-3344   44-4444   44-5555
12-3456   78-9012   34-5678   90-1234   01-2345   67-8901   23-4567   89-0123
--  ----   --  ----   --  ----   --  ----   --  ----   --  ----   --  ----   --  ----
                                                                            KEY 1

                                                                            ENTER

  0011  -  0100  -  0000  -  1101  -  0101  -  0010  -  1010  -  0111   EXIT


22-1022   20-2121   10-0122   20-0131   13-0021   11-3200   02-1130   01-2102
59-6701   11-9287   75-1536   62-5810   02-2844   49-2739   92-9306   66-2145
--  ----   --  ----   --  ----   --  ----   --  ----   --  ----   --  ----   --  ----
01-0000   01-1011   10-1101   11-0111   11-1111   11-1111   10-1111   10-0010   M-2 EXP

11-2122   10-0122   02-2202   00-1010   54-4453   34-3344   45-5355   34-5333
01-5660   74-6917   58-3422   37-4921   06-3947   34-0287   06-1835   51-7946
--  ----   --  ----   --  ----   --  ----   --  ----   --  ----   --  ----   --  ----
                                                                            KEY 2

                                                                            ENTER

  0000  -  0101  -  0001  -  0111  -  0100  -  0011  -  1110  -  0000   EXIT
```

Instead of recovering keybits one S-box at a time, as we did in the one-iteration DES problem, here we are going to recover, or attempt to recover, keybits four S-boxes at a time. That is, we are first going to identify, or attempt to identify, the keybits 01 through 28, the keybits used in the first four S-boxes. Later, in the second part of our attack we can use the same technique and recover, or attempt to recover, the keybits 30 through 57, the keybits used in the last four S-boxes.

Therefore, turning to the first part of the present problem, we can use the contents of the S-boxes in their reverse mode [provided in Appendix F], in order to find the possible keybits used in KEY 1 and KEY 2. Note that to the values found in Appendix F we must add modulo 2 the values of M-1 EXPanded line and the M-2 EXPanded line.

For each of the first four S-boxes we will then have facing us four possible lines of keybits, and our task will be to identify for each S-box the correct line of keybits.

The first four S-boxes and their respective four possible lines of key-bits are as follows:

00–0000	00–0111	11–1111	12–2222	
12–3456	78–9012	34–5678	90–1234	
-- ----	-- ----	-- ----	-- ----	
10–0000	00–0101	00–0111	00–0110	
11–0110	01–0000	01–0100	01–0111	KEY 1
00–0100	10–0111	10–0001	10–0000	
01–0010	11–0100	11–0101	11–0001	
----	----	----	----	
0011	0100	0000	1101	EXIT

11–2122	10–0122	02–2202	00–1010	
01–5660	74–6917	58–3422	37–4921	
-- ----	-- ----	-- ----	-- ----	
01–1110	01–0101	10–0101	11–0111	
00–0000	00–0100	11–0010	10–1110	KEY 2
11–1111	11–0011	00–0100	01–0001	
10–1101	10–0110	01–1101	00–1010	
----	----	----	----	
0000	0101	0001	0111	EXIT

The task of identifying the above keybits 01 through 28 is not especially difficult. Some keybits can be identified immediately. For example, in looking at the possible lines of keybits in KEY 1 it is evident that the keybits 03, 06, 09, 15, and 21 must each be 0. When these identifications are placed in the possible lines of keybits in KEY 2, further keybits can identified. For example, consider the S–2 box of KEY 2:

```
10–0122
74–6917
-- ----
01–0101

00–0100

11–0011

10–0110

----

0101
```

Since keybit 21 has been identified from KEY 1 as being 0, we can see in the S-2 box of KEY 2 that only two of the lines of keybits are actually possible:

```
10-0122
74-6917
-- ----
01-0101
00-0100
```

Looking at the other keybits in this box, we can see confirmation that keybit 06 is 0, and we can make the new identifications that keybit 17 is 0 and keybit 19 is 1.

Analysis continues in the same manner with keybit identifications in one key being placed in and confirmed by the other key. In a sense, the keys are played against each other.

In the described manner it will not take the cryptanalyst very long to identify most of the keybits:

```
00-0000    00-0111    11-1111    12-2222
12-3456    78-9012    34-5678    90-1234
-- ----    -- ----    -- ----    -- ----
11-0110    00-0101    01-0100    11-0001
                      11-0101                    KEY 1


11-2122    10-0122    02-2202    00-1010
01-5660    74-6917    58-3422    37-4921
-- ----    -- ----    -- ----    -- ----
10-1101    01-0101    00-0100    00-1010    KEY 2
```

But note that sometimes not every keybit can uniquely be identified. It can be seen above, for example, in KEY 1 that keybits 13 and 18 cannot be specifically identified, although it can be seen that they are the same. If another couplet with a common key were available, it is very likely that all keybits could be identified. Still, even in this case with only a single couplet available is there perhaps another means of identifying the the keybits 13 and 18? The answer lies in derivation of the master or external key. By putting the recovered keybits into the master or external key we may find some identifiable pattern in the ASCII values therein. It is not inconceivable, therefore, that even in this case we might be able to still identify with some degree of certainty the values of keybits 13 and 18 — but only if there is some pattern in the ASCII values which comprise the master or external key.

The methodology involved with the recovery of the keybits 01 through 28 in the case of a single two-iteration DES problem has been described above. The remaining 28 keybits, the keybits 30 through 57, can be recovered in a similar manner.

With the reader now hopefully well acquainted with the cryptography and analysis of the single-iteration and two-iteration DES ciphering processes, we are in a good position to focus our attention in the next chapter on the cryptography and analysis of the three-iteration DES problem.

Chapter IV
EXERCISE

The following couplet is known:

Plaintext — 68F3AA90B8E3CA15

Ciphertext — AE7002EF86E48D90

Using this couplet, which provides known input and output, the following lines are obtained:

```
22-1022  20-2121  10-0122  20-0131  13-0021  11-3200  02-1130  01-2102
59-6701  11-9287  75-1536  62-5810  02-2844  49-2739  92-9306  66-2145
--  ----  --  ----  --  ----  --  ----  --  ----  --  ----  --  ----  --  ----
01-0111  10-1110  00-0011  10-0111  10-0101  10-0101  10-0110  00-0110  M-1 EXP

00-0000  00-0111  11-1111  12-2222  33-3333  33-3344  44-4444  44-5555
12-3456  78-9012  34-5678  90-1234  01-2345  67-8901  23-4567  89-0123
--  ----  --  ----  --  ----  --  ----  --  ----  --  ----  --  ----  --  ----
                                                                        KEY 1
                                                                        ENTER

   1101  -  0101  -  1110  -  0001  -  0010  -  1110  -  1101  -  1101  EXIT
```

```
22-1022  20-2121  10-0122  20-0131  13-0021  11-3200  02-1130  01-2102
59-6701  11-9287  75-1536  62-5810  02-2844  49-2739  92-9306  66-2145
--  ----  --  ----  --  ----  --  ----  --  ----  --  ----  --  ----  --  ----
11-1111  10-1001  11-0010  00-1011  11-0100  00-1001  11-0001  11-1101  M-2 EXP

11-2122  10-0122  02-2202  00-1010  54-4453  34-3344  45-5355  34-5333
01-5660  74-6917  58-3422  37-4921  06-3947  34-0287  06-1835  51-7946
--  ----  --  ----  --  ----  --  ----  --  ----  --  ----  --  ----  --  ----
                                                                        KEY 2
                                                                        ENTER

   1001  -  0010  -  0111  -  0000  -  0100  -  1111  -  0110  -  0101  EXIT
```

Recover as many possible of the 56 keybits used in the two—iteration DES ciphering process which produced the above couplet.

Chapter V

THE THREE-ITERATION PROBLEM

We turn our attention now to the cryptography and analysis of the three-iteration DES problem. Analysis is no longer quite as trivial as it was earlier. In attacking the three-iteration problem we shall need to use a "trial and error" or brute-force form of attack — although in this case it might be better to term the attack a minor brute-force attack, since the number of trials is rather minimal.

DESCRIPTION OF THE THREE-ITERATION ENCIPHERMENT

An example of three-iteration DES encipherment is the following:

```
64-BIT 'DES' MASTER OR EXTERNAL KEY --
2113355-1025554-0214434-1123334-0012343-2021453-0202435-0110454-
1031975-1176107-2423401-7632789-7452553-0858846-6836043-9495226-
-----------------------------------------------------------------
0000011110100111000100110111000001000101110110100010101000010110

    KEY IN HEXADECIMAL FORM = 07A7137045DA2A16

64-BIT BLOCK OF PLABITS -- (BITS WHICH FORM M-0 AND M-1)
1414042526360303141525142603362525251403252525360314041414030315
7902915780133546248079139157242413684668023546027957803568132491
-----------------------------------------------------------------
0011101111011101000100011001000001001001001101110010100000000010

PLABITS IN HEXADECIMAL FORM = 3BDD119049372802
```

```
-----------------------------------------------------------------------

    3333      3334      4444      4444      4555      5555      5556      6666
    3456      7890      1234      5678      9012      3456      7890      1234
    ----      ----      ----      ----      ----      ----      ----      ----
    0011  -   1100  -   0110  -   0000  -   0100  -   1011  -   1001  -   0110   M-0

    0000      0000      0111      1111      1112      2222      2222      2333
    1234      5678      9012      3456      7890      1234      5678      9012
    ----      ----      ----      ----      ----      ----      ----      ----
    0010  -   0001  -   1100  -   0110  -   0010  -   0010  -   1001  -   1100   M-1

............................................................................

22-1022   20-2121   10-0122   20-0131   13-0021   11-3200   02-1130   01-2102
59-6701   11-9287   75-1536   62-5810   02-2844   49-2739   92-9306   66-2145
-- ----   -- ----   -- ----   -- ----   -- ----   -- ----   -- ----   -- ----
11-0000   00-1010   00-0110   00-0001   10-0101   11-0011   10-1010   00-0001   M-1 EXP

00-0000   00-0111   11-1111   12-2222   33-3333   33-3344   44-4444   44-5555
12-3456   78-9012   34-5678   90-1234   01-2345   67-8901   23-4567   89-0123
-- ----   -- ----   -- ----   -- ----   -- ----   -- ----   -- ----   -- ----
00-1110   01-0010   00-0101   01-0010   00-1000   10-0011   01-0111   10-1011   KEY 1
```

```
11-1110   01-1000   00-0011   01-0011   10-1101   01-0000   11-1101   10-1010   ENTER

   0110  -  1100  -  1110  -  0101  -  0011  -  1010  -  0010  -  1010   EXIT

+  0011  -  1100  -  0110  -  0000  -  0100  -  1011  -  1001  -  0110   M-0

   0000      0000      0111      1111      1112      2222      2222      2333
   1234      5678      9012      3456      7890      1234      5678      9012
   ----      ----      ----      ----      ----      ----      ----      ----
=  0101  -  0000  -  1000  -  0101  -  0111  -  0001  -  1011  -  1100   M-2

................................................................................

22-1022   20-2121   10-0122   20-0131   13-0021   11-3200   02-1130   01-2102
59-6701   11-9287   75-1536   62-5810   02-2844   49-2739   92-9306   66-2145
-- ----   -- ----   -- ----   -- ----   -- ----   -- ----   -- ----   -- ----
11-1010   00-1010   00-0000   01-0100   00-1011   11-0101   10-1010   01-0011   M-2 EXP

11-2122   10-0122   02-2202   00-1010   54-4453   34-3344   45-5355   34-5333
01-5660   74-6917   58-3422   37-4921   06-3947   34-0287   06-1835   51-7946
-- ----   -- ----   -- ----   -- ----   -- ----   -- ----   -- ----   -- ----
01-0101   01-0001   10-1000   10-0000   11-1000   00-0111   10-0011   01-1001   KEY 2

10-1111   01-1011   10-1000   11-0100   11-0011   11-0010   00-1001   00-1010   ENTER

   0000  -  1010  -  1011  -  1010  -  0111  -  0010  -  1100  -  0011   EXIT

+  0010  -  0001  -  1100  -  0110  -  0010  -  0010  -  1001  -  1100   M-1

   0000      0000      0111      1111      1112      2222      2222      2333
   1234      5678      9012      3456      7890      1234      5678      9012
   ----      ----      ----      ----      ----      ----      ----      ----
=  0010  -  1011  -  0111  -  1100  -  0101  -  0000  -  0101  -  1111   M-3

................................................................................

22-1022   20-2121   10-0122   20-0131   13-0021   11-3200   02-1130   01-2102
59-6701   11-9287   75-1536   62-5810   02-2844   49-2739   92-9306   66-2145
-- ----   -- ----   -- ----   -- ----   -- ----   -- ----   -- ----   -- ----
01-0110   00-1110   01-0001   10-1111   11-0101   10-1010   00-0110   00-0100   M-3 EXP

01-2021   12-0220   10-2120   10-0211   43-3435   43-5535   34-3533   45-4444
34-3127   14-7585   84-7016   52-8039   26-1781   19-7672   56-2034   45-0359
-- ----   -- ----   -- ----   -- ----   -- ----   -- ----   -- ----   -- ----
10-1000   10-0001   11-1000   00-1100   01-0100   10-1001   01-1100   01-1110   KEY 3

11-1110   10-1111   10-1001   10-0011   10-0001   00-0011   01-1010   01-1010   ENTER

   0110  -  1111  -  0001  -  0000  -  0010  -  1111  -  0101  -  0110   EXIT

+  0101  -  0000  -  1000  -  0101  -  0111  -  0001  -  1011  -  1100   M-2

   3333      3334      4444      4444      4555      5555      5556      6666
   3456      7890      1234      5678      9012      3456      7890      1234
   ----      ----      ----      ----      ----      ----      ----      ----
=  0011  -  1111  -  1001  -  0101  -  0101  -  1110  -  1110  -  1010   M-4

--------------------------------------------------------------------------------

RESULTING 64-BIT BLOCK OF CIBITS -- (FORMED FROM M-3 AND M-4)

1414042526360303141525142603362525251403252525360314041403031415
7902915780133546248079139157242413684668023546027957803524136891
--------------------------------------------------------------------------------
0010010110111101111101101111100101111101110100101100111001000000

CIBITS IN HEXADECIMAL FORM = 25BDF6F97DD2CE40
```

ANALYZING A THREE-ITERATION PROBLEM

We are given the following three couplets, all having a common key:

COUPLET NO. 1

64-BIT 'DES' MASTER OR EXTERNAL KEY --

```
2113355-1025554-0214434-1123334-0012343-2021453-0202435-0110454-
1031975-1176107-2423401-7632789-7452553-0858846-6836043-9495226-
-----------------------------------------------------------------
```

KEY IN HEXADECIMAL FORM =

64-BIT BLOCK OF PLABITS -- (BITS WHICH FORM M-0 AND M-1)

```
14140425263603031415251426033625252514032525253603140414140303 15
79029157801335462480791391572424136846680235460279578035681324 91
-----------------------------------------------------------------
0111001100111000000100001111101001101011101100111001011000110110
```

PLABITS IN HEXADECIMAL FORM = 733810FA6BB39636

3333	3334	4444	4444	4555	5555	5556	6666	
3456	7890	1234	5678	9012	3456	7890	1234	
----	----	----	----	----	----	----	----	
1100 -	1101 -	0100 -	0010 -	1100 -	1010 -	1000 -	1110	M-0

0000	0000	0111	1111	1112	2222	2222	2333	
1234	5678	9012	3456	7890	1234	5678	9012	
----	----	----	----	----	----	----	----	
1010 -	1110 -	0100 -	1100 -	0011 -	0110 -	1100 -	1111	M-1

. . . .

22-1022	20-2121	10-0122	20-0131	13-0021	11-3200	02-1130	01-2102	
59-6701	11-9287	75-1536	62-5810	02-2844	49-2739	92-9306	66-2145	
-- ----	-- ----	-- ----	-- ----	-- ----	-- ----	-- ----	-- ----	
11-0110	01-1000	01-1011	10-1011	11-0001	11-1010	01-1111	10-1001	M-1 EXP

00-0000	00-0111	11-1111	12-2222	33-3333	33-3344	44-4444	44-5555	
12-3456	78-9012	34-5678	90-1234	01-2345	67-8901	23-4567	89-0123	
-- ----	-- ----	-- ----	-- ----	-- ----	-- ----	-- ----	-- ----	

KEY 1

ENTER

EXIT

| + 1100 - | 1101 - | 0100 - | 0010 - | 1100 - | 1010 - | 1000 - | 1110 | M-0 |

0000	0000	0111	1111	1112	2222	2222	2333	
1234	5678	9012	3456	7890	1234	5678	9012	
----	----	----	----	----	----	----	----	
=								M-2

. . . .

22-1022	20-2121	10-0122	20-0131	13-0021	11-3200	02-1130	01-2102	
59-6701	11-9287	75-1536	62-5810	02-2844	49-2739	92-9306	66-2145	
-- ----	-- ----	-- ----	-- ----	-- ----	-- ----	-- ----	-- ----	
								M-2 EXP

```
11-2122   10-0122   02-2202   00-1010   54-4453   34-3344   45-5355   34-5333
01-5660   74-6917   58-3422   37-4921   06-3947   34-0287   06-1835   51-7946
-- ----   -- ----   -- ----   -- ----   -- ----   -- ----   -- ----   -- ----
                                                                              KEY 2

                                                                              ENTER

    0111  -  1011  -  0011  -  1110  -  1111  -  1011  -  1011  -  0010 EXIT

+ 1010  -  1110  -  0100  -  1100  -  0011  -  0110  -  1100  -  1111 M-1

    0000      0000      0111      1111      1112      2222      2222      2333
    1234      5678      9012      3456      7890      1234      5678      9012
    ----      ----      ----      ----      ----      ----      ----      ----
= 1101  -  0101  -  0111  -  0010  -  1100  -  1101  -  0111  -  1101 M-3

..............................................................................

22-1022   20-2121   10-0122   20-0131   13-0021   11-3200   02-1130   01-2102
59-6701   11-9287   75-1536   62-5810   02-2844   49-2739   92-9306   66-2145
-- ----   -- ----   -- ----   -- ----   -- ----   -- ----   -- ----   -- ----
01-0001   11-1111   10-1101   11-0101   11-1110   00-1100   01-0011   10-1110 M-3 EXP

01-2021   12-0220   10-2120   10-0211   43-3435   43-5535   34-3533   45-4444
34-3127   14-7585   84-7016   52-8039   26-1781   19-7672   56-2034   45-0359
-- ----   -- ----   -- ----   -- ----   -- ----   -- ----   -- ----   -- ----
                                                                              KEY 3

                                                                              ENTER

                                                                              EXIT

+                                                                             M-2

    3333      3334      4444      4444      4555      5555      5556      6666
    3456      7890      1234      5678      9012      3456      7890      1234
    ----      ----      ----      ----      ----      ----      ----      ----
= 1010  -  1001  -  1100  -  1101  -  1010  -  1010  -  1110  -  1010 M-4

------------------------------------------------------------------------------
```

RESULTING 64-BIT BLOCK OF CIBITS -- (FORMED FROM M-3 AND M-4)

```
14140425263603031415251426033625252514032525253603140414030314 15
79029157801335462480791391572424136846680235460279578035241368 91
-------------------------------------------------------------------
1111010110010110101011101101101011110110000110100010110101111001
```

CIBITS IN HEXADECIMAL FORM = F596AEDAF61A2D79

COUPLET NO. 2

64-BIT 'DES' MASTER OR EXTERNAL KEY --

```
2113355-1025554-0214434-1123334-0012343-2021453-0202435-0110454-
1031975-1176107-2423401-7632789-7452553-0858846-6836043-9495226-
-----------------------------------------------------------------
```

KEY IN HEXADECIMAL FORM =

64-BIT BLOCK OF PLABITS -- (BITS WHICH FORM M-0 AND M-1)

```
1414042526360303141525142603362525251403252525360314041414030315
7902915780133546248079139157242413684668023546027957803568132491
----------------------------------------------------------------
0100011111010010000010111011000110001000010100101101101011100111
```

PLABITS IN HEXADECIMAL FORM = 47D20BB18852DAE7

3333		3334		4444		4444		4555		5555		5556		6666	
3456		7890		1234		5678		9012		3456		7890		1234	
----		----		----		----		----		----		----		----	
0100	-	1010	-	1010	-	0011	-	1011	-	0110	-	1001	-	0010	M-0
0000		0000		0111		1111		1112		2222		2222		2333	
1234		5678		9012		3456		7890		1234		5678		9012	
----		----		----		----		----		----		----		----	
1001	-	1011	-	0010	-	1101	-	0010	-	1000	-	1011	-	1100	M-1

. . . .

22-1022	20-2121	10-0122	20-0131	13-0021	11-3200	02-1130	01-2102	
59-6701	11-9287	75-1536	62-5810	02-2844	49-2739	92-9306	66-2145	
-- ----	-- ----	-- ----	-- ----	-- ----	-- ----	-- ----	-- ----	
11-1101	11-1010	01-1000	00-1000	00-0101	11-0100	00-1110	01-0111	M-1 EXP

00-0000	00-0111	11-1111	12-2222	33-3333	33-3344	44-4444	44-5555	
12-3456	78-9012	34-5678	90-1234	01-2345	67-8901	23-4567	89-0123	
-- ----	-- ----	-- ----	-- ----	-- ----	-- ----	-- ----	-- ----	

KEY 1

ENTER

EXIT

+	0100	-	1010	-	1010	-	0011	-	1011	-	0110	-	1001	-	0010	M-0
	0000		0000		0111		1111		1112		2222		2222		2333	
	1234		5678		9012		3456		7890		1234		5678		9012	
	----		----		----		----		----		----		----		----	
=																M-2

. . . .

22-1022	20-2121	10-0122	20-0131	13-0021	11-3200	02-1130	01-2102	
59-6701	11-9287	75-1536	62-5810	02-2844	49-2739	92-9306	66-2145	
-- ----	-- ----	-- ----	-- ----	-- ----	-- ----	-- ----	-- ----	
								M-2 EXP

11-2122	10-0122	02-2202	00-1010	54-4453	34-3344	45-5355	34-5333	
01-5660	74-6917	58-3422	37-4921	06-3947	34-0287	06-1835	51-7946	
-- ----	-- ----	-- ----	-- ----	-- ----	-- ----	-- ----	-- ----	

KEY 2

ENTER

	0010	-	0110	-	1001	-	1001	-	1011	-	0111	-	1100	-	1011	EXIT
+	1001	-	1011	-	0010	-	1101	-	0010	-	1000	-	1011	-	1100	M-1
	0000		0000		0111		1111		1112		2222		2222		2333	
	1234		5678		9012		3456		7890		1234		5678		9012	
	----		----		----		----		----		----		----		----	
=	1011	-	1101	-	1011	-	0100	-	1001	-	1111	-	0111	-	0111	M-3

```
. . . . . . . . . . . . . . . . . . . . . . . . . . . . . . . . . . . . . . . . . . .
  22-1022   20-2121   10-0122   20-0131   13-0021   1I-3200   02-1130   01-2102
  59-6701   11-9287   75-1536   62-5810   02-2844   49-2739   92-9306   66-2145
  -- ----   -- ----   -- ----   -- ----   -- ----   -- ----   -- ----   -- ----
  00-0011   11-0111   11-1011   10-1010   01-0111   10-1111   11-0011   10-1110   M-3 EXP

  01-2021   12-0220   10-2120   10-0211   43-3435   43-5535   34-3533   45-4444
  34-3127   14-7585   84-7016   52-8039   26-1781   19-7672   56-2034   45-0359
  -- ----   -- ----   -- ----   -- ----   -- ----   -- ----   -- ----   -- ----

                                                                                 KEY 3

                                                                                 ENTER

                                                                                 EXIT

 +                                                                               M-2

     3333      3334      4444      4444      4555      5555      5556      6666
     3456      7890      1234      5678      9012      3456      7890      1234
     ----      ----      ----      ----      ----      ----      ----      ----
 = 1010  -  1111  -  0100  -  1110  -  1111  -  0101  -  0000  -  0010   M-4
```

RESULTING 64-BIT BLOCK OF CIBITS -- (FORMED FROM M-3 AND M-4)

```
14140425262636030314152514260336252525140325252536031404140303141S
790291S780133546248079139157242413684668023546027957803524136891
11011000101111101001101000111011101011111101110010111010100110001
```

CIBITS IN HEXADECIMAL FORM = D8BE9A3BAFEE5D31

COUPLET NO. 3

64-BIT 'DES' MASTER OR EXTERNAL KEY --

```
2113355-1025554-0214434-1·123334-0012343-2021453-0202435-0110454-
1031975-1176107-2423401-7632789-7452553-0858846-6836043-9495226-
```

      KEY IN HEXADECIMAL FORM =

64-BIT BLOCK OF PLABITS -- (BITS WHICH FORM M-0 AND M-1)

```
14140425262636030314152514260336252525140325252536031404141403031S
790291S780133546248079139157242413684668023546027957803568132491
100010001010011111101011001010110111101000100000000001100101001
```

PLABITS IN HEXADECIMAL FORM = 88A7EB2B7D100329

```
     3333      3334      4444      4444      4555      5555      5556      6666
     3456      7890      1234      5678      9012      3456      7890      1234
     ----      ----      ----      ----      ----      ----      ----      ----
   0011  -  0100  -  0011  -  1100  -  0010  -  1110  -  0100  -  0000   M-0
```

```
    0000       0000       0111       1111       1112       2222       2222       2333
    1234       5678       9012       3456       7890       1234       5678       9012
    ----       ----       ----       ----       ----       ----       ----       ----
    1101  -    1000  -    1011  -    1100  -    1100- -    0100  -    0111  -    0011   M-1

...............................................................................

22-1022    20-2121    10-0122    20-0131    13-0021    11-3200    02-1130    01-2102
59-6701    11-9287    75-1536    62-5810    02-2844    49-2739    92-9306    66-2145
-- ----    -- ----    -- ----    -- ----    -- ----    -- ----    -- ----    -- ----
00-0000    01-0111    11-1001    11-1110    01-1001    10-1101    11-0100    00-1110   M-1 EXP

00-0000    00-0111    11-1111    12-2222    33-3333    33-3344    44-4444    44-5555
12-3456    78-9012    34-5678    90-1234    01-2345    67-8901    23-4567    89-0123
-- ----    -- ----    -- ----    -- ----    -- ----    -- ----    -- ----    -- ----
                                                                                      KEY  1

                                                                                      ENTER

                                                                                      EXIT
  + 0011  -    0100  -    0011  -    1100  -    0010  -    1110  -    0100  -    0000   M-0
    0000       0000       0111       1111       1112       2222       2222       2333
    1234       5678       9012       3456       7890       1234       5678       9012
    ----       ----       ----       ----       ----       ----       ----       ----
  =                                                                                    M-2

...............................................................................

22-1022    20-2121    10-0122    20-0131    13-0021    11-3200    02-1130    01-2102
59-6701    11-9287    75-1536    62-5810    02-2844    49-2739    92-9306    66-2145
-- ----    -- ----    -- ----    -- ----    -- ----    -- ----    -- ----    -- ----
                                                                                      M-2 EXP

11-2122    10-0122    02-2202    00-1010    54-4453    34-3344    45-5355    34-5333
01-5660    74-6917    58-3422    37-4921    06-3947    34-0287    06-1835    51-7946
-- ----    -- ----    -- ----    -- ----    -- ----    -- ----    -- ----    -- ----
                                                                                      KEY  2

                                                                                      ENTER
  1001  -    0111  -    1100  -    1011  -    1010  -    0010  -    0110  -    1010     EXIT
+ 1101  -    1000  -    1011  -    1100  -    1100  -    0100  -    0111  -    0011     M-1
    0000       0000       0111       1111       1112       2222       2222       2333
    1234       5678       9012       3456       7890       1234       5678       9012
    ----       ----       ----       ----       ----       ----       ----       ----
= 0100  -    1111  -    0111  -    0111  -    0110  -    0110  -    0001  -    1001     M-3

...............................................................................

22-1022    20-2121    10-0122    20-0131    13-0021    11-3200    02-1130    01-2102
59-6701    11-9287    75-1536    62-5810    02-2844    49-2739    92-9306    66-2145
-- ----    -- ----    -- ----    -- ----    -- ----    -- ----    -- ----    -- ----
01-1100    00-1110    01-0110    01-1101    11-1101    11-1000    01-1001    11-1100   M-3 EXP

01-2021    12-0220    10-2120    10-0211    43-3435    43-5535    34-3533    45-4444
34-3127    14-7585    84-7016    52-8039    26-1781    19-7672    56-2034    45-0359
-- ----    -- ----    -- ----    -- ----    -- ----    -- ----    -- ----    -- ----
                                                                                      KEY  3

                                                                                      ENTER

                                                                                      EXIT
  +                                                                                    M-2
```

| 3333 | 3334 | 4444 | 4444 | 4555 | 5555 | 5556 | 6666 |
3456	7890	1234	5678	9012	3456	7890	1234
= 1001 -	0100 -	0100 -	0100 -	0000 -	1001 -	0000 -	0011 M-4

RESULTING 64-BIT BLOCK OF CIBITS -- (FORMED FROM M-3 AND M-4)

14140425263603031415251426033625252514032525253603140414403031415
79029157801335462480791391572424136846680235460279578035241368 91

0011000010010001101000101010101110010011110010010010101000010011010

CIBITS IN HEXADECIMAL FORM = 3091A2AE4F24A89A

Looking at the three-iteration problem, we see immediately that of the five M sequences, only the M-2 sequence is unknown. The sequences M-0 and M-1 are available from the 64 bits of known plaintext and the sequences M-3 and M-4 are available from the 64 bits of known ciphertext. As we might expect, recovery of the M-2 sequence or part of the M-2 sequence plays a major role in the solution of the three-iteration problem.

The solution of the three-iteration problem coming at this time is probably very appropriate because it exemplifies the form of solution that we can likely expect when attacking the Data Encryption Standard when there is a multiplicity of iterations. Very simply, solution of the Data Encryption Standard (DES) after one or two iterations depends upon some form of "trial and error" testing, termed also as a brute-force attack, with the effectiveness of the solution process being measured by the time it takes to accomplish the "tests" or brute-force attack necessary to effect the solution.

With respect to the "trial and error" testing or brute-force attack, we already know that the solution of the Data Encryption Standard (DES) can be accomplished by making 2^{56} trials or tests. This number of trials or tests of course is the worst case scenario — where solution is reached on the last of the 2^{56} trials or tests. But with regard to these trials or tests, it is probably important to make the following statement. While the time necessary to accomplish the trials or tests is of extreme importance, with respect to the DES any reduction of the number of trials or tests to a figure less than 2^{56} is a target to shoot for.

Turning to the solution of Couplet No. 1, by what means can we recover the keybits used to produce the following Couplet No. 1:

Plaintext: 733810FA6BB39636

Ciphertext: F596AEDAF61A2D79

We begin by examining the "outline" of the problem — where known lines of bits are indicated by shading. One way that comes to mind concerns the S-6 box. Look at the following lines from the "outline" that apply to the S-6 box:

```
11-3200                        11-3200
49-2739                        49-2739
-------                        -------
11-1010   M-1 EXP              00-1100   M-3 EXP

33-3344                        43-5535
67-8901                        19-7672
-------                        -------
          KEY 1                          KEY 3

          ENTER                          ENTER

          EXIT                           EXIT

   1010   M-0                            M-2

   2222                          5555
   1234                          3456
   ----                          ----
          M-2                     1010   M-4
```

There are two particular reasons for interest in these lines from the "outline" of the problem. The first is because the value of M-2 in the two parallel columns, above, is the same. The second is because there are three keybits in KEY 1 which are common to the keybits in KEY 3. If we know the identity of nine specific keybits, therefore, we will know both KEY 1 and KEY 3.

The assumption of knowing nine keybits, which identify KEY 1 and KEY 3, provides the foundation for a "trial and error" attack against the three-iteration DES problem. In this attack the value of M-2 plays a key role. As each "trial" is made, two values of M-2 are obtained, one from KEY 1 and one from KEY 3. If the two values of M-2 are the same, it is possible that the assumed nine keybits are correct; but if the two values of M-2 are not the same, we can immediately regard the assumed keybits as being incorrect.

In this "trial and error" form of attack we shall assume the values of nine keybits. The number of trials, therefore, will be 2^9 or 512. Since we can expect an accidental match of two M-2 values to occur every 2^4 or 16 times, we can expect approximately 2^{9-4} or 32 accidental hits or "trials that might be correct" to occur during the course of 512 trials. How then can we find the correct hit out of approximately 32 hits?

The answer lies in the other couplets which we have at our disposal. When we get a hit with Couplet No. 1, we can try or test the same assumed keybits in Couplet No. 2. Since an accidental hit will still likely occur every 2^4 or 16 times when we run the assumed keybits in Couplet No. 2, we can expect approximately 2^{5-4} or two of the assumed keybit values to be good in both Couplet No. 1 and No. 2. We now turn to Couplet No. 3. With this third couplet at our disposal, we can run these final several good keybit values in Couplet No. 3. Whichever keybit value makes a hit in the third couplet will probably represent the nine keybits which we are looking for. That is, we will have found nine keybits that in all three couplets result in hits — where the M-2 value from KEY 1 equals the M-2 value from KEY 3.

While making 2^9 or 512 tests, each with a different set of nine keybits, may appear to be a time consuming process, this is true only from a manual viewpoint. From the viewpoint of using a computer, making 512 trials is rather minor.

The writer has written a simple program in BASIC which performs the "trial and error" test described. A listing of the program of this minor brute-force type of test can be found in Appendix I.

In this test, the trials are made first with respect to Couplet No. 1. Only when a hit occurs, when the two values of M-2 are the same, does the program turn to Couplet No. 2. If no hit occurs in Couplet No. 2, the program returns to the next trial in Couplet No. 1. On the other hand, if a hit occurs in Couplet No. 2, as well as in Couplet No. 1, the program turns to Couplet No. 3 in order to confirm or deny the validity of the hit in Couplet No. 2. If a hit occurs in Couplet No. 3, as well as in Couplets No. 1 and No. 2, there is a high degree of probability that the trial of nine keybits represents the actual correct nine keybits in the key being searched for.

Let us examine now the effectiveness of the described program when it is used against the three-iteration problem given earlier in this chapter. In this problem we were given the following three couplets:

Couplet No. 1 —   Plaintext: 733810FA6BB39636
                   Ciphertext: F596AEDAF61A2D79

Couplet No. 2 —   Plaintext: 47D20BB18852DAE7
                   Ciphertext: D8BE9A3BAFEE5D31

Couplet No. 3 —   Plaintext: 88A7EB2B7D100329
                   Ciphertext: 3091A2AE4F24A89A

For Couplet No. 1 the program performs 2^9 or 512 trials or tests. Each trial or test assumes a different set of values for the nine bits which comprise KEY 1 and KEY 3 of the S-6 box, as shown on page 49. At the same time, again with respect to the S-6 box, the bits forming M-1 EXP, M-0, M-3 EXP, and M-4 are entered into the program. These form the known bits upon which the trial or test is based. While the program might have been written to accept these values, as determined from the "outline" of the couplet, in order to facilitate the use of the program and to make the program easier to use, the program has been written to accept directly the plabits and cibits in hexadecimal form for each couplet; and from these the values of M-1 EXP, M-0, M-3 EXP, and M-4 are determined and used.

The object of the program again is to select those nine keybit combinations which form KEY 1 and KEY 3 (of the S-6 box) so that the two values of M-2 found are the same.

After entering the three given couplets, the program immediately begins to select in Couplet No. 1 those keybit combinations that give rise to a common M-2 value. These are all listed as output to a printer. As each hit occurs in Couplet No. 1, the same keybits are tested in Couplet No. 2. If the same keybits then give rise to a hit also in Couplet No. 2, these are likewise listed under the heading of Couplet No. 2. Finally, if a set of keybits give rise to a hit in both Couplet No. 1 and Couplet No. 2, the keybits are tested in Couplet No. 3; and if these also give rise to a hit in Couplet No. 3, the successful hit is listed under the heading of Couplet No. 3. On the next page is the actual output to the printer in the case of the above three couplets.

COUPLET NO. 1 -- PLAINTEXT = 733810FA6BB39636
CIPHERTEXT = F596AEDAF61A2D79

COUPLET NO. 2 -- PLAINTEXT = 47D20BB18852DAE7
CIPHERTEXT = D8BE9A3BAFEE5D31

COUPLET NO. 3 -- PLAINTEXT = 88A7EB2B7D100329
CIPHERTEXT = 3091A2AE4F24A89A

COUPLET NO. 1

M-2	36	37	-	38	39	40	41	41	39	-	57	56	37	52
1011	0	0	-	0	0	0	0	0	0	-	1	1	0	1
1101	0	0	-	0	0	0	1	1	0	-	0	1	0	0
0100	0	0	-	0	0	1	1	1	0	-	1	1	0	1
1100	0	0	-	0	1	1	0	0	1	-	0	1	0	0
1010	0	0	-	0	1	1	1	1	1	-	0	0	0	1
1000	0	0	-	1	0	0	0	0	0	-	1	0	0	1
0101	0	0	-	1	1	0	0	0	1	-	1	1	0	1
1111	0	0	-	1	1	1	1	1	1	-	1	0	0	1
1110	0	1	-	0	0	0	0	0	0	-	0	1	1	1
0000	0	1	-	0	0	0	1	1	0	-	0	1	1	1
0111	0	1	-	0	1	1	1	1	1	-	0	0	1	1
0101	0	1	-	1	0	0	0	0	0	-	1	1	1	1
1111	0	1	-	1	0	0	1	1	0	-	1	1	1	1
1000	0	1	-	1	1	1	0	0	1	-	1	1	1	1
0010	0	1	-	1	1	1	1	1	1	-	0	0	1	0
0111	1	0	-	0	0	0	0	0	0	-	0	1	0	1
0100	1	0	-	0	0	0	1	1	0	-	1	1	0	1
1011	1	0	-	0	0	1	1	1	0	-	0	0	0	0
1010	1	0	-	0	1	1	0	0	1	-	0	0	0	0
0001	1	0	-	0	1	1	1	1	1	-	0	1	0	0
1000	1	0	-	1	0	0	1	1	0	-	1	0	0	0
1111	1	0	-	1	1	0	1	1	1	-	1	0	0	1
1101	1	0	-	1	1	1	0	0	1	-	1	0	0	0
1001	1	1	-	0	0	0	0	0	0	-	0	1	1	0
1110	1	1	-	0	0	0	1	1	0	-	0	1	1	0
1111	1	1	-	0	1	0	0	0	1	-	1	0	1	1
0100	1	1	-	0	1	1	0	0	1	-	0	1	1	1
1101	1	1	-	0	1	1	1	1	1	-	0	1	1	1
0000	1	1	-	1	0	0	0	0	0	-	1	1	1	0
0101	1	1	-	1	0	0	1	1	0	-	1	1	1	0
0010	1	1	-	1	1	0	1	1	1	-	0	0	1	0
0011	1	1	-	1	1	1	0	0	1	-	1	0	1	0
1000	1	1	-	1	1	1	1	1	1	-	1	1	1	0

COUPLET NO. 2

M-2	36	37	-	38	39	40	41	41	39	-	57	56	37	52
0001	1	0	-	0	0	0	0	0	0	-	0	1	0	1
1101	1	0	-	1	0	0	1	1	0	-	1	0	0	0

COUPLET NO. 3

M-2	36	37	-	38	39	40	41	41	39	-	57	56	37	52
1001	1	0	-	0	0	0	0	0	0	-	0	1	0	1

Examination of the output to the printer shown on the adjacent page shows that the following keybits will provide in all three couplets in the S-6 box a value of M-2 that follows KEY 1 to be the same as the value of M-2 that follows KEY 3:

$$
\begin{array}{ll}
33-3344 & 43-5535 \\
67-8901 & 19-7672 \\
\text{-------} & \text{-------} \\
10-0000 \quad \text{KEY 1} & 00-0101 \quad \text{KEY 3}
\end{array}
$$

We can therefore assume that these are the correct values of the above keybits.

It might be interesting to see the output to the printer if we reverse the given three couplets. That is, we shall consider Couplet No. 3 to now be Couplet No. 1, Couplet No. 2 to be Couplet No. 2, and Couplet No. 1 to now be Couplet No. 3. With this reversal of the couplets, the output to the printer appears as follows:

```
COUPLET NO. 1 --   PLAINTEXT  = 88A7EB2B7D100329
                   CIPHERTEXT = 3091A2AE4F24A89A

COUPLET NO. 2 --   PLAINTEXT  = 47D20BB18852DAE7
                   CIPHERTEXT = D8BE9A3BAFEE5D31

COUPLET NO. 3 --   PLAINTEXT  = 733810FA6BB39636
                   CIPHERTEXT = F596AEDAF61A2D79
```

COUPLET NO. 1

M-2	3 6	3 7	-	3 8	3 9	4 0	4 1	4 1	3 9	-	5 7	5 6	3 7	5 2
1111	0	0	-	0	0	0	1	1	0	-	0	0	0	0
0101	0	0	-	0	0	1	1	1	0	-	1	1	0	1
1110	0	0	-	0	1	0	0	0	1	-	0	0	0	0
1001	0	0	-	0	1	0	1	1	1	-	0	0	0	0
0100	0	0	-	0	1	1	0	0	1	-	0	1	0	1
1101	0	0	-	1	0	1	0	0	0	-	1	0	0	0
0010	0	0	-	1	0	1	1	1	0	-	0	1	0	1
0000	0	0	-	1	1	0	0	0	1	-	1	0	0	0
0111	0	0	-	1	1	0	1	1	1	-	0	1	0	0
1011	0	0	-	1	1	1	0	0	1	-	1	1	0	0
1110	0	1	-	0	0	0	0	0	0	-	0	0	1	1
0011	0	1	-	0	0	1	0	0	0	-	1	1	1	1
1111	0	1	-	0	1	1	1	1	1	-	1	1	1	0
1011	0	1	-	1	0	0	0	0	0	-	1	0	1	0
0111	0	1	-	1	0	0	1	1	0	-	0	0	1	1
0100	0	1	-	1	0	1	0	0	0	-	0	1	1	1
0001	0	1	-	1	0	1	1	1	0	-	0	1	1	1
1101	0	1	-	1	1	0	0	0	1	-	0	0	1	0
1010	0	1	-	1	1	0	1	1	1	-	0	0	1	0
0010	0	1	-	1	1	1	0	0	1	-	0	1	1	0
1100	0	1	-	1	1	1	1	1	1	-	0	1	1	0

```
1001     1  0 - 0  0  0  0        0  0 - 0  1  0  1
1110     1  0 - 0  1  0  1        1  1 - 0  1  0  1
1100     1  0 - 1  0  0  0        0  0 - 1  1  0  1
1000     1  0 - 1  0  1  1        1  0 - 0  0  0  1
0001     1  0 - 1  1  1  0        0  1 - 1  1  0  1
0100     1  0 - 1  1  1  1        1  1 - 0  0  0  1
0101     1  1 - 0  0  0  0        0  0 - 1  0  1  1
0110     1  1 - 0  0  1  0        0  0 - 1  1  1  0
1101     1  1 - 0  0  1  1        1  0 - 1  0  1  0
1111     1  1 - 0  1  0  0        0  1 - 0  1  1  1
0011     1  1 - 0  1  1  1        1  1 - 1  0  1  0
1011     1  1 - 1  0  1  0        0  0 - 1  0  1  0
0111     1  1 - 1  0  1  1        1  0 - 0  0  1  1
1100     1  1 - 1  1  1  0        0  1 - 1  0  1  1
1010     1  1 - 1  1  1  1        1  1 - 0  0  1  0
```

COUPLET NO. 2

```
          3  3 - 3  3  4  4        4  3 - 5  5  3  5
   M-2    6  7 - 8  9  0  1        1  9 - 7  6  7  2
   ----   ------------------       ------------------
   0100   0  0 - 0  1  1  0        0  1 - 0  1  0  1
   0100   0  1 - 0  0  0  0        0  0 - 0  0  1  1
   1011   0  1 - 1  0  0  1        1  0 - 0  0  1  1
   0001   1  0 - 0  0  0  0        0  0 - 0  1  0  1
   1001   1  1 - 0  1  1  1        1  1 - 1  0  1  0
```

COUPLET NO. 3

```
          3  3 - 3  3  4  4        4  3 - 5  5  3  5
   M-2    6  7 - 8  9  0  1        1  9 - 7  6  7  2
   ----   ------------------       ------------------
   0111   1  0 - 0  0  0  0        0  0 - 0  1  0  1
```

Entering the couplets into the search program in a different order has no effect on the final result or effectiveness of the search program. The nine keybits which comprise KEY 1 and KEY 3 in the S-6 box are found to be the same as previously found.

To continue the solution of the three-iteration problem from this point is fairly simple. With knowledge of nine of the 28 keybits which comprise the second set of keybits, those used in the S-5, S-6, S-7, and S-8 boxes, there are any number of ways to identify additional keybits.

The described method of attacking the three-iteration problem is one that the writer found when he first looked at the "outline" of the problem where known lines of bits are shaded. But there are other various and potential "wedges" that the analyst might use when attacking the three-iteration problem. The reader might look for other methods of attacking the same problem.

Before leaving this problem, the writer would like to point out also the effectiveness of using a yellow or other light-colored marking pen of the type used for underlining. He has found such a marking pen to be almost indispensable when examining the "outlines" of DES problems, particularly those that contain a large number of iterations. The marking pen can be used not only to indicate known lines of bits, but also known or assumed to be known values of keybits, etc.

In the next chapter we shall look at the cryptography and analysis of the four-iteration problem. As might be expected, the four-iteration DES problem is signficantly more difficult than the problems which we have looked at up to this point.

Chapter V
QUESTIONS

Fill in the Blanks.

1. In the case of the three-iteration problem, one of five M sequences is unknown. That sequence is _____.

2. In a three-iteration encipherment the resulting 64-bit block of cibits is formed from two M sequences, _____ and _____.

3. Assuming knowledge of nine keybits would require making _____ trials or tests.

4. Assuming knowledge of 56 keybits would require making _____ trials or tests.

5. We are going to assume knowlege of ten keybits. This will require making 2^{10} or 1024 trials or tests. At the same time we are going to disprove an assumption by four bits not being the same. Only if the four bits are the same can the assumption be considered as possibly correct. When the four bits are the same we say that a "hit" has taken place. By accident, therefore, a hit will occur on the average every 2^4 or 16 trials or tests. In making 2^{10} trials or tests we can expect _____ trials or tests to occur by accident.

6. We are going to assume knowlege of eight keybits. When three bits match, a hit occurs. In running 2^8 trials or tests, by accident a hit can be expected to occur every 2^3 times. Therefore, with respect to one couplet we can expect 2^5 accidental hits. But if we have available two couplets, where the second couplet is capable of disproving an accidental hit found in the first couplet, on the average we will end up with _____ hits in both couplets.

7. There are _____ M sequences in a three-iteration encipherment.

8. With known plaintext there are two known M sequences, _____ and M-1.

9. In the case of 16-iterations there are a total of _____ M sequences.

10. In every DES problem we will always know _____ M sequences.

Chapter VI

THE FOUR-ITERATION PROBLEM

We have finally reached that point in our analysis of the Data Encryption Standard (DES) where the solution is no longer simple and easy, sometimes described even as trivial. With analysis of the four-iteration problem the reader will begin to see and to appreciate the difficulties facing the analyst when he attacks analytically the 16-iteration problem. But the writer must hasten to add that the four-iteration problem is not equal, nor even close, to the 16-iteration DES problem with respect to analysis. In fact, in terms of a solution to the DES, the four-iteration problem is relatively easy — although in comparison to the analysis and solution of the one, two, and three-iteration problems already covered, the four-iteration problem is much more difficult.

DESCRIPTION OF THE FOUR-ITERATION ENCIPHERMENT

An example of four-iteration DES encipherment is the following:

```
64-BIT 'DES' MASTER OR EXTERNAL KEY --
2113355-1025554-0214434-1123334-0012343-2021453-0202435-0110454-
1031975-1176107-2423401-7632789-7452553-0858846-6836043-9495226-
------------------------------------------------------------------
0000011110100111000100110111000001000101110110100010101000010110

     KEY IN HEXADECIMAL FORM = 07A7137045DA2A16


64-BIT BLOCK OF PLABITS -- (BITS WHICH FORM M-0 AND M-1)

1414042526360303141525142603362525251403252525360314041414030315
7902915780133546248079139157242413684668023546027957803568132491
------------------------------------------------------------------
0011101111011101000100011001000001001001001101110010100000000010

PLABITS IN HEXADECIMAL FORM = 3BDD119049372802
```

```
----------------------------------------------------------------------

    3333      3334      4444      4444      4555      5555      5556      6666
    3456      7890      1234      5678      9012      3456      7890      1234
    ----      ----      ----      ----      ----      ----      ----      ----
    0011   -  1100   -  0110   -  0000   -  0100   -  1011   -  1001   -  0110   M-0

    0000      0000      0111      1111      1112      2222      2222      2333
    1234      5678      9012      3456      7890      1234      5678      9012
    ----      ----      ----      ----      ----      ----      ----      ----
    0010   -  0001   -  1100   -  0110   -  0010   -  0010   -  1001   -  1100   M-1

    .........................................................................
```

```
22-1022  20-2121  10-0122  20-0131  13-0021  11-3200  02-1130  01-2102
59-6701  11-9287  75-1536  62-5810  02-2844  49-2739  92-9306  66-2145
-- ----  -- ----  -- ----  -- ----  -- ----  -- ----  -- ----  -- ----
11-0000  00-1010  00-0110  00-0001  10-0101  11-0011  10-1010  00-0001  M-1 EXP

00-0000  00-0111  11-1111  12-2222  33-3333  33-3344  44-4444  44-5555
12-3456  78-9012  34-5678  90-1234  01-2345  67-8901  23-4567  89-0123
-- ----  -- ----  -- ----  -- ----  -- ----  -- ----  -- ----  -- ----
00-1110  01-0010  00-0101  01-0010  00-1000  10-0011  01-0111  10-1011  KEY 1

11-1110  01-1000  00-0011  01-0011  10-1101  01-0000  11-1101  10-1010  ENTER

  0110  -  1100  -  1110  -  0101  -  0011  -  1010  -  0010  -  1010  EXIT

+ 0011  -  1100  -  0110  -  0000  -  0100  -  1011  -  1001  -  0110  M-0

  0000     0000     0111     1111     1112     2222     2222     2333
  1234     5678     9012     3456     7890     1234     5678     9012
  ----     ----     ----     ----     ----     ----     ----     ----
= 0101  -  0000  -  1000  -  0101  -  0111  -  0001  -  1011  -  1100  M-2

.............................................................................

22-1022  20-2121  10-0122  20-0131  13-0021  11-3200  02-1130  01-2102
59-6701  11-9287  75-1536  62-5810  02-2844  49-2739  92-9306  66-2145
-- ----  -- ----  -- ----  -- ----  -- ----  -- ----  -- ----  -- ----
11-1010  00-1010  00-0000  01-0100  00-1011  11-0101  10-1010  01-0011  M-2 EXP

11-2122  10-0122  02-2202  00-1010  54-4453  34-3344  45-5355  34-5333
01-5660  74-6917  58-3422  37-4921  06-3947  34-0287  06-1835  51-7946
-- ----  -- ----  -- ----  -- ----  -- ----  -- ----  -- ----  -- ----
01-0101  01-0001  10-1000  10-0000  11-1000  00-0111  10-0011  01-1001  KEY 2

10-1111  01-1011  10-1000  11-0100  11-0011  11-0010  00-1001  00-1010  ENTER

  0000  -  1010  -  1011  -  1010  -  0111  -  0010  -  1100  -  0011  EXIT

+ 0010  -  0001  -  1100  -  0110  -  0010  -  0010  -  1001  -  1100  M-1

  0000     0000     0111     1111     1112     2222     2222     2333
  1234     5678     9012     3456     7890     1234     5678     9012
  ----     ----     ----     ----     ----     ----     ----     ----
= 0010  -  1011  -  0111  -  1100  -  0101  -  0000  -  0101  -  1111  M-3

.............................................................................

22-1022  20-2121  10-0122  20-0131  13-0021  11-3200  02-1130  01-2102
59-6701  11-9287  75-1536  62-5810  02-2844  49-2739  92-9306  66-2145
-- ----  -- ----  -- ----  -- ----  -- ----  -- ----  -- ----  -- ----
01-0110  00-1110  01-0001  10-1111  11-0101  10-1010  00-0110  00-0100  M-3 EXP

01-2021  12-0220  10-2120  10-0211  43-3435  43-5535  34-3533  45-4444
34-3127  14-7585  84-7016  52-8039  26-1781  19-7672  56-2034  45-0359
-- ----  -- ----  -- ----  -- ----  -- ----  -- ----  -- ----  -- ----
10-1000  10-0001  11-1000  00-1100  01-0100  10-1001  01-1100  01-1110  KEY 3

11-1110  10-1111  10-1001  10-0011  10-0001  00-0011  01-1010  01-1010  ENTER

  0110  -  1111  -  0001  -  0000  -  0010  -  1111  -  0101  -  0110  EXIT

+ 0101  -  0000  -  1000  -  0101  -  0111  -  0001  -  1011  -  1100  M-2

  0000     0000     0111     1111     1112     2222     2222     2333
  1234     5678     9012     3456     7890     1234     5678     9012
  ----     ----     ----     ----     ----     ----     ----     ----
= 0011  -  1111  -  1001  -  0101  -  0101  -  1110  -  1110  -  1010  M-4

.............................................................................
```

```
22-1022   20-2121   10-0122   20-0131   13-0021   11-3200   02-1130   01-2102
59-6701   11-9287   75-1536   62-5810   02-2844   49-2739   92-9306   66-2145
-- ----   -- ----   -- ----   -- ----   -- ----   -- ----   -- ----   -- ----
11-1111   10-1100   01-0011   10-1110   00-0101   10-0111   11-0001   11-1011   M-4 EXP

10-2101   11-0201   02-0020   12-1122   44-5553   54-4455   43-5444   33-3334
58-7961   40-2348   94-5387   21-6765   89-3202   53-0614   46-6215   94-5107
-- ----   -- ----   -- ----   -- ----   -- ----   -- ----   -- ----   -- ----
01-1001   00-0111   00-1100   00-1000   10-1111   11-1100   01-0011   00-0001   KEY 4

10-0110   10-1011   01-1111   10-0110   10-1010   01-1011   10-0010   11-1010   ENTER

  0010  -   0110  -   0001  -   0111  -   1100  -   1110  -   1011  -   1001   EXIT

+ 0010  -   1011  -   0111  -   1100  -   0101  -   0000  -   0101  -   1111   M-3

  3333      3334      4444      4444      4555      5555      5556      6666
  3456      7890      1234      5678      9012      3456      7890      1234
  ----      ----      ----      ----      ----      ----      ----      ----
= 0000  -   1101  -   0110  -   1011  -   1001  -   1110  -   1110  -   0110   M-5
```

RESULTING 64-BIT BLOCK OF CIBITS -- (FORMED FROM M-4 AND M-5)

```
14140425262636030314152514260336252525140325252536031404140303141 5
790291578013354624807913915724241368466802354602795780352413689 1
```

```
0101101100111010101011011011001111111101111110001100111011000000 0
```

CIBITS IN HEXADECIMAL FORM = 5B3AADB3FBF19DC0

Just as the single-iteration ciphering process uses one sub-key, KEY 1, the two-iteration ciphering process two sub-keys, KEY 1 and KEY 2, and the three-iteration ciphering process three sub-keys, KEY 1, KEY 2, and KEY 3, the four-iteration ciphering process uses four sub-keys, KEY 1, KEY 2, KEY 3, and KEY 4. As previously mentioned, keybits 01 through 28 are used exclusively for the first four S-boxes and keybits 30 through 57 are used exclusively for the last four S-boxes. This fact provides a means which we might attack the four-iteration DES problem.

ANALYZING A FOUR-ITERATION PROBLEM

We are given the following three couplets having a common key:

Couplet No. 1 —   Plaintext: 26955F6835AF609A
                  Ciphertext: 50316E3B9923E51F

Couplet No. 2 —   Plaintext: 18D4900AC328772F
                  Ciphertext: DA6417A32621DCF6

Couplet No. 3 —   Plaintext: 0000000000000000
Ciphertext: BF42B25C497FC424

As a first step we can begin our analysis by looking at Couplet No. 1 with its known lines of bits shaded.

COUPLET NO. 1

64-BIT 'DES' MASTER OR EXTERNAL KEY --

2113355-1025554-0214434-1123334-0012343-2021453-0202435-0110454-
1031975-1176107-2423401-7632789-7452553-0858846-6836043-9495226-
----

    KEY IN HEXADECIMAL FORM =

64-BIT BLOCK OF PLABITS -- (BITS WHICH FORM M-0 AND M-1)

1414042526360303141525142603362525251403252525360314041414030315
7902915780133546248079139157242413684668023546027957803568132491

0010011010010101010111110110100000110101101011110110000010011010

PLABITS IN HEXADECIMAL FORM = 26955F6835AF609A

3333	3334	4444	4444	4555	5555	5556	6666	
3456	7890	1234	5678	9012	3456	7890	1234	
----	----	----	----	----	----	----	----	
1011 -	0110 -	1011 -	0100 -	0100 -	0001 -	0110 -	1110	M-0
0000	0000	0111	1111	1112	2222	2222	2333	
1234	5678	9012	3456	7890	1234	5678	9012	
----	----	----	----	----	----	----	----	
0100 -	1000 -	0110 -	0011 -	0011 -	0011 -	1111 -	0101	M-1

. . . .

22-1022	20-2121	10-0122	20-0131	13-0021	11-3200	02-1130	01-2102	
59-6701	11-9287	75-1536	62-5810	02-2844	49-2739	92-9306	66-2145	
-- ----	-- ----	-- ----	-- ----	-- ----	-- ----	-- ----	-- ----	
10-1010	00-0010	01-0111	11-1001	11-1010	01-1100	00-1010	01-0101	M-1 EXP

00-0000	00-0111	11-1111	12-2222	33-3333	33-3344	44-4444	44-5555	
12-3456	78-9012	34-5678	90-1234	01-2345	67-8901	23-4567	89-0123	
-- ----	-- ----	-- ----	-- ----	-- ----	-- ----	-- ----	-- ----	

KEY 1

ENTER

EXIT

+ 1011 -	0110 -	1011 -	0100 -	0100 -	0001 -	0110 -	1110	M-0
0000	0000	0111	1111	1112	2222	2222	2333	
1234	5678	9012	3456	7890	1234	5678	9012	
----	----	----	----	----	----	----	----	
=								M-2

. . . .

```
22-1022  20-2121  10-0122  20-0131  13-0021  11-3200  02-1130  01-2102
59-6701  11-9287  75-1536  62-5810  02-2844  49-2739  92-9306  66-2145
-- ----  -- ----  -- ----  -- ----  -- ----  -- ----  -- ----  -- ----

                                                                        M-2 EXP

11-2122  10-0122  02-2202  00-1010  54-4453  34-3344  45-5355  34-5333
01-5660  74-6917  58-3422  37-4921  06-3947  34-0287  06-1835  51-7946
-- ----  -- ----  -- ----  -- ----  -- ----  -- ----  -- ----  -- ----

                                                                        KEY 2

                                                                        ENTER

                                                                        EXIT

+ 0100  - 1000  - 0110  - 0011  - 0011  - 0011  - 1111  - 0101   M-1

   0000     0000     0111     1111     1112     2222     2222     2333
   1234     5678     9012     3456     7890     1234     5678     9012
   ----     ----     ----     ----     ----     ----     ----     ----
=                                                                       M-3

. . . . . . . . . . . . . . . . . . . . . . . . . . . . . . . . . . . . .

22-1022  20-2121  10-0122  20-0131  13-0021  11-3200  02-1130  01-2102
59-6701  11-9287  75-1536  62-5810  02-2844  49-2739  92-9306  66-2145
-- ----  -- ----  -- ----  -- ----  -- ----  -- ----  -- ----  -- ----

                                                                        M-3 EXP

01-2021  12-0220  10-2120  10-0211  43-3435  43-5535  34-3533  45-4444
34-3127  14-7585  84-7016  52-8039  26-1781  19-7672  56-2034  45-0359
-- ----  -- ----  -- ----  -- ----  -- ----  -- ----  -- ----  -- ----

                                                                        KEY 3

                                                                        ENTER

                                                                        EXIT

+                                                                       M-2

   0000     0000     0111     1111     1112     2222     2222     2333
   1234     5678     9012     3456     7890     1234     5678     9012
   ----     ----     ----     ----     ----     ----     ----     ----
= 0100  - 1010  - 0010  - 0110  - 0110  - 1110  - 0010  - 0111   M-4

. . . . . . . . . . . . . . . . . . . . . . . . . . . . . . . . . . . . .

22-1022  20-2121  10-0122  20-0131  13-0021  11-3200  02-1130  01-2102
59-6701  11-9287  75-1536  62-5810  02-2844  49-2739  92-9306  66-2145
-- ----  -- ----  -- ----  -- ----  -- ----  -- ----  -- ----  -- ----
00-0101  10-0000  01-0110  01-1110  01-1001  11-1100  01-1010  00-1100   M-4 EXP

10-2101  11-0201  02-0020  12-1122  44-5553  54-4455  43-5444  33-3334
58-7961  40-2348  94-5387  21-6765  89-3202  53-0614  46-6215  94-5107
-- ----  -- ----  -- ----  -- ----  -- ----  -- ----  -- ----  -- ----

                                                                        KEY 4

                                                                        ENTER

                                                                        EXIT

+                                                                       M-3

   3333     3334     4444     4444     4555     5555     5556     6666
   3456     7890     1234     5678     9012     3456     7890     1234
   ----     ----     ----     ----     ----     ----     ----     ----
= 1101  - 1111  - 0101  - 1000  - 1010  - 0100  - 0110  - 0110   M-5
```

RESULTING 64-BIT BLOCK OF CIBITS -- (FORMED FROM M-4 AND M-5)

1414042526360303141525142603362525251403252525360314041403031415
7902915780133546248079139157242413684668023546027957803524136891

0101000000110001011011100011101110011001001000111110010100011111

CIBITS IN HEXADECIMAL FORM = 50316E3B9923E51F

Looking at Couplet No. 1 now before us, we see that there are four sub-keys unknown, KEY 1, KEY 2, KEY 3, and KEY 4, plus two M sequences likewise unknown, M-2 and M-3.

The direction that our cryptanalytic attack will take can generally be expected to follow the line of attack taken in the previous case of the three-iteration DES problem. That is — we shall endeavor to prove or disprove the validity of a surmised or assumed number of bits. In the case of the three-iteration DES problem, we surmised or assumed knowledge of the values of nine bits. This gave us 2^9 or 512 possible choices for the values of the nine bits. We then tried or tested these possible choices, one after another, using a computer of course, until we reached a choice which gave us some positive result. Since we were surmising or assuming knowledge of keybits, we were able to test the same keybits in another couplet, thus confirming the positive result from the first couplet. In the present problem we are going to endeavor to use the same approach towards solution.

While we might surmise or assume knowledge of bits contained in either or both of the sequences M-2 and M-3, such an approach would narrow our solution to dependency solely on one couplet, since the sequences M-2 and M-3 are different in each couplet. A better approach would be to make our solution dependent on surmised or assumed knowledge of keybits, since each couplet uses the same keybits.

The question then arises regarding which keybits shall we surmise or assume knowledge of. Obviously, we would like to surmise or assume knowledge of a minimal number of keybits. The fewer the keybits we surmise or assume knowledge of the fewer will be the number of "trials" necessary to prove or disprove the validity of values of the surmised or assumed keybits.

One fact seems to stand out with respect to the Data Encryption Standard

(DES). The keybits 01 through 28 affect exclusively the bits which enter the first four S-boxes, S-1, S-2, S-3, and S-4. On the other hand, the keybits 30 through 57 affect exclusively the bits which enter the last four S-boxes, S-5, S-6, S-7, and S-8. On the surface this would appear to be an inherent weakness in the cryptography of the DES. However, whether or not it really affects the cryptographic security of the DES is something else. Perhaps the best that we can say is that the phenomenon of the keybits being divided into two groups or classes, those keybits 01 through 28 and those keybits 30 through 57, and the effect that these two distinctive groups or classes have respectively on the first four S-boxes and the last four S-boxes _may_ potentially provide the cryptanalyst with a "wedge" that he _might_ take advantage of.

Concerning the present four-iteration problem, let us therefore surmise or assume knowledge of 28 keybits, the keybits 01 through 28. With the knowledge of these 28 keybits, will we be able to deduce or reconstruct the total unknown 56 keybits which comprise the effective bits of the initial, master or external key?

While 2^{28} or 268,435,456 may appear to be at first glance an enormously large number, and it is, with respect to 2^{56} it is fairly small. It is important to remember also that the "trials" and tests being discussed here are those that in the pragmatic world of analysis will be done by high-speed computers making a great number of parallel computations at the same time. Moreover, with care in the selection of the known keybits, 2^{28} may even be reduced to 2^{27} which will reduce the potential number of "trials" to 134,217,728 — a reduction of 50%.

Therefore, let us look at Couplet No. 1 with the keybits 01 through 28 being known. It follows that the first 16 bits comprising M-2 and M-3 now become known, as well as a number of bits in M-2 EXP and M-3 EXP. The "outline" of Couplet No. 1 appears as follows:

```
64-BIT 'DES' MASTER OR EXTERNAL KEY --

2113355-1025554-0214434-1123334-0012343-2021453-0202435-0110454-
1031975-1176107-2423401-7632789-7452553-0858846-6836043-9495226-
-----------------------------------------------------------------

    KEY IN HEXADECIMAL FORM =
```

64-BIT BLOCK OF PLABITS -- (BITS WHICH FORM M-0 AND M-1)

```
141404252636030314152514260336252525140325252536031404141403031 5
790291578013354624807913915724241368466802354602795780356813249 1
---------------------------------------------------------------
0010011010010101010111110110100001101011010111101100001001101 0
```

PLABITS IN HEXADECIMAL FORM = 26955F6835AF609A

```
   3333      3334      4444      4444      4555      5555      5556      6666
   3456      7890      1234      5678      9012      3456      7890      1234
   ----      ----      ----      ----      ----      ----      ----      ----
   1011  -   0110  -   1011  -   0100  -   0100  -   0001  -   0110  -   1110   M-0

   0000      0000      0111      1111      1112      2222      2222      2333
   1234      5678      9012      3456      7890      1234      5678      9012
   ----      ----      ----      ----      ----      ----      ----      ----
   0100  -   1000  -   0110  -   0011  -   0011  -   0011  -   1111  -   0101   M-1
```

. . . .

```
22-1022   20-2121   10-0122   20-0131   13-0021   11-3200   02-1130   01-2102
59-6701   11-9287   75-1536   62-5810   02-2844   49-2739   92-9306   66-2145
--  ----  --  ----  --  ----  --  ----  --  ----  --  ----  --  ----  --  ----
10-1010   00-0010   01-0111   11-1001   11-1010   01-1100   00-1010   01-0101   M-1 EXP

00-0000   00-0111   11-1111   12-2222   33-3333   33-3344   44-4444   44-5555
12-3456   78-9012   34-5678   90-1234   01-2345   67-8901   23-4567   89-0123
--  ----  --  ----  --  ----  --  ----  --  ----  --  ----  --  ----  --  ----
11-1100   11-0000   00-0001   11-0000                                          KEY 1

01-0110   11-0010   01-0110   00-1001                                          ENTER

   1101  -   1010  -   0110  -   0010                                          EXIT

 + 1011  -   0110  -   1011  -   0100  -   0100  -   0001  -   0110  -   1110   M-0

   0000      0000      0111      1111      1112      2222      2222      2333
   1234      5678      9012      3456      7890      1234      5678      9012
   ----      ----      ----      ----      ----      ----      ----      ----
 = 0110  -   1100  -   1101  -   0110                                          M-2
```

. . . .

```
22-1022   20-2121   10-0122   20-0131   13-0021   11-3200   02-1130   01-2102
59-6701   11-9287   75-1536   62-5810   02-2844   49-2739   92-9306   66-2145
--  ----  --  ----  --  ----  --  ----  --  ----  --  ----  --  ----  --  ----
   -00     0- 1      1-01      1-1  1    1- 10 1   1 -  11   1 - 0 1   10- 00   M-2 EXP

11-2122   10-0122   02-2202   00-1010   54-4453   34-3344   45-5355   34-5333
01-5660   74-6917   58-3422   37-4921   06-3947   34-0287   06-1835   51-7946
--  ----  --  ----  --  ----  --  ----  --  ----  --  ----  --  ----  --  ----
00-1011   01-0101   00-0010   11-0001                                          KEY 2

..-10..   .1-.0..   .1-01..   .0-1..0                                          ENTER

   1111  -   0001  -   1010  -   0001                                          EXIT

 + 0100  -   1000  -   0110  -   0011  -   0011  -   0011  -   1111  -   0101   M-1

   0000      0000      0111      1111      1112      2222      2222      2333
   1234      5678      9012      3456      7890      1234      5678      9012
   ----      ----      ----      ----      ----      ----      ----      ----
 = 1011  -   1001  -   1100  -   0010                                          M-3
```

22-1022	20-2121	10-0122	20-0131	13-0021	11-3200	02-1130	01-2102
59-6701	11-9287	75-1536	62-5810	02-2844	49-2739	92-9306	66-2145
-- ----	-- ----	-- ----	-- ----	-- ----	-- ----	-- ----	-- ----
-00	1- 0	1-11	0-1 1	1 -01 0	0 - 11	1 - 0 0	00- 01	M-3 EXP

01-2021	12-0220	10-2120	10-0211	43-3435	43-5535	34-3533	45-4444
34-3127	14-7585	84-7016	52-8039	26-1781	19-7672	56-2034	45-0359
-- ----	-- ----	-- ----	-- ----	-- ----	-- ----	-- ----	-- ----
10-0100	00-1100	11-1000	01-1101					KEY 3

..-01..	.1-.1..	.0=01..	.1-0..0	ENTER
0010 -	0110 -	1111 -	0000	EXIT
+ 0110 -	1100 -	1101 -	0110	M-2

0000	0000	0111	1111	1112	2222	2222	2333
1234	5678	9012	3456	7890	1234	5678	9012
----	----	----	----	----	----	----	----
= 0100 -	1010 -	0010 -	0110 -	0110 -	1110 -	0010 -	0111	M-4

. . . .

22-1022	20-2121	10-0122	20-0131	13-0021	11-3200	02-1130	01-2102
59-6701	11-9287	75-1536	62-5810	02-2844	49-2739	92-9306	66-2145
-- ----	-- ----	-- ----	-- ----	-- ----	-- ----	-- ----	-- ----
00-0101	10-0000	01-0110	01-1110	01-1001	11-1100	01-1010	00-1100	M-4 EXP

10-2101	11-0201	02-0020	12-1122	44-5553	54-4455	43-5444	33-3334
58-7961	40-2348	94-5387	21-6765	89-3202	53-0614	46-6215	94-5107
-- ----	-- ----	-- ----	-- ----	-- ----	-- ----	-- ----	-- ----
01-1100	00-1011	00-0101	00-0011					KEY 4

01-1001	10-1011	01-0011	01-1101	ENTER
0110 -	0110 -	1001 -	1010	EXIT
+ 1011 -	1001 -	1100 -	0010	M-3

3333	3334	4444	4444	4555	5555	5556	6666
3456	7890	1234	5678	9012	3456	7890	1234
----	----	----	----	----	----	----	----
= 1101 -	1111 -	0101 -	1000 -	1010 -	0100 -	0110 -	0110	M-5

RESULTING 64-BIT BLOCK OF CIBITS -- (FORMED FROM M-4 AND M-5)

14140425263603031415251426033625252514032525253603140414030314151415
79029157801335462480791391572424136846680235460279578035241368917

0101000000011000101101110001110111001100100100011111100101000011111

CIBITS IN HEXADECIMAL FORM = 50316E3B9923E51F

Knowledge of the keybits 01 through 28 permit us by means of the first sub-key, KEY 1, to recover the first half or the first 16 bits of M-2. Likewise, knowledge of the same keybits permit us by means of the last sub-key, KEY 4, to recover the first half or the first 16 bits of M-3. Even with this seemingly abundant amount of knowledge, solution of the four-iteration problem does not arrive easily. There is still an amount of careful analysis that must be done in order to recover all 56 keybits used to encipher the given couplets.

One important factor in favor of the analyst is that the bits of M-2 and M-3 are dispersed and expanded in a known manner to form M-2 EXP and M-3 EXP. Consider the 16 known bits of M-2, those designated as 01 through 16. Since two bits of each block of four appear twice in the expansion, the 16 known bits of M-2 in M-2 EXP amount to 24 known bits. Very interestingly, the 24 known bits in M-2 EXP divide themselves into ten known bits in the first half of M-2 EXP and 14 known bits in the second half of M-2 EXP. The same holds true of the 16 known bits of M-3. As the first 16 bits of M-3 they divide themselves exactly in the same fashion, ten known bits in the first half of M-3 EXP and 14 known bits in the second half of M-3 EXP. It is evident also that the manner in which the bits are dispersed and expanded is not the result of accident. Great care by the creators of the Data Encryption Standard (DES) was taken to insure that the method of dispersion and expansion was spread through the eight blocks of six bits each — each block affecting a particular S-block — so that the analyst would have a maximum of difficulty in finding what we might term a "thread of opportunity" which might run through the 16 iterations which comprise the Data Encryption Standard (DES).

That ten known bits occur in he first half of the expanded M sequence vs. 14 known bits in the second half of the expanded M sequence — when given the first half of a M sequence — is not accidental. Analysis is distinctively made more difficult. But in spite of these roadblocks or barricades, let us see how we might prove or disprove the validity of the values selected for the first 28 keybits, 01 through 28.

Let us look at the following four lines from the "outline" just made:

```
22-1022   20-2121   10-0122   20-0131   13-0021   11-3200   02-1130   01-2102
59-6701   11-9287   75-1536   62-5810   02-2844   49-2739   92-9306   66-2145
--  ----   --  ----   --  ----   --  ----   --  ----   --  ----   --  ----   --  ----
    -00     0- 1     1-01      1-1  1     1 -10 1    1 -  11    1 - 0 1    10- 00     M-2 EXP

11-2122   10-0122   02-2202   00-1010   54-4453   34-3344   45-5355   34-5333
01-5660   74-6917   58-3422   37-4921   06-3947   34-0287   06-1835   51-7946
--  ----   --  ----   --  ----   --  ----   --  ----   --  ----   --  ----   --  ----
00-1011   01-0101   00-0010   11-0001                                          KEY 2

..-10..   .1-.0..   .1-01..   .0-1..0                                          ENTER

  1111  -   0001   -  1010   -  0001                                           EXIT
```

Our analysis now will focus on those bits which affect the first four S-boxes:

22-1022	20-2121	10-0122	20-0131	
59-6701	11-9287	75-1536	62-5810	
-- ----	-- ----	-- ----	-- ----	
-00	0- 1	1-01	1-1 1	M-2 EXP
11-2122	10-0122	02-2202	00-1010	
01-5660	74-6917	58-3422	37-4921	
-- ----	-- ----	-- ----	-- ----	
00-1011	01-0101	00-0010	11-0001	KEY 2
..-10..	.1-.0..	.1-01..	.0-1..0	ENTER
1111 —	0001 —	1010 —	0001	EXIT

We shall attempt to recover the unknown bits in the above sequence of bits which comprise the first half of M-2 EXP. By looking at the contents of the first four S-boxes in their <u>reverse mode</u>, which are provided in Appendix F, we can attempt to find the bits which enter the S-boxes even though we have only partial identifications of the values which actually entered the boxes.

Using the above EXIT values, let us take a look at the possible ENTER values from the Contents of the S-boxes in their <u>reverse mode</u>:

00-0101	00-0001	00-0000	00-1000
01-0001	01-1010	01-0111	01-1100
10-1000	10-0000	10-1101	10-1001
11-<u>0000</u>	11-<u>0011</u>	11-<u>0001</u>	11-<u>0101</u>
1111	0001	1010	0001

In the case of the S-1 box, it is evident that the ENTER value must be 10-1000. Likewise, in the case of the S-3 box, it is evident that the ENTER value must be 01-0111; and in the case of the S-4 box, it is evident that the ENTER value must be 00-1000. Only in the case of the S-2 box is there a question of values. Two values seem to fit: 01-1010 and 11-0011.

If we enter into the S-1 box, the S-3 box, and the S-4 box, the above known ENTER values <u>and add (modulo 2) the values of KEY 2</u>, the result will be recovered bit values in M-2 EXP. Moreover, since there are repeated and similar bits in M-2 EXP, when we look at the values in M-2 EXP there will confirmation that our selected 28 keybits, 01 through 28, are correct.

The sequence of bits comprising the first half of M-2 EXP *after* entering into the S-1 box, the S-3 box, and the S-4 box, the determined ENTER values which fit the given partial bit patterns, termed adumbrations, and *after* adding (modulo 2) the values of KEY 2 is as follows:

22-1022	20-2121	10-0122	20-0131	
59-6701	11-9287	75-1536	62-5810	
-- ----	-- ----	-- ----	-- ----	
10-0011	0- 1	01-0101	11-1001	M-2 EXP

The repeated and similar bits in M-2 EXP all appear to confirm the validity of the selected 28 keybits. Note also that several new identified bits, based on repeated and similar bits in the adjacent groups, can now be added, so that M-2 EXP appears as follows:

22-1022	20-2121	10-0122	20-0131	
59-6701	11-9287	75-1536	62-5810	
-- ----	-- ----	-- ----	-- ----	
10-0011	10-01 0	01-0101	11-1001	M-2 EXP

Going back to the two values which seemed to fit the ENTER value for the S-2 box, 01-1010 and 11-0011, after adding (modulo 2) the value of the bits of KEY 2 which affect the S-2 box (01-0101), the two possible values for the bits in M-2 EXP can be obtained: 00-1111 and 10-0110. Of these two values it is evident that 10-0110 fits nicely into the above adumbration, so that the first half of M-2 EXP appears as follows:

22-1022	20-2121	10-0122	20-0131	
59-6701	11-9287	75-1536	62-5810	
-- ----	-- ----	-- ----	-- ----	
10-0011	10-0110	01-0101	11-1001	M-2 EXP

That we have a seemingly valid sequence of bits for the first half of M-2 EXP does not provide proof that the selected 28 keybits (01 through 28) are correct. Where the number of trials in a "trial and error" test or brute-force attack is large, the test or attack being performed of course by means of a computer, there will always be results which appear to be correct yet are actually only the result of chance. Many an analyst has lost days of time following an elusive lead that might occur only once in 500,000 trials. But if you are making 10,000,000 trials, how many results of chance can you expect?

Therefore, in the present case, although the first half of M-2 EXP, above, appears to confirm the validity of the selected keybits, we still need much more evidence to really confirm that the values selected for the keybits 01 through 28 are correct.

Perhaps the first place we can turn to with respect to the confirmation process is to again look at the "outline" of Couplet No. 1 where keybits 01 through 28 are assumed to be known. This time, however, let us focus our attention on the following four lines:

```
22-1022   20-2121   10-0122   20-0131   13-0021   11-3200   02-1130   01-2102
59-6701   11-9287   75-1536   62-5810   02-2844   49-2739   92-9306   66-2145
--  ----  --  ----  --  ----  --  ----  --  ----  --  ----  --  ----  --  ----
    -00      1- 0      1-11      0-1 1    1 -01 0   0 -  11   1 - 0 0   00- 01    M-3 EXP

01-2021   12-0220   10-2120   10-0211   43-3435   43-5535   34-3533   45-4444
34-3127   14-7585   84-7016   52-8039   26-1781   19-7672   56-2034   45-0359
--  ----  --  ----  --  ----  --  ----  --  ----  --  ----  --  ----  --  ----
10-0100   00-1100   11-1000   01-1101                                           KEY 3

..-01..   .1-.1..   .0-01..   .1-0..0                                           ENTER

 0010   -   0110   -   1111   -   0000                                          EXIT
```

It is immediately evident that we are faced with a problem similar to that just discussed. This time, however, instead of recovering bits in M-2 EXP, we shall recover bits in M-3 EXP. Bits which affect the first four S-boxes followed by the possible ENTER values (from the Contents of the S-boxes in their reverse mode) based on the given EXIT values follow:

```
22-1022          20-2121          10-0122          20-0131
59-6701          11-9287          75-1536          62-5810
--  ----         --  ----         --  ----         --  ----
    -00              1- 0             1-11             0-1  1      M-3 EXP

01-2021          12-0220          10-2120          10-0211
34-3127          14-7585          84-7016          52-8039
--  ----         --  ----         --  ----         --  ----
10-0100          00-1100          11-1000          01-1101        KEY 3

..-01..          .1-.1..          .0-01..          .1-0..0        ENTER

 0010      -      0110      -      1111      -      0000          EXIT

00-0100          00-0100          00-0110          00-0100
01-0101          01-1100          01-1110          01-0110
10-0110          10-1011          10-0101          10-0011
11-0011          11-1001          11-1001          11-0010
 0010            0110            1111             0000
```

A look at the above possible ENTER values quickly shows that identifying the four adumbrations of the ENTER line will not be quite as easy as it was previously. Only in the case of the S-2 box is there a set of unique bits. In the S-3 and S-4 boxes there are two sets of bits which fit the adumbrations of the ENTER line, while in the S-1 box there are three sets of bits which fit the adumbration of the ENTER line.

Let us now look at the known bits on the M-3 EXP line, together with the possible ENTER values (from the Contents of the S-boxes in their _reverse_ _mode_ based on the given EXIT values) with the bits of KEY 3 added (modulo 2). That is, the possible ENTER values will now be in terms of the M-3 EXP bits, as follows:

22-1022	20-2121	10-0122	20-0131	
59-6701	11-9287	75-1536	62-5810	
-- ----	-- ----	-- ----	-- ----	
-00	1- 0	1-11	0-1 1	M-3 EXP
10-0000	00-1000	11-1110	01-1001	
11-0001	01-0000	10-0110	00-1011	
00-0010	10-0111	01-1101	11-1110	
01-0111	11-0101	00-0001	10-1111	
0010	0110	1111	0000	

From this point we can extend the unique set of bits found in the S-2 box to M-3 EXP, and at the same time eliminate the impossible sets of bits in the other S-boxes which will not fit the remaining three adumbrations:

22-1022	20-2121	10-0122	20-0131	
59-6701	11-9287	75-1536	62-5810	
-- ----	-- ----	-- ----	-- ----	
-00	01-0000	1-11	0-1 1	M-3 EXP
10-0000				
11-0001		11-1110	00-1011	
00-0010	01-0000	01-1101	10-1111	
0010	0110	1111	0000	

From the above possible ENTER values, now in terms of the M-3 EXP bits, while there is still no actual proof of the validity of the selected 28 keybits, on the plus side there is nothing to disprove their validity.

Can we now go further in filling in the gaps in the above adumbrations? The answer is affirmative. Since there are a number of repeated or similar bits in M-3 EXP, we can use these repetitions to good advantage.

Examination of the groups of bits in an expanded line, such as M–3 EXP, shows that _four_ bits of each group are repeated in adjacent groups. More specifically, two bits of each group are repeated in the group immediately to the right and two bits of each group are repeated in the group immediately to the left.

In the case of the group of bits in M–3 EXP which affect the S–2 box, the bits numbered 21 and 29 are repeated in the group of bits which affect the S–1 box and the bits numbered 01 and 17 are repeated in the group of bits which affect the S–3 box. Since we know the bits in M–3 EXP which affect the S–2 box, we can easily pass two identifications to the groups of bits adjacent on each side. Actually, in the case at hand, since the bit numbered 01 is already identified in two groups, we can only pass a total of three identifications to adjacent groups. The M–3 EXP line plus the possible ENTER values, in terms of the M–3 EXP bits, therefore, now appears as follows:

22–1022	20–2121	10–0122	20–0131	
59–6701	11–9287	75–1536	62–5810	
-- ----	-- ----	-- ----	-- ----	
0–00 0	01–0000	01–11	0–1 1	M–3 EXP

10–0000				
11–0001		11–1110	00–1011	
00–0010	01–0000	01–1101	10–1111	
0010	0110	1111	0000	

With two new bits in the group of bits in M–3 EXP which affect the S–1 box and one additional new bit in the group of bits in M–3 EXP which affect the S–3 box, the possible ENTER values, above, in the S–1 box are reduced to two; and in the S–3 box are reduced to one. The group of bits in M–3 EXP which affect the M–3 box, therefore, are identified as 01–1101. With the bit number 26 identified as 1, the group of bits in M–3 EXP affecting the S–4 box must be 10–1111. In short, we have identified M–3 EXP now as:

22–1022	20–2121	10–0122	20–0131	
59–6701	11–9287	75–1536	62–5810	
-- ----	-- ----	-- ----	-- ----	
0–00 0	01–0000	01–1101	10–1111	M–3 EXP

Only the group of bits in M–3 EXP which affect the S–1 box remain as a group unidentified; although even in this group of bits, we know four of the six bits plus the knowledge that bits 25 and 20 are of opposite value.

With respect to analysis of Couplet No. 1, up to this point, as we have gone through the somewhat mechanical steps of recovering all or most of the bits in the first halves of M-2 EXP and M-3 EXP, there have been no conflicts. This, however, still does not leave us with a solution to the four-iteration DES problem. On the other hand, since no conflicts have arisen, at least we can feel with a certain amount of confidence that the selected keybits 01 through 28 are correct. Keep in mind, of course, that if this were an actual problem which we were attacking by means of a computer, at the moment of any conflict or impossibility with regard to the bits of M-2 EXP or M-3 EXP, we would turn immediately to another selection of keybits 01 through 28.

With the assumption that we have selected the correct keybits 01 through 28 and that we have recovered all or most of the bits comprising the first halves of M-2 EXP and M-3 EXP, let us continue with the solution process.

GOING AFTER THE KEYBITS 30 THROUGH 57

This time let us go back to that point where we recovered the bits which comprise the first half of M-2 EXP. Note that the newly identified bits in M-2 EXP are actually bits which have come from the expansion of the bits in the second half of M-2. Therefore, after putting these bits back into M-2, and after identifying various bits in the previous EXIT line, since the bits of M-0 are known, the lines between M-1 EXP and M-2 appear as the following:

22-1022	20-2121	10-0122	20-0131	13-0021	11-3200	02-1130	01-2102	
59-6701	11-9287	75-1536	62-5810	02-2844	49-2739	92-9306	66-2145	
-- ----	-- ----	-- ----	-- ----	-- ----	-- ----	-- ----	-- ----	
10-1010	00-0010	01-0111	11-1001	11-1010	01-1100	00-1010	01-0101	M-1 EXP
00-0000	00-0111	11-1111	12-2222	33-3333	33-3344	44-4444	44-5555	
12-3456	78-9012	34-5678	90-1234	01-2345	67-8901	23-4567	89-0123	
-- ----	-- ----	-- ----	-- ----	-- ----	-- ----	-- ----	-- ----	
11-1100	11-0000	00-0001	11-0000					KEY 1
01-0110	11-0010	01-0110	00-1001					ENTER
1101 -	1010 -	0110 -	0010 -	01.1 -	1.0. -	10.1 -	1.1.	EXIT
+ 1011 -	0110 -	1011 -	0100 -	0100 -	0001 -	0110 -	1110	M-0
0000	0000	0111	1111	1112	2222	2222	2333	
1234	5678	9012	3456	7890	1234	5678	9012	
----	----	----	----	----	----	----	----	
= 0110 -	1100 -	1101 -	0110 -	00 1 -	1 0 -	11 1 -	0 0	M-2

Given the adumbrations formed by the bits exiting the last four S-boxes, assisted also by similar adumbrations formed in the fourth iteration, provides the analyst with a means to recover the keybits 30 through 57. Moreover, while the analyst might recover the last 28 keybits by carefully playing possible six-bit key values back and forth between KEY 1 and Key 4, plus working in the keybits found in KEY 2 and KEY 3, the analyst has also has another weapon available which will greatly aid recovery of the keybits. This weapon is the availability of additional couplets. Thus, before even trying to recover the remaining 28 keybits using Couplet No. 1, the analyst probably would attack Couplet No. 2, using the same procedure used in the case of Couplet No. 1. That is, the same selected keybits 01 through 28 would be applied to Couplet No. 2 and assuming no conflicts occurred, the first halves of M-2 EXP and M-3 EXP would be totally or partially recovered. The attack against Couplet No. 2 would serve, therefore, not only to verify the correctness of the selected 28 keybits 01 through 28, but also to provide additional adumbrations to identify the keybits 30 through 57. The reader might also keep in mind that there is even a third couplet available which will further provide verification of the correctness of the selected 28 keybits 01 through 28, plus providing more material to work with when looking for the values of the last 28 keybits.

It should now be evident that the four-iteration problem provides no particular difficulties if we can make the assumption of knowing the 28 keybits 01 through 28. While 2^{28} is a large number, when using a computer, and especially a computer with a multiplicity of processors, the search for 28 keybits is not particularly a difficult task. In fact, when compared to the search for 2^{56} keybits, the search for 2^{28} keybits may even border on the trivial.

EXERCISE

A form of brute—force attack has been devised to be used against a four—iteration DES problem. The attack depends upon the correct selection of 28 keybits, the keybits 01 through 28. In the course of the attack against three given couplets, all having a common key, a particular selection of 28 keybits has been found which offers no conflicts in the three couplets. With respect to this particular selection of 28 keybits, the recovered bits in M—2 EXP are passed back to the last half of M—2. Looking at the S—7 box in the first iteration, three of four bits have been identified in the four—bit value which exits the S—7 box. Since in this case we have data or material from three couplets, it seems likely that we will be able to re—cover the keybits of KEY 1 which affect the S—7 box. Therefore, given the following lines of data from M—1 EXP to M—2 with respect to the given three couplets, recover the six bits of KEY 1 which affect the S—7 box in the first iteration.

Couplet No. 1	Couplet No. 2	Couplet No. 3	
02—1130	02—1130	02—1130	
92—9306	92—9306	92—9306	
—— ————	—— ————	—— ————	
00—1010	11—1101	00—0000	M—1 EXP
44—4444	44—4444	44—4444	
23—4567	23—4567	23—4567	
—— ————	—— ————	—— ————	
			KEY 1
			ENTER
10.1	00.1	11.1	EXIT
0110	0001	0000	M—0
2222	2222	2222	
5678	5678	5678	
————	————	————	
11 1	00 0	11 1	M—2

Chapter VII

CONCLUSION

The methodology used in analyzing the Data Encryption Standard (DES) with a limited number of iterations has been shown in some detail in the preceding chapters. The reader will note that the writer only went up to the analysis of the four-iteration problem — and even in this latter case it might be questioned whether he really covered the analysis very well since he did have to assume knowledge of 28 bits. But even if the analysis of the four-iteration problem proved to be as easy as the three-iteration problem, it is evident that the greater the number of iterations, the more difficult is analysis. We can say, therefore, that following this form of analysis, without some form of additional help the only method of practical attack against the Data Encryption Standard (DES) is that which already has been mentioned a number of times — the brute force attack.

In the above paragraph the writer used the words "without some form of additional help". What these words mean is that a successful analysis, other than the brute force attack, requires either a different analytical approach or we must find in the S-boxes some relationship in the bits which comprise the S-boxes, such that we can determine at least one or all of the four bits which exit a S-box using less than the six bits which normally enter a S-box. In other words, as a minimum can we determine, for example, in a given S-box the first bit of the four bits which exit given only five entering bits? In such a case, one bit of the entering bits will have no effect upon our recognizing one or all of the four bits which exit the S-box.

The technique used by the writer in his analysis of the S-boxes is as follows: he assumed that one of the six bits entering an S-box was an in-active bit. The remaining five bits provided, therefore, two possible four bit combinations which might exit the S-box. That is, the inactive bit might be either 0 or 1, and each would provide a different four bit combination which might exit the S-box. He now compared the two possible four bit exit combinations — looking for similar bits in the same positions. This was done by subtracting the two four bit exit combinations, one from the other, looking for 0 in the result. Let us look now at the S-4 box and the possibility that from five of the entering bits we can determine at least one or all of the bits which exit the box. Using the program which is provided in Appendix J, the results concerning the S-4 box are provided in Appendix K.

An explanation of the results provided in Appendix K is probably in order. Let us turn to the first of the results, that which assumes the first bit of the entering bits is inactive. The first line of these is as follows:

```
S-4 BOX
(32) 16 - 8 4 2 1
0 = 0111    32 = 1010    ---    1101
```

Here the entering bits are assumed to be 00-0000 and 10-0000. Note that the first bit (the bit having a value of 32) can be either 0 or 1. When the first bit is 0, the value of the entering bits is 0, but when the first bit is 1, the value of the entering bits is 32. These two possible enter values provide two possible exit values, 0111 or 1010. Subtracting these provides the value 1101. Since a 0 is in the third position of this value, we know that regardless of the first bit, if the last five bits of the enter value are 0-0000, that the third bit of the exit value will be 1. We next assume the same five enter bits are 0-0001. These provide two possible enter values, 00-0001 and 10-0001. From these the next line of the results is obtained:

```
1 = 1101    33 = 0110    ---    1011
```

The complete chart provides the known bits in the four-bit exit value (by a 0 in the subtracted value) for all possible enter values (where the first enter bit is inactive and can be either 0 or 1).

At the bottom of the chart is a count by position of the number of 0's in the resulting subtracted values. For example, it will be seen that of the 32 possible last five bits in the enter value, only 10 will provide the analyst of knowledge of the first bit of the four bits comprising the exit value. Likewise, the same is true of the other three positions of the exit value. We can conclude, therefore, that only the last five bits of the entering bits in the S-4 box will not consistently lead to knowledge of any bits in the four bits which exit the S-4 box.

To this point we have been discussing only the S-4 box where the first of the six bits to enter is assumed to be inactive; that is, the first bit is assumed to be either 0 or 1. The results of this assumption are shown on the chart with the title (32) 16 - 8 4 2 1. But since an inactive bit might be any of the remaining five bits (which enter the S-4 box), these have been considered on their own charts in Appendix K.

The charts of Appendix K seem to indicate that knowledge of five bits alone (of the six enter bits) will not lead with any uniform consistency to the knowledge of one or more of the four bits that exit the S-4 box.

The reader might note the seemingly non-randomness in the results shown in the charts of Appendix K. It seems evident that the bits (or values) selected for the S-boxes were not chosen randomly. They were selected so that it would be difficult for the analyst to determine with any uniform or definitive pattern the bits that exit an S-box with fewer than than the six bits that enter an S-box.

Perhaps the greatest threat against the Data Encryption Standard (DES) is the already often mentioned brute-force attack. With computers becoming faster and faster each year and especially the use of parallel processing, plus perhaps the use of a simplified DES algorithm, such as that described in this book, the Data Encryption Standard (DES) can hardly be described as a highly secure cryptographic system. Very simply, the security of this system seems to depend upon how rapidly couplets can be tested, and even here, improvements in the "testing process" are always being made. For example, a test of a "key" can be made in as few as eight iterations, with the test beginning at the front with the assumed plaintext while at the same time the test has begun at the end (at the 16th iteration) with the known ciphertext — meeting at the middle after eight iterations to prove or disprove the "key" being tested.

Finally, the writer would like to comment that opportunities abound for further study regarding the Data Encryption Standard (DES) and who knows, someone may come up with a better solution. He hopes that this book, which is only an introductory text, will be a stepping-stone in that direction.

APPENDIX A

FIPS PUB **46**

FEDERAL INFORMATION
PROCESSING STANDARDS PUBLICATION
1977 JANUARY 15

U.S. DEPARTMENT OF COMMERCE / National Bureau of Standards

DATA ENCRYPTION STANDARD

CATEGORY: ADP OPERATIONS
SUBCATEGORY: COMPUTER SECURITY

(1)

U.S. DEPARTMENT OF COMMERCE • Elliot L. Richardson, *Secretary*

Edward O. Vetter, *Under Secretary*

Dr. Betsy Ancker-Johnson, *Assistant Secretary for Science and Technology*

NATIONAL BUREAU OF STANDARDS • Ernest Ambler, *Acting Director*

Foreword

The Federal Information Processing Standards Publication Series of the National Bureau of Standards is the official publication relating to standards adopted and promulgated under the provisions of Public Law 89-306 (Brooks Bill) and under Part 6 of Title 15, Code of Federal Regulations. These legislative and executive mandates have given the Secretary of Commerce important responsibilities for improving the utilization and management of computers and automatic data processing systems in the Federal Government. To carry out the Secretary's responsibilities, the NBS, through its Institute for Computer Sciences and Technology, provides leadership, technical guidance, and coordination of government efforts in the development of technical guidelines and standards in these areas.

The series is used to announce Federal Information Processing Standards, and to provide standards information of general interest and an index of relevant standards publications and specifications. Publications that announce adoption of standards provide the necessary policy, administrative, and guidance information for effective standards implementation and use. The technical specifications of the standard are usually attached to the publication, otherwise a reference source is cited.

Comments covering Federal Information Processing Standards and Publications are welcomed, and should be addressed to the Associate Director for ADP Standards, Institute for Computer Sciences and Technology, National Bureau of Standards, Washington, D.C. 20234. Such comments will be either considered by NBS or forwarded to the responsible activity as appropriate.

ERNEST AMBLER, *Acting Director*

Abstract

The selective application of technological and related procedural safeguards is an important responsibility of every Federal organization in providing adequate security to its ADP systems. This publication provides a standard to be used by Federal organizations when these organizations specify that cryptographic protection is to be used for sensitive or valuable computer data. Protection of computer data during transmission between electronic components or while in storage may be necessary to maintain the confidentiality and integrity of the information represented by that data. The standard specifies an encryption algorithm which is to be implemented in an electronic device for use in Federal ADP systems and networks. The algorithm uniquely defines the mathematical steps required to transform computer data into a cryptographic cipher. It also specifies the steps required to transform the cipher back to its original form. A device performing this algorithm may be used in many applications areas where cryptographic data protection is needed. Within the context of a total security program comprising physical security procedures, good information management practices and computer system/network access controls, the Data Encryption Standard is being made available for use by Federal agencies.

Key Words: ADP security; computer security; encryption; Federal Information Processing Standard.

Nat. Bur. Stand. (U.S.), Fed. Info. Process. Stand. Publ. (FIPS PUB) 46, 17 pages (1977)
CODEN: FIPPAT

(2)

Federal Information Processing Standards Publication 46

1977 January 15

ANNOUNCING THE

DATA ENCRYPTION STANDARD

Federal Information Processing Standards are issued by the National Bureau of Standards pursuant to the Federal Property and Administrative Services Act of 1949, as amended, Public Law 89-306 (79 Stat 1127), Executive Order 11717 (38 FR 12315, dated May 11, 1973), and Part 6 of Title 15 Code of Federal Regulations (CFR).

Name of Standard: Data Encryption Standard (DES).

Category of Standard: Operations, Computer Security.

Explanation: The Data Encryption Standard (DES) specifies an algorithm to be implemented in electronic hardware devices and used for the cryptographic protection of computer data. This publication provides a complete description of a mathematical algorithm for encrypting (enciphering) and decrypting (deciphering) binary coded information. Encrypting data converts it to an unintelligible form called cipher. Decrypting cipher converts the data back to its original form. The algorithm described in this standard specifies both enciphering and deciphering operations which are based on a binary number called a key. The key consists of 64 binary digits ("0"s or "1"s) of which 56 bits are used directly by the algorithm and 8 bits are used for error detection.

Binary coded data may be cryptographically protected using the DES algorithm in conjunction with a key. The key is generated in such a way that each of the 56 bits used directly by the algorithm are random and the 8 error detecting bits are set to make the parity of each 8-bit byte of the key odd, i.e., there is an odd number of "1"s in each 8-bit byte. Each member of a group of authorized users of encrypted computer data must have the key that was used to encipher the data in order to use it. This key, held by each member in common, is used to decipher the data received in cipher form from other members of the group. The encryption algorithm specified in this standard is commonly known among those using the standard. The unique key chosen for use in a particular application makes the results of encrypting data using the algorithm unique. Selection of a different key causes the cipher that is produced for any given set of inputs to be different. The cryptographic security of the data depends on the security provided for the key used to encipher and decipher the data.

Data can be recovered from cipher only by using exactly the same key used to encipher it. Unauthorized recipients of the cipher who know the algorithm but do not have the correct key cannot derive the original data algorithmically. However, anyone who does have the key and the algorithm can easily decipher the cipher and obtain the original data. A standard algorithm based on a secure key thus provides a basis for exchanging encrypted computer data by issuing the key used to encipher it to those authorized to have the data. Additional FIPS guidelines for implementing and using the DES are being developed and will be published by NBS.

Approving Authority: Secretary of Commerce.

Maintenance Agency: Institute for Computer Sciences and Technology, National Bureau of Standards.

Applicability: This standard will be used by Federal departments and agencies for the cryptographic protection of computer data when the following conditions apply:

(3)

1. An authorized official or manager responsible for data security or the security of any computer system decides that cryptographic protection is required; and

2. The data is not classified according to the National Security Act of 1947, as amended, or the Atomic Energy Act of 1954, as amended.

However, Federal agencies or departments which use cryptographic devices for protecting data classified according to either of these acts can use those devices for protecting unclassified data in lieu of the standard.

In addition, this standard may be adopted and used by non-Federal Government organizations. Such use is encouraged when it provides the desired security for commercial and private organizations.

Data that is considered sensitive by the responsible authority, data that has a high value, or data that represents a high value should be cryptographically protected if it is vulnerable to unauthorized disclosure or undetected modification during transmission or while in storage. A risk analysis should be performed under the direction of a responsible authority to determine potential threats. FIPS PUB 31 (Guidelines for Automatic Data Processing Physical Security and Risk Management) and FIPS PUB 41 (Computer Security Guidelines for Implementing the Privacy Act of 1974) provide guidance for making such an analysis. The costs of providing cryptographic protection using this standard as well as alternative methods of providing this protection and their respective costs should be projected. A responsible authority then should make a decision, based on these analyses, whether or not to use cryptographic protection and this standard.

Applications: Data encryption (cryptography) may be utilized in various applications and in various environments. The specific utilization of encryption and the implementation of the DES will be based on many factors particular to the computer system and its associated components. In general, cryptography is used to protect data while it is being communicated between two points or while it is stored in a medium vulnerable to physical theft. Communication security provides protection to data by enciphering it at the transmitting point and deciphering it at the receiving point. File security provides protection to data by enciphering it when it is recorded on a storage medium and deciphering it when it is read back from the storage medium. In the first case, the key must be available at the transmitter and receiver simultaneously during communication. In the second case, the key must be maintained and accessible for the duration of the storage period.

Hardware Implementation: The algorithm specified in this standard is to be implemented in computer or related data communication devices using hardware (not software) technology. The specific implementation may depend on several factors such as the application, the environment, the technology used, etc. Implementations which comply with this standard include Large Scale Integration (LSI) "chips" in individual electronic packages, devices built from Medium Scale Integration (MSI) electronic components, or other electronic devices dedicated to performing the operations of the algorithm. Micro-processors using Read Only Memory (ROM) or micro-programmed devices using microcode for hardware level control instructions are examples of the latter. Hardware implementations of the algorithm which are tested and validated by NBS will be considered as complying with the standard. Procedures for testing and validating equipment for conformance with this standard are available from the Systems and Software Division, National Bureau of Standards, Washington, D.C. 20234. Software implementations in general purpose computers are not in compliance with this standard. Information regarding devices which have been tested and validated will be made available to all FIPS points of contact.

Export Control: Cryptographic devices and technical data regarding them are subject to Federal Government export controls as specified in Title 22, Code of Federal Regulations, Parts 121 through 128. Cryptographic devices implementing this standard and technical data regarding them must comply with these Federal regulations.

(4)

Patents: Crytographic devices implementing this standard may be covered by U.S. and foreign patents issued to the International Business Machines Corporation. However, IBM has granted nonexclusive, royalty-free licenses under the patents to make, use and sell apparatus which complies with the standard. The terms, conditions and scope of the licenses are set out in notices published in the May 13, 1975 and August 31, 1976 issues of the Official Gazette of the United States Patent and Trademark Office (934 O. G. 452 and 949 O. G. 1717).

Alternative Modes of Using the DES: The "Guidelines for Implementing and Using the Data Encryption Standard" describe two different modes for using the algorithm described in this standard. Blocks of data containing 64 bits may be directly entered into the device where 64-bit cipher blocks are generated under control of the key. This is called the electronic code book mode. Alternatively, the device may be used as a binary stream generator to produce statistically random binary bits which are then combined with the clear (unencrypted) data (1-64 bits) using an "exclusive-or" logic operation. In order to assure that the enciphering device and the deciphering device are synchronized, their inputs are always set to the previous 64 bits of cipher that were transmitted or received. This second mode of using the encryption algorithm is called the cipher feedback (CFB) mode. The electronic codebook mode generates blocks of 64 cipher bits. The cipher feedback mode generates cipher having the same number of bits as the plain text. Each block of cipher is independent of all others when the electronic codebook mode is used while each byte (group of bits) of cipher depends on the previous 64 cipher bits when the cipher feedback mode is used. The modes of operation briefly described here are further explained in the FIPS "Guidelines for Implementing and Using the Data Encryption Standard."

Implementation of this standard: This standard becomes effective six months after the publication date of this FIPS PUB. It applies to all Federal ADP systems and associated telecommunications networks under development as well as to installed systems when it is determined that cryptographic protection is required. Each Federal department or agency will issue internal directives for the use of this standard by their operating units based on their data security requirement determinations.

NBS will provide assistance to Federal organizations by developing and issuing additional technical guidelines on computer security and by providing technical assistance in using data encryption. A data encryption testbed has been established within NBS for use in providing this technical assistance. The National Security Agency assists Federal departments and agencies in communications security and in determining specific security requirements. Instructions and regulations for procuring data processing equipment utilizing this standard will be provided by the General Services Administration.

Specifications: Federal Information Processing Standard (FIPS 46) Data Encryption Standard (DES) (affixed).

Cross Index:

    a. FIPS PUB 31, "Guidelines to ADP Physical Security and Risk Management"

    b. FIPS PUB 39, "Glossary for Computer Systems Security"

    c. FIPS PUB 41, "Computer Security Guidelines for Implementing the Privacy Act of 1974"

    d. FIPS PUB—, "Guidelines for Implementing and Using the Data Encryption Standard" (to be published)

    e. Other FIPS and Federal Standards are applicable to the implementation and use of this standard. In particular, the American Standard Code for Information Interchange (FIPS PUB 1)

(5)

and other related data storage media or data communications standards should be used in conjunction with this standard. A list of currently approved FIPS may be obtained from the Office of ADP Standards Management, Institute for Computer Sciences and Technology, National Bureau of Standards, Washington, D.C. 20234.

Qualifications: The cryptographic algorithm specified in this standard transforms a 64-bit binary value into a unique 64-bit binary value based on a 56-bit variable. If the complete 64-bit input is used (i.e., none of the input bits should be predetermined from block to block) and if the 56-bit variable is randomly chosen, no technique other than trying all possible keys using known input and output for the DES will guarantee finding the chosen key. As there are over 70,000,000,000,000,000 (seventy quadrillion) possible keys of 56 bits, the feasibility of deriving a particular key in this way is extremely unlikely in typical threat environments. Moreover, if the key is changed frequently, the risk of this event is greatly diminished. However, users should be aware that it is theoretically possible to derive the key in fewer trials (with a correspondingly lower probability of success depending on the number of keys tried) and should be cautioned to change the key as often as practical. Users must change the key and provide it a high level of protection in order to minimize the potential risks of its unauthorized computation or acquisition. The feasibility of computing the correct key may change with advances in technology. A more complete description of the strength of this algorithm against various threats will be contained in the Guidelines for Implementing and Using the DES.

When correctly implemented and properly used, this standard will provide a high level of cryptographic protection to computer data. NBS, supported by the technical assistance of Government agencies responsible for communication security, has determined that the algorithm specified in this standard will provide a high level of protection for a time period beyond the normal life cycle of its associated ADP equipment. The protection provided by this algorithm against potential new threats will be reviewed within five years to assess its adequacy. In addition, both the standard and possible threats reducing the security provided through the use of this standard will undergo continual review by NBS and other cognizant Federal organizations. The new technology available at that time will be evaluated to determine its impact on the standard. In addition, the awareness of any breakthrough in technology or any mathematical weakness of the algorithm will cause NBS to reevaluate this standard and provide necessary revisions.

Comments: Comments and suggestions regarding this standard and its use are welcomed and should be addressed to the Associate Director for ADP Standards, Institute for Computer Sciences and Technology, National Bureau of Standards, Washington, D.C. 20234.

Waiver Procedure: The head of a Federal agency may waive the provisions of this FIPS PUB after the conditions and justifications for the waiver have been coordinated with the National Bureau of Standards. A waiver is necessary if cryptographic devices performing an algorithm other than that which is specified in this standard are to be used by a Federal agency for data subject to cryptographic protection under this standard. No waiver is necessary if classified communications security equipment is to be used. Software implementations of this algorithm for operational use in general purpose computer systems do not comply with this standard and each such implementation must also receive a waiver. Implementation of the algorithm in software for testing or evaluation does not require waiver approval. Implementation of other special purpose cryptographic algorithms in software for limited use within a computer system (e.g., encrypting password files) or implementations of cryptographic algorithms in software which were being utilized in computer systems before the effective date of this standard do not require a waiver. However, these limited uses should be converted to the use of this standard when the system or equipment involved is upgraded or redesigned to include general cryptographic protection of computer data. Letters describing the nature of and reasons for the waiver should be addressed to the Associate Director for ADP Standards as previously noted.

(6)

Sixty days should be allowed for review and response by NBS. The waiver shall not be approved until a response from NBS is received; however, the final decision for granting the waiver is the responsibility of the head of the particular agency involved.

Where to Obtain Copies of the Standard:

Copies of this publication are for sale by the National Technical Information Service, U. S. Department of Commerce, 5285 Port Royal Road, Springfield, Virginia 22161. Order by FIPS PUB number and title. Prices are published by NTIS in current catalogs and other issuances. Payment may be made by check, money order, deposit account or charged to a credit card accepted by NTIS.

(7)

**Federal Information
Processing Standards Publication 46**

1977 January 15

SPECIFICATIONS FOR THE

DATA ENCRYPTION STANDARD

The Data Encryption Standard (DES) shall consist of the following Data Encryption Algorithm to be implemented in special purpose electronic devices. These devices shall be designed in such a way that they may be used in a computer system or network to provide cryptographic protection to binary coded data. The method of implementation will depend on the application and environment. The devices shall be implemented in such a way that they may be tested and validated as accurately performing the transformations specified in the following algorithm.

DATA ENCRYPTION ALGORITHM

Introduction

The algorithm is designed to encipher and decipher blocks of data consisting of 64 bits under control of a 64-bit key. Deciphering must be accomplished by using the same key as for enciphering, but with the schedule of addressing the key bits altered so that the deciphering process is the reverse of the enciphering process. A block to be enciphered is subjected to an initial permutation IP, then to a complex key-dependent computation and finally to a permutation which is the inverse of the initial permutation IP^{-1}. The key-dependent computation can be simply defined in terms of a function f, called the cipher function, and a function KS, called the key schedule. A description of the computation is given first, along with details as to how the algorithm is used for encipherment. Next, the use of the algorithm for decipherment is described. Finally, a definition of the cipher function f is given in terms of primitive functions which are called the selection functions S_i and the permutation function P. S_i, P and KS of the algorithm are contained in the Appendix.

The following notation is convenient: Given two blocks L and R of bits, LR denotes the block consisting of the bits of L followed by the bits of R. Since concatenation is associative $B_1B_2 \ldots B_N$, for example, denotes the block consisting of the bits of B_1 followed by the bits of $B_2 \ldots$ followed by the bits of B_N.

Enciphering

A sketch of the enciphering computation is given in figure 1.

(8)

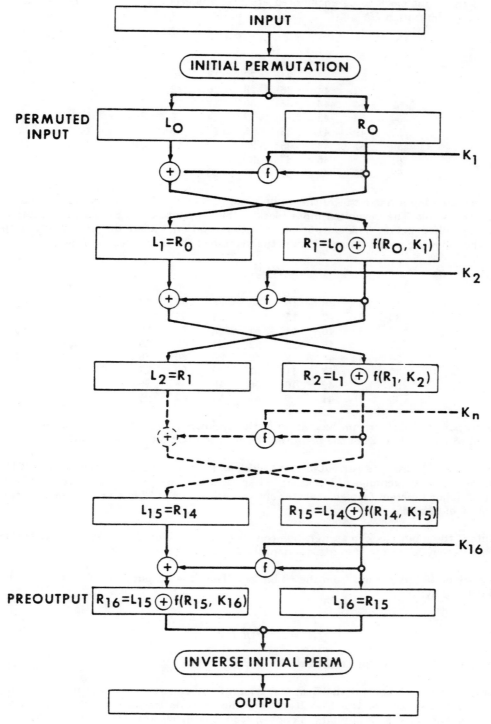

FIGURE 1. *Enciphering computation.*

(9)

The 64 bits of the input block to be enciphered are first subjected to the following permutation, called the initial permutation IP:

$$IP$$

58	50	42	34	26	18	10	2
60	52	44	36	28	20	12	4
62	54	46	38	30	22	14	6
64	56	48	40	32	24	16	8
57	49	41	33	25	17	9	1
59	51	43	35	27	19	11	3
61	53	45	37	29	21	13	5
63	55	47	39	31	23	15	7

That is the permuted input has bit 58 of the input as its first bit, bit 50 as its second bit, and so on with bit 7 as its last bit. The permuted input block is then the input to a complex key-dependent computation described below. The output of that computation, called the preoutput, is then subjected to the following permutation which is the inverse of the initial permutation:

$$IP^{-1}$$

40	8	48	16	56	24	64	32
39	7	47	15	55	23	63	31
38	6	46	14	54	22	62	30
37	5	45	13	53	21	61	29
36	4	44	12	52	20	60	28
35	3	43	11	51	19	59	27
34	2	42	10	50	18	58	26
33	1	41	9	49	17	57	25

That is, the output of the algorithm has bit 40 of the preoutput block as its first bit, bit 8 as its second bit, and so on, until bit 25 of the preoutput block is the last bit of the output.

The computation which uses the permuted input block as its input to produce the preoutput block consists, but for a final interchange of blocks, of 16 iterations of a calculation that is described below in terms of the cipher function f which operates on two blocks, one of 32 bits and one of 48 bits, and produces a block of 32 bits.

Let the 64 bits of the input block to an iteration consist of a 32 bit block L followed by a 32 bit block R. Using the notation defined in the introduction, the input block is then LR.

Let K be a block of 48 bits chosen from the 64-bit key. Then the output $L'R'$ of an iteration with input LR is defined by:

(1)
$$L' = R$$
$$R' = L \oplus f(R,K)$$

where $\oplus$ denotes bit-by-bit addition modulo 2.

As remarked before, the input of the first iteration of the calculation is the permuted input block. If $L'R'$ is the output of the 16th iteration then $R'L'$ is the preoutput block. At each iteration a different block K of key bits is chosen from the 64-bit key designated by KEY.

(10)

With more notation we can describe the iterations of the computation in more detail. Let KS be a function which takes an integer n in the range from 1 to 16 and a 64-bit block KEY as input and yields as output a 48-bit block K_n which is a permuted selection of bits from KEY. That is

(2)
$$K_n = KS(n, KEY)$$

with K_n determined by the bits in 48 distinct bit positions of KEY. KS is called the key schedule because the block K used in the n'th iteration of (1) is the block K_n determined by (2).

As before, let the permuted input block be LR. Finally, let L_0 and R_0 be respectively L and R and let L_n and R_n be respectively L' and R' of (1) when L and R are respectively L_{n-1} and R_{n-1} and K is K_n; that is, when n is in the range from 1 to 16,

(3)
$$L_n = R_{n-1}$$
$$R_n = L_{n-1} \oplus f(R_{n-1}, K_n)$$

The preoutput block is then $R_{16}L_{16}$.

The key schedule KS of the algorithm is described in detail in the Appendix. The key schedule produces the 16 K_n which are required for the algorithm.

Deciphering

The permutation IP^{-1} applied to the preoutput block is the inverse of the initial permutation IP applied to the input. Further, from (1) it follows that:

(4)
$$R = L'$$
$$L = R' \oplus f(L', K)$$

Consequently, to *decipher* it is only necessary to apply the *very same algorithm to an enciphered message block*, taking care that at each iteration of the computation *the same block of key bits* K *is used* during decipherment as was used during the encipherment of the block. Using the notation of the previous section, this can be expressed by the equations:

(5)
$$R_{n-1} = L_n$$
$$L_{n-1} = R_n \oplus f(L_n, K_n)$$

where now $R_{16}L_{16}$ is the permuted input block for the deciphering calculation and $L_0 R_0$ is the preoutput block. That is, for the decipherment calculation with $R_{16}L_{16}$ as the permuted input, K_{16} is used in the first iteration, K_{15} in the second, and so on, with K_1 used in the 16th iteration.

The Cipher Function f

A sketch of the calculation of $f(R, K)$ is given in figure 2.

(11)

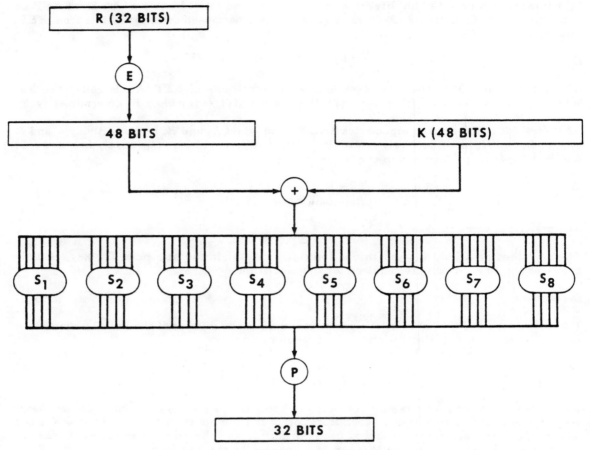

FIGURE 2. *Calculation of* f (R, K).

Let E denote a function which takes a block of 32 bits as input and yields a block of 48 bits as output. Let E be such that the 48 bits of its output, written as 8 blocks of 6 bits each, are obtained by selecting the bits in its inputs in order according to the following table:

E BIT-SELECTION TABLE

32	1	2	3	4	5
4	5	6	7	8	9
8	9	10	11	12	13
12	13	14	15	16	17
16	17	18	19	20	21
20	21	22	23	24	25
24	25	26	27	28	29
28	29	30	31	32	1

Thus the first three bits of $E(R)$ are the bits in positions 32, 1 and 2 of R while the last 2 bits of $E(R)$ are the bits in positions 32 and 1.

(12)

Each of the unique selection functions $S_1, S_2, \ldots, S_8$ takes a 6-bit block as input and yields a 4-bit block as output and is illustrated by using a table containing the recommended S_1:

$$\underline{S_1}$$

Column Number

Row No.	0	1	2	3	4	5	6	7	8	9	10	11	12	13	14	15
0	14	4	13	1	2	15	11	8	3	10	6	12	5	9	0	7
1	0	15	7	4	14	2	13	1	10	6	12	11	9	5	3	8
2	4	1	14	8	13	6	2	11	15	12	9	7	3	10	5	0
3	15	12	8	2	4	9	1	7	5	11	3	14	10	0	6	13

If S_1 is the function defined in this table and B is a block of 6 bits, then $S_1(B)$ is determined as follows: The first and last bits of B represent in base 2 a number in the range 0 to 3. Let that number be i. The middle 4 bits of B represent in base 2 a number in the range 0 to 15. Let that number be j. Look up in the table the number in the i'th row and j'th column. It is a number in the range 0 to 15 and is uniquely represented by a 4 bit block. That block is the output $S_1(B)$ of S_1 for the input B. For example, for input 011011 the row is 01, that is row 1, and the column is determined by 1101, that is column 13. In row 1 column 13 appears 5 so that the output is 0101. Selection functions $S_1, S_2, \ldots, S_8$ of the algorithm appear in the Appendix.

The permutation function P yields a 32-bit output from a 32-bit input by permuting the bits of the input block. Such a function is defined by the following table:

$$\underline{P}$$

16	7	20	21
29	12	28	17
1	15	23	26
5	18	31	10
2	8	24	14
32	27	3	9
19	13	30	6
22	11	4	25

The output $P(L)$ for the function P defined by this table is obtained from the input L by taking the 16th bit of L as the first bit of $P(L)$, the 7th bit as the second bit of $P(L)$, and so on until the 25th bit of L is taken as the 32nd bit of $P(L)$. The permutation function P of the algorithm is repeated in the Appendix.

Now let $S_1, \ldots, S_8$ be eight distinct selection functions, let P be the permutation function and let E be the function defined above.

To define $f(R, K)$ we first define $B_1, \ldots, B_8$ to be blocks of 6 bits each for which

$$(6) \qquad B_1 B_2 \ldots B_8 = K \oplus E(R)$$

The block $f(R, K)$ is then defined to be

$$(7) \qquad P(S_1(B_1) S_2(B_2) \ldots S_8(B_8))$$

(13)

Thus $K \oplus E(R)$ is first divided into the 8 blocks as indicated in (6). Then each B_i is taken as an input to S_i and the 8 blocks $S_1(B_1)$, $S_2(B_2)$, ..., $S_8(B_8)$ of 4 bits each are consolidated into a single block of 32 bits which forms the input to P. The output (7) is then the output of the function f for the inputs R and K.

$$(14)$$

APPENDIX

PRIMITIVE FUNCTIONS FOR THE
DATA ENCRYPTION ALGORITHM

The choice of the primitive functions KS, S_1, ..., S_8 and P is critical to the strength of an encipherment resulting from the algorithm. Specified below is the recommended set of functions, describing S_1, ..., S_8 and P in the same way they are described in the algorithm. For the interpretation of the tables describing these functions, see the discussion in the body of the algorithm.

The primitive functions S_1, ..., S_8 are:

S_1

14	4	13	1	2	15	11	8	3	10	6	12	5	9	0	7
0	15	7	4	14	2	13	1	10	6	12	11	9	5	3	8
4	1	14	8	13	6	2	11	15	12	9	7	3	10	5	0
15	12	8	2	4	9	1	7	5	11	3	14	10	0	6	13

S_2

15	1	8	14	6	11	3	4	9	7	2	13	12	0	5	10
3	13	4	7	15	2	8	14	12	0	1	10	6	9	11	5
0	14	7	11	10	4	13	1	5	8	12	6	9	3	2	15
13	8	10	1	3	15	4	2	11	6	7	12	0	5	14	9

S_3

10	0	9	14	6	3	15	5	1	13	12	7	11	4	2	8
13	7	0	9	3	4	6	10	2	8	5	14	12	11	15	1
13	6	4	9	8	15	3	0	11	1	2	12	5	10	14	7
1	10	13	0	6	9	8	7	4	15	14	3	11	5	2	12

S_4

7	13	14	3	0	6	9	10	1	2	8	5	11	12	4	15
13	8	11	5	6	15	0	3	4	7	2	12	1	10	14	9
10	6	9	0	12	11	7	13	15	1	3	14	5	2	8	4
3	15	0	6	10	1	13	8	9	4	5	11	12	7	2	14

S_5

2	12	4	1	7	10	11	6	8	5	3	15	13	0	14	9
14	11	2	12	4	7	13	1	5	0	15	10	3	9	8	6
4	2	1	11	10	13	7	8	15	9	12	5	6	3	0	14
11	8	12	7	1	14	2	13	6	15	0	9	10	4	5	3

S_6

12	1	10	15	9	2	6	8	0	13	3	4	14	7	5	11
10	15	4	2	7	12	9	5	6	1	13	14	0	11	3	8
9	14	15	5	2	8	12	3	7	0	4	10	1	13	11	6
4	3	2	12	9	5	15	10	11	14	1	7	6	0	8	13

(15)

$$S_7$$

4	11	2	14	15	0	8	13	3	12	9	7	5	10	6	1
13	0	11	7	4	9	1	10	14	3	5	12	2	15	8	6
1	4	11	13	12	3	7	14	10	15	6	8	0	5	9	2
6	11	13	8	1	4	10	7	9	5	0	15	14	2	3	12

$$S_8$$

13	2	8	4	6	15	11	1	10	9	3	14	5	0	12	7
1	15	13	8	10	3	7	4	12	5	6	11	0	14	9	2
7	11	4	1	9	12	14	2	0	6	10	13	15	3	5	8
2	1	14	7	4	10	8	13	15	12	9	0	3	5	6	11

The primitive function P is:

16	7	20	21
29	12	28	17
1	15	23	26
5	18	31	10
2	8	24	14
32	27	3	9
19	13	30	6
22	11	4	25

Recall that K_n, for $1 \leq n \leq 16$, is the block of 48 bits in (2) of the algorithm. Hence, to describe KS, it is sufficient to describe the calculation of K_n from KEY for $n = 1, 2, \ldots, 16$. That calculation is illustrated in figure 3. To complete the definition of KS it is therefore sufficient to describe the two permuted choices, as well as the schedule of left shifts. One bit in each 8-bit byte of the KEY may be utilized for error detection in key generation, distribution and storage. Bits 8, 16, . . ., 64 are for use in assuring that each byte is of odd parity.

Permuted choice 1 is determined by the following table:

$$PC-1$$

57	49	41	33	25	17	9
1	58	50	42	34	26	18
10	2	59	51	43	35	27
19	11	3	60	52	44	36
63	55	47	39	31	23	15
7	62	54	46	38	30	22
14	6	61	53	45	37	29
21	13	5	28	20	12	4

The table has been divided into two parts, with the first part determining how the bits of C_0 are chosen, and the second part determining how the bits of D_0 are chosen. The bits of KEY are numbered 1 through 64. The bits of C_0 are respectively bits 57, 49, 41, . . ., 44 and 36 of KEY, with the bits of D_0 being bits 63, 55, 47, . . ., 12 and 4 of KEY.

With C_0 and D_0 defined, we now define how the blocks C_n and D_n are obtained from the blocks C_{n-1} and D_{n-1}, respectively, for $n = 1, 2, \ldots, 16$. That is accomplished by adhering to the following schedule of left shifts of the individual blocks:

(16)

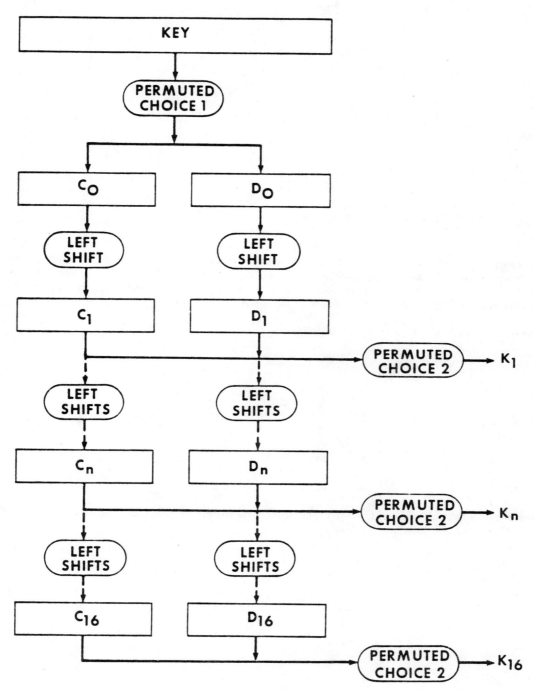

FIGURE 3. *Key schedule calculation.*

(17)

Iteration Number	Number of Left Shifts
1	1
2	1
3	2
4	2
5	2
6	2
7	2
8	2
9	1
10	2
11	2
12	2
13	2
14	2
15	2
16	1

For example, C_3 and D_3 are obtained from C_2 and D_2, respectively, by two left shifts, and C_{16} and D_{16} are obtained from C_{15} and D_{15}, respectively, by one left shift. In all cases, by a single left shift is meant a rotation of the bits one place to the left, so that after one left shift the bits in the 28 positions are the bits that were previously in positions 2, 3, . . ., 28, 1.

Permuted choice 2 is determined by the following table:

PC-2

14	17	11	24	1	5
3	28	15	6	21	10
23	19	12	4	26	8
16	7	27	20	13	2
41	52	31	37	47	55
30	40	51	45	33	48
44	49	39	56	34	53
46	42	50	36	29	32

Therefore, the first bit of K_n is the 14th bit of $C_n D_n$, the second bit the 17th, and so on with the 47th bit the 29th, and the 48th bit the 32nd.

(18)

APPENDIX B

COMPUTER SCIENCE & TECHNOLOGY:

VALIDATING THE CORRECTNESS OF HARDWARE IMPLEMENTATIONS OF THE NBS DATA ENCRYPTION STANDARD

Revised September 1980

NBS Special Publication 500-20

U.S. DEPARTMENT OF COMMERCE
National Bureau of Standards

COMPUTER SCIENCE & TECHNOLOGY

Validating the Correctness of Hardware Implementations of the NBS Data Encryption Standard

Jason Gait

Center for Programming Science and Technology
Institute for Computer Sciences and Technology
National Bureau of Standards
Washington, D.C. 20234

U.S. DEPARTMENT OF COMMERCE, Philip M. Klutznick, Secretary

Luther H. Hodges, Jr., Deputy Secretary
Jordan J. Baruch, Assistant Secretary for Productivity, Technology and Innovation

NATIONAL BUREAU OF STANDARDS, Ernest Ambler, Director

Revised September 1980

Reports on Computer Science and Technology

The National Bureau of Standards has a special responsibility within the Federal Government for computer science and technology activities. The programs of the NBS Institute for Computer Sciences and Technology are designed to provide ADP standards, guidelines, and technical advisory services to improve the effectiveness of computer utilization in the Federal sector, and to perform appropriate research and development efforts as foundation for such activities and programs. This publication series will report these NBS efforts to the Federal computer community as well as to interested specialists in the academic and private sectors. Those wishing to receive notices of publications in this series should complete and return the form at the end of this publication.

National Bureau of Standards Special Publication 500-20

Nat. Bur. Stand. (U.S.), Spec. Publ. 500-20, 46 pages (Revised Sept. 1980)
CODEN: XNBSAV

Library of Congress Catalog Card Number: 77-16067

U.S. GOVERNMENT PRINTING OFFICE
WASHINGTON: 1980

TABLE OF CONTENTS

-iii-

LIST OF FIGURES

Validating the Correctness of Hardware Implementations of the NBS Data Encryption Standard

Jason Gait

This publication describes the design and operation of the NBS testbed that is used for the validation of hardware implementations of the Federal Information Processing Data Encryption Standard (DES). A particular implementation is verified if it correctly performs a set of 291 test cases that have been defined to exercise every basic element of the algorithm. As a further check on the correctness of the implementation an extensive Monte-Carlo test is performed. This publication includes the full specification of the DES algorithm, a complete listing of the DES test set and a detailed description of the interface to the testbed.

Key words: Communications security; computer security; cryptography; encryption standard; interface requirements; Monte-Carlo testing; testbed; test cases; validating correctness.

1. INTRODUCTION

The National Bureau of Standards has built a hardware testbed facility to validate manufacturer's implementations of the Federal Information Processing Data Encryption Standard (DES) [3]. The facility includes a hardware implementation of the DES built by NBS in TTL logic and capable of performing an encryption or decryption in 8 micro-seconds. The NBS DES unit is controlled by a microcomputer, which is downstream-loaded with the test program by a time-shared program (currently running on a PDP-11/45 **). When a manufacturer submits a DES device for validation, the device is interfaced to a microcomputer in parallel with the NBS DES unit and its correctness is evaluated by comparison with the NBS DES unit. The device and the NBS DES unit are run

----
** The designations of computer products contained in this report are included for technical accuracy and completeness. The National Bureau of Standards does not endorse the products of any particular computer manufacturer.

(1)

simultaneously and synchronously as the test cases are computed.

Nineteen encryptions and comparisons are required to fully exercise the non-linear substitution tables, or S-boxes. The key schedule is exercised by presenting 56 basis vectors for both encryption and decryption, an additional 112 tests. The initial and final permutations are tested by presenting to each permutation 64 basis vectors, for 128 more tests during which the expansion operator E is automatically verified. The permutation P is verified by performing 32 more encryptions. Thus, a total of 235 encryptions and 56 decryptions are used in the DES test set.

At his option, a manufacturer of a DES implementation may provide an interface to the DES testbed when he submits his device for validation, or NBS will construct the interface from a full specification of device characteristics provided by the manufacturer. If the submitter elects to provide his own interface, he should design it in accordance with the specifications given in this document.

2. DESCRIPTION OF ALGORITHM

The Federal Information Processing Data Encryption Standard published on January 15, 1977 [3] is a complex non-linear ciphering algorithm that was designed with a view to efficient hardware implementation. Although there have been software implementations, they do not comply with the standard and they are generally quite inefficient compared to hardware versions [6]. The DES algorithm operates on 64 bits of plaintext to produce 64 bits of ciphertext under the action of a 56-bit keying parameter. With the exception of initial and final permutations, the algorithm is a series connection of sixteen rounds, one of which is depicted in figure 1. Each round uses 48 bits of the key in a sequence determined by a key schedule. With the exception of this difference in the round keys, the sixteen rounds are identical to one another. Each round receives an input of 64 bits; the 32-bit right half is expanded by the linear operator E to 48 bits and the result is mod two added to the round key; the 48 bit sum is divided into eight 6-bit blocks, each of which determines a 4-bit S-box entry; the resulting 32 bits are added mod two to the left half and the two halves are interchanged, thus producing 64 bits of output for the round. Sixteen rounds connected in series, each

(2)

using a different round key as determined by the key schedule, together with initial and final permutations make up the DES algorithm. Despite its complexity the DES is capable of operating at high speed when implemented in hardware...for example, an encryption or decryption of one 64-bit block on the NBS DES unit takes 6 micro-seconds. Guidelines on the proper usage of the DES are published in [8].

An example of round-by-round encryption for a given key and plaintext is shown in figure 4. Appendix A contains a complete functional description of the DES algorithm parameters, i. e., permutations, S-boxes and key schedule.

2.1   The Permutations

The role of the permutations is to thoroughly mix the data bits so they cannot be traced back through the S-boxes. Most of the permutations have been designed for efficient hardware realization. In particular, the initial and final permutations are byte oriented, and the controlling microcomputer outputs data to the DES hardware eight bits at a time to take advantage of this feature. In addition to performing a permutation, the operator E expands its 32 bit input to a 48 bit output that is added mod 2 to the round key. The permutation P intermixes the bits that result from the S-box substitution in a complex way to prevent bit tracing. The permutations in the key-schedule intermix the key bits among the round keys in such a way as to equalize key-bit utilization...no key bit is used more than 15 times nor less than 12 times.

Each permutation is a linear operator, and so can be thought of as an n x m matrix and can be completely validated if it operates correctly on an appropriate set of basis vectors. The set of tests for the permutation operators is founded on this principle, and the test cases have been constructed to present a complete set of basis vectors to each operator.

2.2   The S-boxes

The non-linear substitution tables, or S-boxes, constitute the most important part of the algorithm. The purpose of the S-boxes is to ensure that the algorithm is not linear, and hence too weak to stand up under cryptanalytic attack [1,2]. Each of the eight S-boxes, such as is shown in

(3)

figure 2, contains 64 entries, organized as a 4x16 matrix.
Each entry is a four bit binary number, represented as 0-15
in figure 2, so the output of the parallel connection of
eight S-boxes is 32 bits. A particular entry in a single
S-box is selected by six bits, two of which select a row and
four select a column. The entry in the corresponding row
and column is the output for that input. Each row in each
S-box is a permutation of the numbers 0-15, so no entry is
repeated in any one row.

There is no obvious small set of inputs that could be
used to verify the S-boxes, so an extensive series of
Monte-Carlo experiments was performed to discover a relatively small set of inputs that would exercise every S-box
entry at least once. Nearly 200 separate trials were made,
and among these were several test sets of 19 inputs which
exercised every S-box entry. One of these sets is used as
the DES test set for the S-boxes.

2.3   The Key Schedule

The purpose of the key schedule is to provide a
thorough intermixing of the key bits for each round. Figure
3 shows how the key schedule determines the sixteen 48-bit
round keys from the 56-bit encryption key. The key schedule
is linear, so its implementation can be verified by presenting 56 basis vectors as keys, encrypting known input and
comparing with known output. The encryption process depends
on left shifts in the key schedule, but decryption depends
on right shifts, so an additional 56 decryptions are required to test this. The key schedule is extremely important
to the security of the algorithm: it has been shown [4] that
similar algorithms without key schedules are substantially
weaker, even if they have much larger keys.

3.   COMPONENTS OF THE TEST BED

The data encryption testbed has been established within
the Institute for Computer Sciences and Technology at the
National Bureau of Standards. In order to provide a validation service for DES implementations, the testbed was

(4)

conceived and developed as a joint effort of ICST's Center for Programming Science and Technology and the Center for Computer Systems Engineering.

The data encryption testbed was developed in three phases. During phase one the DES algorithm was implemented in readily available TTL hardware technology. Two units are presently in operation. Phase two incorporated these units in a communication channel between a high speed computer terminal and the ICST Computer Facility. A microcomputer is used to interface the NBS DES unit to the data communications channel, as in figure 5. Phase three provided a method of validating commercial data encryption devices implementing the DES.

The most important component of the testbed is the DES algorithm implemented in standard TTL logic. This device performs an encryption or decryption in eight micro-seconds, and takes 26 micro-seconds to load key or plaintext or to unload ciphertext. This is in contrast to execution times on the order of 30-100 milli-seconds for known software implementations. Figure 6 shows the DES testbed set up for the validation of a manufacturer's DES device. The testbed uses a microcomputer, the NBS DES unit, the proprietary DES device and its interface to the microcomputer port, an operator's terminal (CRT) and a connection to the NBS computer (PDP-11/45). The latter operates in time-sharing mode using the UNIX operating system. The microcomputer contains a small monitor program in read-only memory that is used to permit downstream-loading of the validation software and test data from (PDP-11/45) files under control of the operator's terminal. The current version of the validation software was written and compiled on the PDP-11/45 using an in-house cross-assembler.

(5)

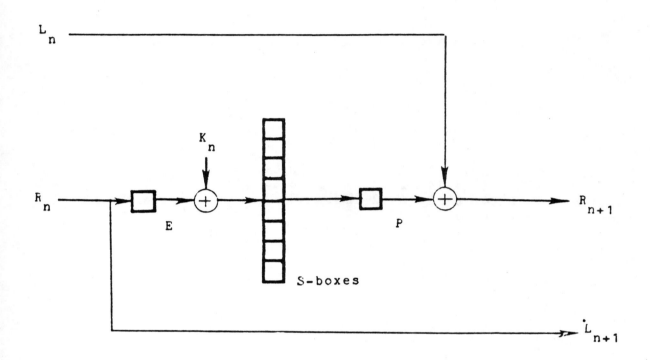

Figure 1 . One of sixteen rounds of the DES. The sixteen rounds
are connected in series and have an initial and
final permutation.A key schedule determines the round keys.

(6)

Figure 2: One of the eight S-boxes in the DES. An S-box entry is determined by a six bit input, four of which determine a column and two determine a row. The output is the four bit S-box entry specified by the row and column. The eight S-boxes are connected in parallel, and are used in each of the sixteen rounds of the DES.

$$S_1$$

```
14   4 13  1  2 15 11  8  3 10  6 12  5  9  0  7
 0 15  7  4 14  2 13  1 10  6 12 11  9  5  3  8
 4  1 14  8 13  6  2 11 15 12  9  7  3 10  5  0
15 12  8  2  4  9  1  7  5 11  3 14 10  0  6 13
```

(7)

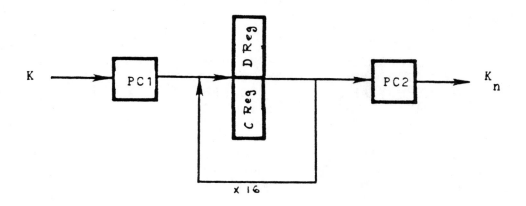

Figure 3 . The key schedule for the DES. The operator PC1
strips away the parity bits from the 64-bit key
to produce the 56-bit active key.This is split into
two 28 bit registors which are rotated by one or two
bits during each round.The operator PC2 produces the
48-bit round key after the bits have been permuted
in the registers.

(8)

Figure 4: Sample round outputs for the DES. For this example the key is 10316E028C8F3B4A and the plaintext is 0000000000000000.

L	R
00000000	47092B5B
47092B5B	53F372AF
53F372AF	9F1D158B
9F1D158B	8109CBEE
8109CBEE	60448698
60448698	29EBB1A4
29EBB1A4	620CC3A3
620CC3A3	DEEB3D8A
DEEB3D8A	A1A0354D
A1A0354D	9F0303DC
9F0303DC	FD898EE8
FD898EE8	2D1AE1DD
2D1AE1DD	CBC829FA
CBC829FA	B367DEC9
B367DEC9	3F6C3EFD
3F6C3EFD	5A1E5228

OUTPUT

82DCBAFBDEAB6602

(9)

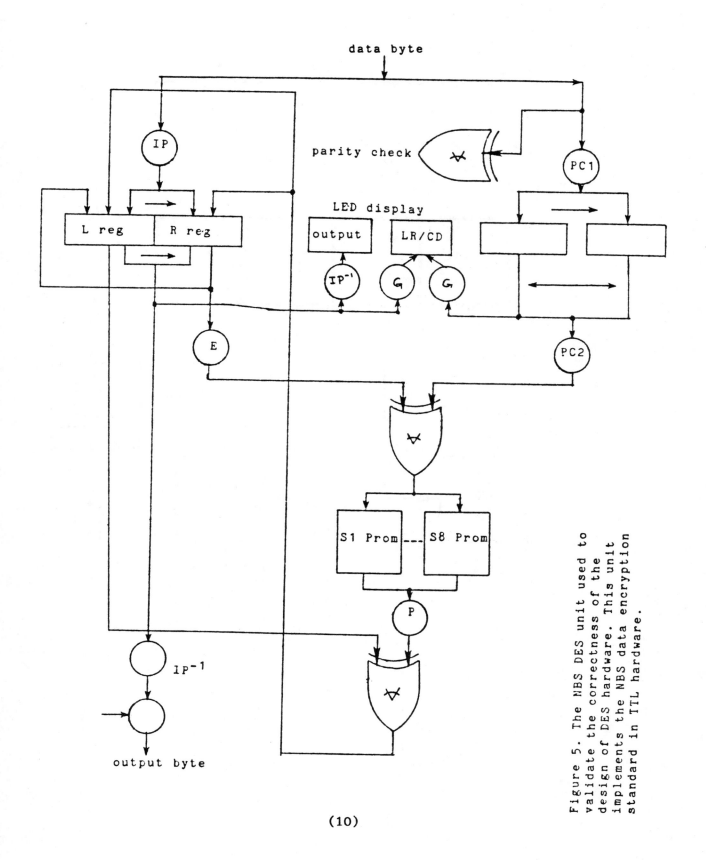

Figure 5. The NBS DES unit used to validate the correctness of the design of DES hardware. This unit implements the NBS data encryption standard in TTL hardware.

(10)

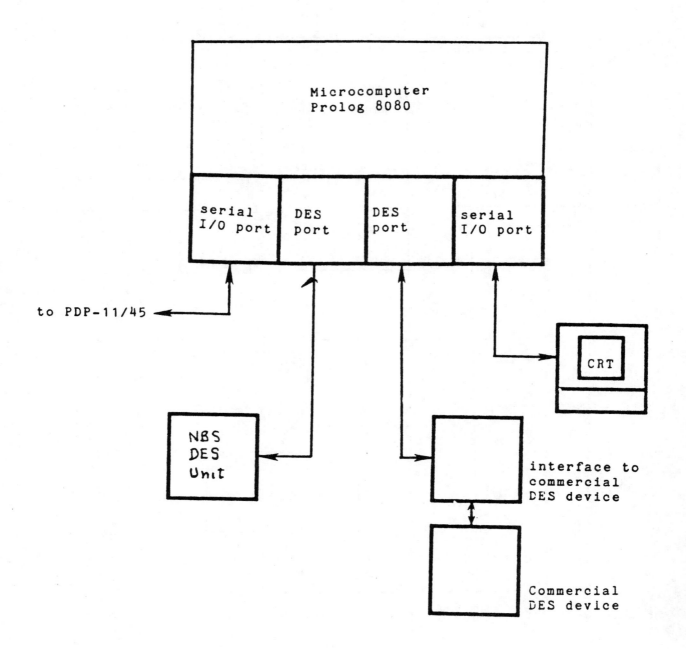

Figure 6 . Current architecture of the validation testbed.
The interface can be provided to NBS with the
hardware, or it can be built by NBS at cost from
specifications of the proprietary hardware.

(11)

Figure 7: Sample validation certificate. This certificate is provided by NBS for encryption hardware implementing the DES that has been tested successfully. A prospective vendor of DES encryption equipment to Federal agencies must obtain a certificate of validation.

VALIDATION CERTIFICATE

The National Bureau of Standards has tested an encryption device, identified as............. manufactured by............... in accordance with the specifications of the Data Encryption Standard (FIPS Pub 46) and in accordance with the procedures specified in NBS Special Publication 500-20.

The device has passed the DES test set, and in addition has passed a Monte Carlo test that lasted four million iterations. For the Monte Carlo test the initial value of the key was................... and the initial value of the input was...................... The final value of the key was................ and the final value of the output was..................

Devices bearing the same identification and manufactured to the same design specifications may be labeled as complying with the standard. No reliability test has been performed and no warranty of the devices by the National Bureau of Standards is either expressed or implied.

Dated...................

Signed................

(Director, Center for Programming Science
 and Technology
Institute for Computer Sciences and
Technology, National Bureau of
Standards)

(12)

4. THE DEVICE VALIDATION PROCEDURE

The device validation procedure verifies that the manufacturer's hardware design of the DES correctly performs the algorithm. To do this a manufacturer submits a single device from his production line for testing. The validation procedure confirms that the device submitted correctly performs the DES algorithm. Quality control of devices from the production line is the responsibility of the manufacturer. NBS does not certify the reliability of DES devices, only the correctness of the way they implement the DES.

An interface can be provided by NBS for the device submitted or the manufacturer can provide his own interface. The device runs under microcomputer control while performing the encryptions and decryptions of the DES test set, the results being compared to known results in the microcomputer. This test takes less than five minutes. The Monte Carlo test is performed by the commercial device and the NBS device in parallel. This test may run as long as eight hours. The successful completion of the tests will result in the issuance of a validation certificate for the manufacturer's implementation of the DES, and Federal agencies may then purchase identical devices from the manufacturer which are in conformity with the standard.

4.1 The Device/Test-bed Interface

An interface must be designed specifically for each proprietary implementation submitted for validation. This is the most time consuming aspect of the testbed procedure and the manufacturer is required to submit detailed characteristics of his device with regard to voltage levels and operating requirements to facilitate this phase.

The NBS microcomputer interface is designed for use with the NBS DES unit, which uses TTL MSI logic. Firms with commercial implementations of the algorithm that are to be validated by NBS may, at their option, have NBS design and build the necessary interface logic and make necessary software changes to the microcomputer program or they may design their own interface logic that will make their device appear to be identical to the NBS device.

In the former case, it will be necessary to supply adequate documentation to NBS on the operation of the commercial device so that NBS can design the necessary interface logic and software modifications. This documentation should

(13)

include a definition of all I/O leads, their pin numbers and a narrative description of the operation of the device and of the particular signals needed to operate it. Signal specifications should include the technology to be used by the external circuits (TTL, CMOS, etc.), any external pull-up resistors required, fan out limitations and any unique voltage levels. All power supply voltages needed should be specified. If any of this information is proprietary, this should be so noted.

Full details of the interfacing requirements are included as Appendix C.

4.2 Validating the Implementation

The testbed verifies the correctness of an implementation by performing a series of tests on the device submitted. The tests are chosen to present basis vectors to each of the matrix operators in the algorithm and to exercise every element in each S-box.

4.2.1 Test Procedure. The NBS standard test consists of 291 individual sets of key, plaintext, and ciphertext. The data are stored in a (PDP-11/45) file with each line in the file containing one individual test, e. g.,

K0101010101010101   P13213AB764588787   S8000000000000000.

The source text of the test program currently resides on a PDP-11/45, and must first be cross-assembled for the PROLOG microcomputer. The resulting object module is downstream loaded into the PROLOG microcomputer via an RS-232 interface. The down-stream loading occurs using a special, almost transparent IO handler on the PROLOG which reads a character from one port (the terminal) and passes it through to the other port (PDP-11/45) and vice versa.

Currently, a program on the PDP-11/45 is executed which starts a process on the PROLOG by sending a special character that starts execution of the test program. The (PDP-11/45) process sends the PROLOG the test data one line at a time. The data is sent in hexadecimal ASCII format . Each line is separated into three sections by tabs and special control characters appear at the beginning of each of these sections. A 'K' at the beginning of the first column indicates that the following 16 characters represent the key. The control character in the second column indicates which operation is to be performed, a 'P' for encryption and a 'S' for decryption. The control character in the third column is the complement of that in the second, indicating

(14)

that the data following is plaintext or ciphertext.

Once the data has been received, the microcomputer program then loads the test device with the key, followed by the data, and initiates the test. It receives the encrypted or decrypted data back from the test device, and compares it with the expected result. Any deviation in the comparison results in an error message being printed at the console, indicating which individual test failed. The rest of the test is continued. The normal execution time of this test is 3-5 minutes, but it is mainly dependent on the transfer time of the test data, which is transmitted to the PROLOG microcomputer at 2400 bits per second.

4.2.2 DES Test Set. The tests have been constructed to validate each of the following components of the algorithm:

1. Initial permutation, IP
2. Inverse permutation, IP^{-1}
3. Expansion matrix, E
4. Data Permutation, P
5. Key Permutation, PC1
6. Key Permutation, PC2
7. Substitution tables: $S_1, S_2, \ldots, S_8$

TEST 1: Set Key=0 and encrypt the 64-bit data vectors

e^i: i=1,...,64; a set of basis vectors.

Basis vectors have all zeros except for a single 1 in the ith position. Compare the resulting cipher c^i with the known results.

CONCLUSIONS: Correct operation verifies the initial permutation, IP. As a full set of basis vectors is also presented to the expansion matrix, E, this operation is also verified.

TEST 2: Set Key=0 and encrypt the results c^i obtained in TEST 1.

CONCLUSIONS: As the set of basis vectors are recovered, each e^i is presented to the inverse permutation, IP^{-1}, thus verifying it.

TEST 3: To test the permutation operator P, set the plaintext to zero and process the 32 keys in PTEST. This presents a complete set of basis vectors to P.

TEST 4: part 1: Set Data=0 and use the keys e^i: i=1,...,64 ignoring i=8,16,...,64.

(15)

Since the 56 possible basis vectors which yield unique keys are used, this is a complete set of basis vectors for PC1. Compare the results to the known values.

CONCLUSIONS: The key permutation, PC1, is verified. Since the key schedule consists of left shifts, as i ranges over the index set, a complete set of basis vectors is also presented to PC2, so this is verified.

Part 2: set data=c^i from part 1 and use the keys e^i: i=1,...,64 ignoring i=8,16,...64. Then decipher. This tests the right shifts in the key schedule during deciphering.

TEST 5: Set Data and Key equal to the inputs defined in the Substitution Table test. These are a set of 19 key-data pairs that result in every entry of all eight substitution tables being used at least once. Compare the results to the known values.

CONCLUSIONS: The eight substitution tables of 64 entries each are verified.

Appendix B contains a listing of the complete set of standard tests described above.

4.3 Monte-Carlo Testing

Since the test set is known to all, an additional series of tests is performed using pseudo-random data to verify that the device has not been designed just to pass the test set. In addition a successful series of Monte Carlo tests give some assurance that an anomalous combination of inputs does not exist that would cause the device to hang or otherwise malfunction for reasons not directly due to the implementation of the algorithm. While the purpose of the DES test set is to insure that the commercial device performs the DES algorithm accurately, the Monte Carlo test is needed to provide assurance that the commercial device was not built expressly to satisfy the announced tests.

(16)

Each device that is submitted for testing is subjected to a Monte-Carlo test on pseudo-random data that will run for a fixed number of iterations for all proprietary devices submitted. An additional purpose of this test is to verify that no undesirable condition within the device will cause the key or plaintext to be exposed in place of ciphertext due to a design error. The Monte-Carlo test is not a reliability test but merely checks for the presence of an apparent operational error. The pseudo-random data is initialized by the test operator at the console, and the test is terminated after a predetermined number of iterations unless there is a failure, in which case the data causing the failure is displayed at the console. The pseudo-random inputs required for the test are produced by the DES itself, used as a pseudo-random number generator. It was shown in [5] that the DES is a statistically good pseudo-random number generator, and the likelihood of cycling is very low during observable time periods.

The Monte-Carlo test, unlike the DES test , runs only on the PROLOG microcomputer. However, the source program is currently kept on a PDP-11/45 and must be cross-assembled and downstream loaded to the PROLOG. Once the program has been loaded, its execution begins immediately. Dialogue consists of prompting the operator for the initial key and seed (plaintext). These are entered as 16 hexadecimal characters. Once this initialization is complete the test begins.

The Monte-Carlo test consists of eight million encryptions and four million decryptions, with one decryption and two encryptions making up a single test. Each of the four million tests is run on both the test device and the NBS DES unit, with comparisons being made after each operation. Each individual test consists of enciphering the plaintext on both the NBS and test devices, comparing the results, enciphering the ciphertext on both the NBS and test device, comparing these results, then deciphering the output of the second encryption on the test device, and comparing this with the first ciphertext. The key remains the same, while the output of the second encryption becomes the new plaintext, as this process is repeated 10,000 times. At this time a new key is generated from the output of the first encryption that occurred in the 10,000th iteration of the preceding group of tests. A message is printed out at the console indicating that the nth group of 10,000 iterations has been completed. This series runs until completion, or until an error is detected. If an error is detected, the current key, the plaintext, the result from the NBS device and the result from the test device is printed out at the console. The error message states whether the error was in

(17)

the first encryption, the second encryption or the decryption.

This test is allowed to run until four million complete tests, comprising 8 million encipherments and 4 million decipherments , have been generated on the test device. Each group of 10,000 iterations takes approximately one minute to complete, but there will be variations from one proprietary device to another.

4.4   Procedure for Requesting Validation
      Service

The general policy for validation test procedures is specified in Part 200 of title 15, Code of Federal Regulations, and in the publication "Calibration and Test Services of the National Bureau of Standards" (NBS Special Pub. 250 [7]). Procedures for formally requesting validation services, shipping, testing and preparation and use of the validation certificate are included. Specific instructions for a manufacturer desiring a formal DES validation are provided below.

A formal request for a validation should be sent prior to the time a device is shipped to NBS. This should provide clear identification of the device being submitted, identification of the individual acting as technical representative for the test (i. e., name, address and telephone no.) and instructions for the return of the device. The formal request should also contain authorization to operate the device and authorization to charge for the test. The name and address of the individual to whom the bill should be sent should also be included.

The request for validation, complete specifications of the device to be tested (sufficient for interfacing the device to the DES testbed) and the device itself should be sent to:

Director, Center for Programming Science and Technology
Institute for Computer Sciences and Technology
A-247 Technology Building
National Bureau of Standards
Washington, D. C.,20234

(18)

The three items should be sent under separate cover. Inquiries regarding the test should be similarly addressed(or tel. 301-921-3531). The request and specifications should be sent first and the device shipped only after NBS has responded with an estimated cost of validation and a tentative testing schedule.

Insofar as possible, NBS personnel will work jointly with the manufacturer's technical representative in performing a timely test. Special provisions for testing devices that have been integrated into larger electronics equipment will be made as appropriate. Validation of DES devices only assures that the devices correctly implement the DES. The validation procedures do not include reliability testing.

Any device shipped to NBS should be sent in a reuseable container packed to minimize the potential for damage in transit. Shipping and insurance costs must be paid by the manufacturer. NBS will assume no responsibility for damage during shipment, handling or in testing.

A validation certificate will be issued to the manufacturer when the tests are successfully completed. Notification will be made to the technical representative if the tests for any reason cannot be carried out. The tests may be terminated at the request of the manufacturer at any time prior to completion and a bill for costs will be issued.

NBS does not approve, recommend or endorse any commercial product. NBS in no way guarantees that devices similar to the device validated can or will pass the validation tests. However, a manufacturer may certify that devices identical to and bearing the same identification as the device validated implement the DES. Such a claim will make the devices eligible for procurement and use by government agencies. However, no expressed or implied agreement for such procurement is made by NBS.

In accordance with Federal law (15 United States Code 275a), fees are charged for all measurement services performed by the National Bureau of Standards. Fees will include the cost of labor and materials used in performing the validation tests and in issuing a validation certificate. Labor costs will include administrative, engineering and programming personnel participating in the test. Labor rates will be determined by the cost of the personnel, including applicable overhead. Materials cost will be actual cost to NBS. Travel costs, when necessary, will be actual costs to NBS. Bills will be issued upon completion or termination of the test. A validation certificate will be issued upon

(19)

receipt of payment.

5. PREPARATION OF DEVICE VALIDATION REPORT

Each manufacturer who submits an implementation for validation will receive a validation certificate detailing the results of the standard test and of the Monte-Carlo test. The successful performance of the tests and the submission of a properly completed validation certificate on the part of the manufacturer is required by the Federal Government in all cases where procurement is being considered by a Federal agency or department. A typical validation certificate will state that the device submitted by the manufacturer satisfied the DES test set, and will also give the starting parameters and final results for the Monte-Carlo test, so the test can be exactly repeated in the future should any question arise. A sample validation certificate is shown in figure 7.

ACKNOWLEDGEMENTS

Dana Crubb and Lou Palombo, of the Center for Computer Systems Engineering, designed and constructed the NBS DES unit. Joe Sokol, of the Center for Programming Science and Technology, was responsible for the production of the testbed software. William Truitt, of the Center for Computer Systems Engineering, adapted and interfaced the microcomputer for the testbed.

Dennis Branstad, of the Center for Programming Science and Technology, was responsible for the conception and overall design of the DES testbed. Seymour Jeffery, Director of the Center for Programming Science and Technology, has provided consistent support for the project since its inception.

Thomas N. Pyke, Jr., Director of the Center for Computer Systems Engineering, provided guidance on the design of the validation certificate. Gordon Fields, Staff Attorney in the NBS Legal Office, provided many suggestions.

(20)

APPENDICES

(21)

6. Appendix A: The DES Algorithm Specification

For the convenience of the reader, this appendix contains a complete specification of the parameters involved in the definition of the DES algorithm.

The DES acts on a 64 bit block of plaintext, which is first permuted by IP:

IP

```
58 50 42 34 26 18 10 2
60 52 44 36 28 20 12 4
62 54 46 38 30 22 14 6
64 56 48 40 32 24 16 8
57 49 41 33 25 17  9 1
59 51 43 35 27 19 11 3
61 53 45 37 29 21 13 5
63 55 47 39 31 23 15 7
```

(e. g., bit one of the output is bit 58 of the input and bit two is bit 50, etc.)

The result is separated into two 32 bit registers, L and R, and then passed through the sixteen rounds as in figure Al. The final 64 bit result is operated on by the inverse of IP, IP^{-1}:

IP^{-1}

```
40  8 48 16 56 24 64 32
39  7 47 15 55 23 63 31
38  6 46 14 54 22 62 30
37  5 45 13 53 21 61 29
36  4 44 12 52 20 60 28
35  3 43 11 51 19 59 27
34  2 42 10 50 18 58 26
33  1 41  9 49 17 57 25
```

(22)

The round keys K_n are determined by the key schedule that is diagrammed in figure 3. There are three parameters to be specified, PC1, PC2 and the shift schedule:

PC1

```
57 49 41 33 25 17  9
 1 58 50 42 34 26 18
10  2 59 51 43 35 27
19 11  3 60 52 44 36
63 55 47 39 31 23 15
 7 62 54 46 38 30 22
14  6 61 53 45 37 29
21 13  5 28 20 12  4
```

PC2

```
14 17 11 24  1  5
 3 28 15  6 21 10
23 19 12  4 26  8
16  7 27 20 13  2
41 52 31 37 47 55
30 40 51 45 33 48
44 49 39 56 34 53
46 42 50 36 29 32
```

and the shift schedule is:

Iteration	Number of shifts
1	1
2	1
3	2
4	2

(23)

```
                        5                    2
                        6                    2
                        7                    2
                        8                    2
                        9                    1
                       10                    2
                       11                    2
                       12                    2
                       13                    2
                       14                    2
                       15                    2
                       16                    1
```

For a single round the expansion operator E and the permutation P need to be specified:

E

```
32   1   2   3   4   5
 4   5   6   7   8   9
 8   9  10  11  12  13
12  13  14  15  16  17
16  17  18  19  20  21
20  21  22  23  24  25
24  25  26  27  28  29
28  29  30  31  32   1
```

P

```
16   7  20  21
29  12  28  17
 1  15  23  26
 5  18  31  10
 2   8  24  14
32  27   3   9
19  13  30   6
22  11   4  25
```

There remain only the S-boxes:

(24)

(S$_1$ is figure 2.)

S$_2$

```
15   1   8  14   6  11   3   4   9   7   2  13  12   0   5  10
 3  13   4   7  15   2   8  14  12   0   1  10   6   9  11   5
 0  14   7  11  10   4  13   1   5   8  12   6   9   3   2  15
13   8  10   1   3  15   4   2  11   6   7  12   0   5  14   9
```

S$_3$

```
10   0   9  14   6   3  15   5   1  13  12   7  11   4   2   8
13   7   0   9   3   4   6  10   2   8   5  14  12  11  15   1
13   6   4   9   8  15   3   0  11   1   2  12   5  10  14   7
 1  10  13   0   6   9   8   7   4  15  14   3  11   5   2  12
```

S$_4$

```
 7  13  14   3   0   6   9  10   1   2   8   5  11  12   4  15
13   8  11   5   6  15   0   3   4   7   2  12   1  10  14   9
10   6   9   0  12  11   7  13  15   1   3  14   5   2   8   4
 3  15   0   6  10   1  13   8   9   4   5  11  12   7   2  14
```

S$_5$

```
 2  12   4   1   7  10  11   6   8   5   3  15  13   0  14   9
14  11   2  12   4   7  13   1   5   0  15  10   3   9   8   6
 4   2   1  11  10  13   7   8  15   9  12   5   6   3   0  14
11   8  12   7   1  14   2  13   6  15   0   9  10   4   5   3
```

S$_6$

```
12   1  10  15   9   2   6   8   0  13   3   4  14   7   5  11
```

(25)

```
10 15  4  2  7 12  9  5  6  1 13 14  0 11  3  8
 9 14 15  5  2  8 12  3  7  0  4 10  1 13 11  6
 4  3  2 12  9  5 15 10 11 14  1  7  6  0  8 13
```

$$S_7$$

```
 4 11  2 14 15  0  8 13  3 12  9  7  5 10  6  1
13  0 11  7  4  9  1 10 14  3  5 12  2 15  8  6
 1  4 11 13 12  3  7 14 10 15  6  8  0  5  9  2
 6 11 13  8  1  4 10  7  9  5  0 15 14  2  3 12
```

$$S_8$$

```
13  2  8  4  6 15 11  1 10  9  3 14  5  0 12  7
 1 15 13  8 10  3  7  4 12  5  6 11  0 14  9  2
 7 11  4  1  9 12 14  2  0  6 10 13 15  3  5  8
 2  1 14  7  4 10  8 13 15 12  9  0  3  5  6 11
```

The reader is referred to [3] for the official specification of these parameters.

(26)

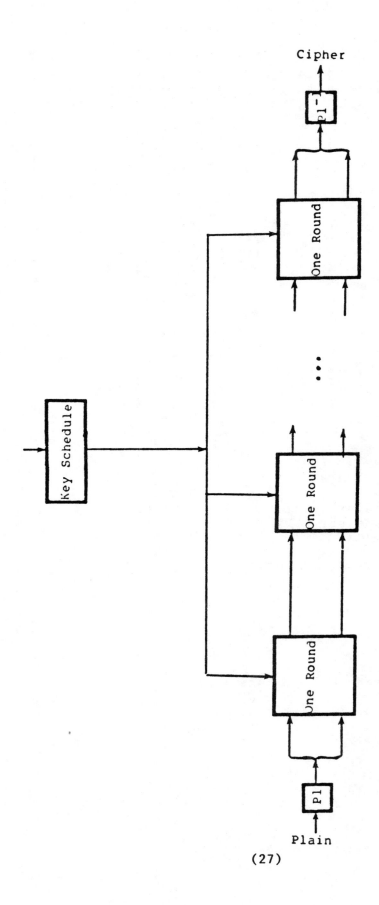

Figure A1. The sixteen rounds of the DES. The rounds are connected in series with initial and final permutations. The round keys are determined by a key schedule that is described elsewhere.

(27)

- 128 -

7. Appendix B: The DES Test Set

IP AND E TEST

KEY	PLAIN	CIPHER
0101010101010101	95F8A5E5DD31D900	8000000000000000
0101010101010101	DD7F121CA5015619	4000000000000000
0101010101010101	2E8653104F3834EA	2000000000000000
0101010101010101	4BD388FF6CD81D4F	1000000000000000
0101010101010101	20B9E767B2FB1456	0800000000000000
0101010101010101	55579380D77138EF	0400000000000000
0101010101010101	6CC5DEFAAF04512F	0200000000000000
0101010101010101	0D9F279BA5D87260	0100000000000000
0101010101010101	D9031B0271BD5A0A	0080000000000000
0101010101010101	424250B37C3DD951	0040000000000000
0101010101010101	B8061B7ECD9A21E5	0020000000000000
0101010101010101	F15D0F286B65BD28	0010000000000000
0101010101010101	ADD0CC8D6E5DEBA1	0008000000000000
0101010101010101	E6D5F82752AD63D1	0004000000000000
0101010101010101	ECBFE3BD3F591A5E	0002000000000000
0101010101010101	F356834379D165CD	0001000000000000
0101010101010101	2B9F982F20037FA9	0000800000000000
0101010101010101	889DE068A16F0BE6	0000400000000000
0101010101010101	E19E275D846A1298	0000200000000000
0101010101010101	329A8ED523D71AEC	0000100000000000
0101010101010101	E7FCE22557D23C97	0000080000000000
0101010101010101	12A9F5817FF2D65D	0000040000000000
0101010101010101	A484C3AD38DC9C19	0000020000000000
0101010101010101	FBE00A8A1EF8AD72	0000010000000000
0101010101010101	750D079407521363	0000008000000000
0101010101010101	64FEED9C724C2FAF	0000004000000000
0101010101010101	F02B263B328E2B60	0000002000000000
0101010101010101	9D64555A9A10B852	0000001000000000
0101010101010101	D106FF0BED5255D7	0000000800000000
0101010101010101	E1652C6B138C64A5	0000000400000000
0101010101010101	E428581186EC8F46	0000000200000000
0101010101010101	AEB5F5EDE22D1A36	0000000100000000
0101010101010101	E943D7568AEC0C5C	0000000080000000
0101010101010101	DF98C8276F54B04B	0000000040000000
0101010101010101	B160E4680F6C696F	0000000020000000
0101010101010101	FA0752B07D9C4AB8	0000000010000000
0101010101010101	CA3A2B036DBC8502	0000000008000000
0101010101010101	5E0905517BB59BCF	0000000004000000
0101010101010101	814EEB3B91D90726	0000000002000000
0101010101010101	4D49DB1532919C9F	0000000001000000

(28)

```
0101010101010101    25EB5FC3F8CF0621    0000000000800000
0101010101010101    AB6A20C0620D1C6F    0000000000400000
0101010101010101    79E90DBC98F92CCA    0000000000200000
0101010101010101    866ECEDD8072BB0E    0000000000100000
0101010101010101    8B54536F2F3E64A8    0000000000080000
0101010101010101    EA51D3975595B86B    0000000000040000
0101010101010101    CAFFC6AC4542DE31    0000000000020000
0101010101010101    8DD45A2DDF90796C    0000000000010000
0101010101010101    1029D55E880EC2D0    0000000000008000
0101010101010101    5D86CB23639DBEA9    0000000000004000
0101010101010101    1D1CA853AE7C0C5F    0000000000002000
0101010101010101    CE332329248F3228    0000000000001000
0101010101010101    8405D1ABE24FB942    0000000000000800
0101010101010101    E643D78090CA4207    0000000000000400
0101010101010101    48221B9937748A23    0000000000000200
0101010101010101    DD7C0BBD61FAFD54    0000000000000100
0101010101010101    2FBC291A570DB5C4    0000000000000080
0101010101010101    E07C30D7E4E26E12    0000000000000040
0101010101010101    0953E2258E8E90A1    0000000000000020
0101010101010101    5B711BC4CEEBF2EE    0000000000000010
0101010101010101    CC083F1E6D9E85F6    0000000000000008
0101010101010101    D2FD8867D50D2DFE    0000000000000004
0101010101010101    06E7EA22CE92708F    0000000000000002
0101010101010101    166B40B44ABA4BD6    0000000000000001
```

(29)

PC1 AND PC2 TEST

KEY   PLAIN   CIPHER

8001010101010101   0000000000000000   95A8D72813DAA94D
4001010101010101   0000000000000000   0EEC1487DD8C26D5
2001010101010101   0000000000000000   7AD16FFB79C45926
1001010101010101   0000000000000000   D3746294CA6A6CF3
0801010101010101   0000000000000000   809F5F873C1FD761
0401010101010101   0000000000000000   C02FAFFEC989D1FC
0201010101010101   0000000000000000   4615AA1D33E72F10
0180010101010101   0000000000000000   2055123350C00858
0140010101010101   0000000000000000   DF3B99D6577397C8
0120010101010101   0000000000000000   31FE17369B5288C9
0110010101010101   0000000000000000   DFDD3CC64DAE1642
0108010101010101   0000000000000000   178C83CE2B399D94
0104010101010101   0000000000000000   50F636324A9B7F80
0102010101010101   0000000000000000   A8468EE3BC18F06D
0101800101010101   0000000000000000   A2DC9E92FD3CDE92
0101400101010101   0000000000000000   CAC09F797D031287
0101200101010101   0000000000000000   90BA680B22AEB525
0101100101010101   0000000000000000   CE7A24F350E280B6
0101080101010101   0000000000000000   882BFF0AA01A0B87
0101040101010101   0000000000000000   25610288924511C2
0101020101010101   0000000000000000   C71516C29C75D170
0101018001010101   0000000000000000   5199C29A52C9F059
0101014001010101   0000000000000000   C22F0A294A71F29F
0101012001010101   0000000000000000   EE371483714C02EA
0101011001010101   0000000000000000   A81FBD448F9E522F
0101010801010101   0000000000000000   4F644C92E192DFED
0101010401010101   0000000000000000   1AFA9A66A6DF92AE
0101010201010101   0000000000000000   B3C1CC715CB879D8
0101010180010101   0000000000000000   19D032E64AB0BD8B
0101010140010101   0000000000000000   3CFAA7A7DC8720DC
0101010120010101   0000000000000000   B7265F7F447AC6F3
0101010110010101   0000000000000000   9DB73B3C0D163F54
0101010108010101   0000000000000000   8181B65BABF4A975
0101010104010101   0000000000000000   93C9B64042EAA240
0101010102010101   0000000000000000   5570530829705592
0101010180800101   0000000000000000   8638809E878787A0
0101010101400101   0000000000000000   41B9A79AF79AC208
0101010101200101   0000000000000000   7A9BE42F2009A892
0101010101100101   0000000000000000   29038D56BA6D2745
0101010101080101   0000000000000000   5495C6ABF1E5DF51
0101010101040101   0000000000000000   AE13DBD561488933
0101010101020101   0000000000000000   024D1FFA8904E389

(30)

```
0101010101018001    0000000000000000    D1399712F99BF02E
0101010101014001    0000000000000000    14C1D7C1CFFEC79E
0101010101012001    0000000000000000    1DE5279DAE3BED6F
0101010101011001    0000000000000000    E941A33F85501303
0101010101010801    0000000000000000    DA99DBBC9A03F379
0101010101010401    0000000000000000    B7FC92F91D8E92E9
0101010101010201    0000000000000000    AE8E5CAA3CA04E85
0101010101010180    0000000000000000    9CC62DF43B6EED74
0101010101010140    0000000000000000    D863DBB5C59A91A0
0101010101010120    0000000000000000    A1AB2190545B91D7
0101010101010110    0000000000000000    0875041E64C570F7
0101010101010108    0000000000000000    5A594528BEBEF1CC
0101010101010104    0000000000000000    FCDB3291DE21F0C0
0101010101010102    0000000000000000    869EFD7F9F265A09
```

(31)

PTEST

KEY	PLAIN	CIPHER
1046913489980131	0000000000000000	88D55E54F54C97B4
1007103489988020	0000000000000000	0C0CC00C83EA48FD
10071034C8980120	0000000000000000	83BC8EF3A6570183
1046103489988020	0000000000000000	DF725DCAD94EA2E9
1086911519190101	0000000000000000	E652B53B550BE8B0
1086911519580101	0000000000000000	AF527120C485CBB0
5107B01519580101	0000000000000000	0F04CE393DB926D5
1007B01519190101	0000000000000000	C9F00FFC74079067
3107915498080101	0000000000000000	7CFD82A593252B4E
3107919498080101	0000000000000000	CB49A2F9E91363E3
10079115B9080140	0000000000000000	00B588BE70D23F56
3107911598080140	0000000000000000	406A9A6AB43399AE
1007D01589980101	0000000000000000	6CB773611DCA9ADA
9107911589980101	0000000000000000	67FD21C17DBB5D70
9107D01589190101	0000000000000000	9592CB4110430787
1007D01598980120	0000000000000000	A6B7FF68A318DDD3
1007940498190101	0000000000000000	4D102196C914CA16
0107910491190401	0000000000000000	2DFA9F4573594965
0107910491190101	0000000000000000	B46604816C0E0774
0107940491190401	0000000000000000	6E7E6221A4F34E87
19079210981A0101	0000000000000000	AA85E74643233199
1007911998190801	0000000000000000	2E5A19DB4D1962D6
10079119981A0801	0000000000000000	23A866A809D30894
1007921098190101	0000000000000000	D812D961F017D320
1007911598190108	0000000000000000	055605816E58608F
1004801598190101	0000000000000000	ABD88E8B1B7716F1
1004801598190102	0000000000000000	537AC95BE69DA1E1
1004801598190108	0000000000000000	AED0F6AE3C25CDD8
1002911598100104	0000000000000000	B3E35A5EE53E7B8D
1002911598190104	0000000000000000	61C79C71921A2EF8
1002911598100201	0000000000000000	E2F5728F0995013C
1002911698100101	0000000000000000	1AEAC39A61F0A464

(32)

19 Key data pairs which exercise every S-box entry.

KEY	PLAIN	CIPHER
7CA110454A1A6E57	01A1D6D039776742	690F5B0D9A26939B
0131D9619DC1376E	5CD54CA83DEF57DA	7A389D10354BD271
07A1133E4A0B2686	0248D43806F67172	868EBB51CAB4599A
3849674C2602319E	51454B582DDF440A	7178876E01F19B2A
04B915BA43FEB5B6	42FD443059577FA2	AF37FB421F8C4095
0113B970FD34F2CE	059B5E0851CF143A	86A560F10EC6D85B
0170F175468FB5E6	0756D8E0774761D2	0CD3DA020021DC09
43297FAD38E373FE	762514B829BF486A	EA676B2CB7DB2B7A
07A7137045DA2A16	3BDD119049372802	DFD64A815CAF1A0F
04689104C2FD3B2F	26955F6835AF609A	5C513C9C4886C088
37D06BB516CB7546	164D5E404F275232	0A2AEEAE3FF4AB77
1F08260D1AC2465E	6B056E18759F5CCA	EF1BF03E5DFA575A
584023641ABA6176	004BD6EF09176062	88BF0DB6D70DEE56
025816164629B007	480D39006EE762F2	A1F9915541020B56
49793EBC79B3258F	437540C8698F3CFA	6FBF1CAFCFFD0556
4FB05E1515AB73A7	072D43A077075292	2F22E49BAB7CA1AC
49E95D6D4CA229BF	02FE55778117F12A	5A6B612CC26CCE4A
018310DC409B26D6	1D9D5C5018F728C2	5F4C038ED12B2E41
1C587F1C13924FEF	305532286D6F295A	63FAC0D034D9F793

(33)

8.   Appendix C: Interface Specifications

A manufacturer providing his own interface logic should use the following description and attached diagrams . In some cases, it will be relatively easy to provide hardwired logic that will make the device appear to be identical to the NBS device. However, there may be cases where it will not be feasible to make the device appear identical without software modifications in the microcomputer. In these cases, NBS personnel will make the necessary changes on a cost reimbursable basis.

Interface Design

The interface uses TTL logic levels (high-level output voltage of at least plus 2.4 volts and low-level of not more than plus 0.4 volts). The cabling normally provides a twisted pair return on three control lines to minimize the effect of noise. If further noise problems should arise, there are connector pins already allocated for twisted pair returns on the other lines. The connector uses an ELCO plug, part number 00-8016-056-000-819. In most cases it will be easier if NBS provides the connector plug and wires it as per the pin assignments of the proprietary device. If desired, the submitter may use a different connector, provided that he supplies NBS with a mate to the connector for cabling to the ELCO on the NBS microcomputer.

The lines used in the interface are shown in figure C1 and salient interface logic in figure C2. These lines are used for transferring a byte of data or key into the device from the microcomputer, for transferring a byte of data from the device back to the microcomputer and for various other control functions.

The mode of operation is controlled by the two lines: DATA/KEY and ENCIPHER/DECIPHER DATA. These levels will be stationary during a given operation. Thus, the proprietary device may either sample them at the time the first byte is loaded (data or key) or merely use them as levels for control of the process. (NBS uses the first alternative in its implementation to avoid the chance of any noise on the lines causing a malfunction.) The DATA/KEY line is low when a block of data is to be enciphered or deciphered. It is high when the key is entered. The ENCIPHER/DECIPHER DATA line is examined by the device only when data is to be enciphered or deciphered; otherwise it must be ignored. The key is

(34)

always loaded in the clear in the validation tests, so any proprietary features for enciphering or deciphering of the key should be inactive during the tests. (However, each option of the proprietary device may be tested by making special arrangements with NBS.)

The RESET EXCEPT KEY level is set by the microcomputer program and then reset by a subsequent instruction. It is used to reset the controls in the device. It may, optionally, be used to reset the LR Register, though this is not necessary. The RESET ALL signal (level) was used in the NBS implementation as a convenience for demonstration purposes and need not be implemented.

PARITY ERROR is a level from the proprietary device that indicates that one or more bytes of the key have even parity. However, it does not have to be implemented. Some devices may have available additional status indicators like BUSY and CONTROL ERROR. The tests do not make use of these indicators.

The lines for loading a byte of data or key into the device are DATA READY 1, its twisted pair return and the 8 INPUT lines. The NBS microcomputer sets up the 8 INPUT lines and, in a subsequent instruction, fires a one shot to give an approximate one microsecond pulse for DATA READY 1. The device should use DATA READY 1 to strobe the 8 INPUT lines into the device. No response from the device to the microcomputer is needed. The 8 INPUT lines should be loaded as data or as key depending on the status of the DATA/KEY control line described previously. This process is repeated for each of the 8 bytes required for the 64 bits of data or key to be loaded into the device.

The lines for transferring a byte of data back to the microcomputer are DATA READY 2, ACCEPT 2, their twisted pair returns, and the 8 OUTPUT lines. This transfer is asynchronous due to the much slower speed of the microcomputer. The sequence is: DATA READY 2 goes active (high) from the device after the 8 OUTPUT lines are stabilized; the DATA READY 2 line is polled by the program; a subsequent instruction fires a one shot to give an approximately one microsecond pulse for ACCEPT 2 (active low) to the device; and the device brings DATA READY 2 inactive (low) in response to ACCEPT 2. This process is repeated for each of the 8 bytes required for a 64 bit block transfer.

The input data, input key and output data byte numbering are shown in the figures C3 and C4.

(35)

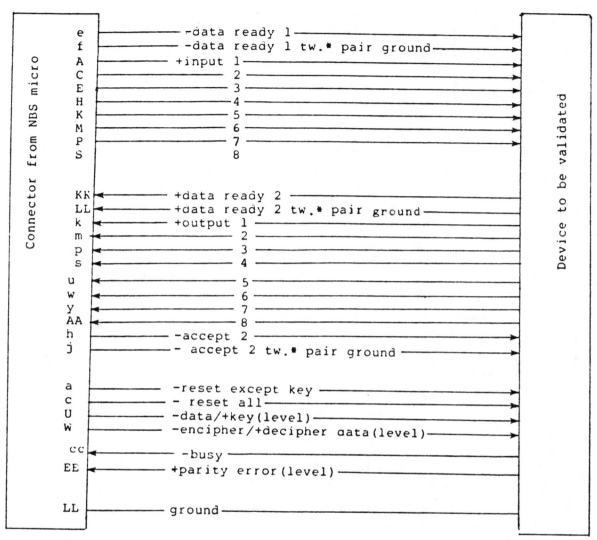

*twisted

Figure C1 . Interface line specifications or the NBS
data encryption testbed.

Cable plug; ELCO 00-8016-056-000-819

Chassis socket: ELCO 00-8016-056-000-707

(36)

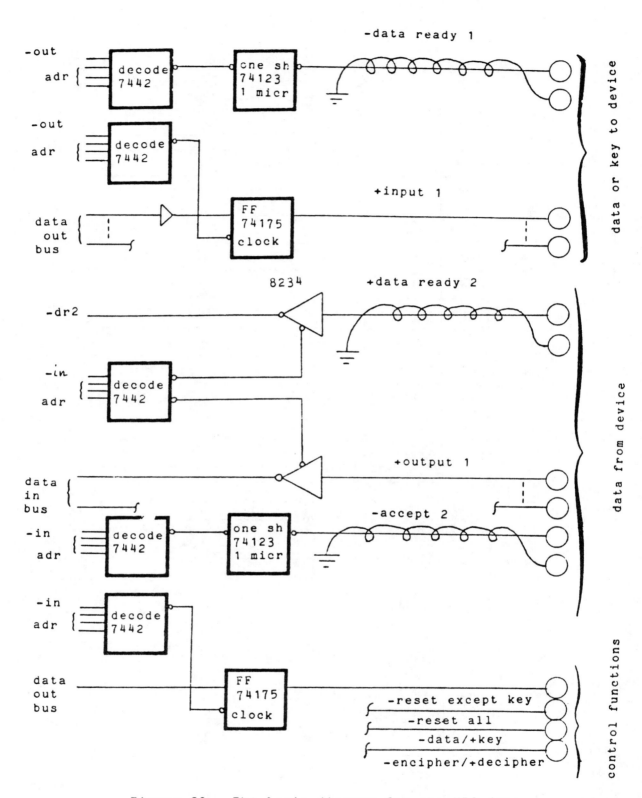

Figure C2 . The logic diagram for the NBS data encryption
testbed interface.

(37)

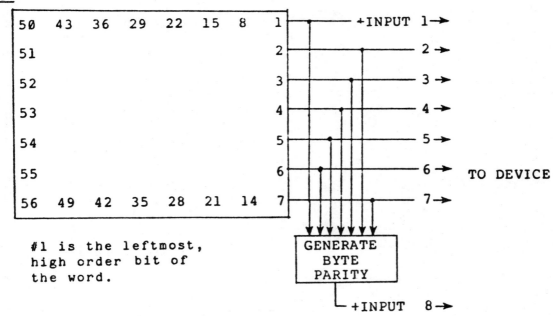

DATA

57	49	41	33	25	17	9	1	→+INPUT 1→
58							2	2→
59							3	3→
60							4	4→
61							5	5→
62							6	6→ TO DEVICE
63							7	7→
64	56	48	40	32	24	16	8	8→

KEY

50	43	36	29	22	15	8	1	+INPUT 1→
51							2	2→
52							3	3→
53							4	4→
54							5	5→
55							6	6→ TO DEVICE
56	49	42	35	28	21	14	7	7→

#1 is the leftmost,
high order bit of
the word.

GENERATE
BYTE
PARITY

+INPUT 8→

Figure C3 . Input data and input key byte numbering
        for the NBS data encryption standard
        testbed interface.

(38)

- 139 -

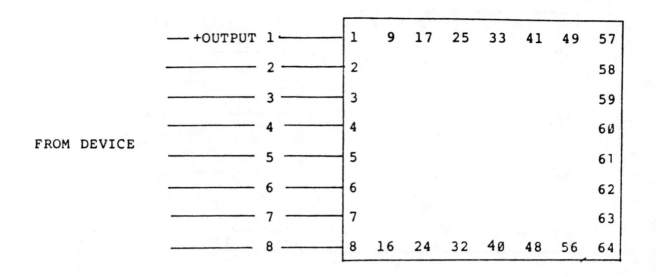

FROM DEVICE

#1 is the leftmost,high order bit
of the 64-bit data block.

Figure C4 . Output data byte numbering for the NBS data
encryption testbed interface.

(39)

REFERENCES

1. Meyer, C., Enciphering Data for Secure Transmission, Computer Design,(April, 1974)129-34.

2. Meyer, C. and W. Tuchman, Pseudo-random Codes Can Be Cracked, Elect. Design,vol. 23(1972)74-6.

3. Data Encryption Standard, FIPS PUB 46, Jan. 15, 1977.

4. Grossman, E. and B. Tuckerman, Analysis of a Feistel-like Cipher Weakened by Having No Rotating Key, IBM Rpt c6375, 1977.

5. Gait, J., A New Non-Linear Pseudo-random Number Generator, IEEE Transactions on Software Engineering, Sept.,1977.

6. Bright, H. and R. Ennison, Cryptography Using Modular Software Elements, National Computer Conf.,1976,113-23.

7. Calibration and Test Services of NBS,Spec.Pub. 250,1970.

8. DES Guidelines,NBS Special Publication 500-xx (In preparation).

(40)

APPENDIX C

FIRST 24 KEYBITS OF EACH SUB-KEY

KEYBITS OF FIRST FOUR S-BOXES

	S-1						S-2						S-3						S-4					
KEY 1	01	02	03	04	05	06	07	08	09	10	11	12	13	14	15	16	17	18	19	20	21	22	23	24
KEY 2	10	11	25	16	26	20	17	04	06	19	21	27	05	28	23	24	02	22	03	07	14	09	12	01
KEY 3	03	14	23	01	22	17	11	24	07	25	28	05	18	04	27	10	21	06	15	02	08	20	13	19
KEY 4	15	08	27	19	06	11	14	10	02	23	04	18	09	24	05	03	28	07	12	21	16	17	26	25
KEY 5	12	16	05	25	07	14	08	03	21	27	24	09	20	10	18	15	04	02	13	28	01	11	22	23
KEY 6	13	01	18	23	02	08	16	15	28	05	10	20	17	03	09	12	24	21	26	04	19	14	06	27
KEY 7	26	19	09	27	21	16	01	12	04	18	03	17	11	15	20	13	10	28	22	24	25	08	07	05
KEY 8	22	25	20	05	28	01	19	13	24	09	15	11	14	12	17	26	03	04	06	10	23	16	02	18
KEY 9	09	15	07	26	08	10	03	05	01	06	23	21	28	27	02	18	25	16	20	19	12	24	11	22
KEY 10	20	12	02	22	16	03	15	18	19	07	27	28	04	05	21	09	23	01	17	25	13	10	14	06
KEY 11	17	13	21	06	01	15	12	09	25	02	05	04	24	18	28	20	27	19	11	23	26	03	08	07
KEY 12	11	26	28	07	19	12	13	20	23	21	18	24	10	09	04	17	05	25	14	27	22	15	16	02
KEY 13	14	22	04	02	25	13	26	17	27	28	09	10	03	20	24	11	18	23	08	05	06	12	01	21
KEY 14	08	06	24	21	23	26	22	11	05	04	20	03	15	17	10	14	09	27	16	18	07	13	19	28
KEY 15	16	07	10	28	27	22	06	14	18	24	17	15	12	11	03	08	20	05	01	09	02	26	25	04
KEY 16	24	17	19	08	13	09	20	28	22	01	02	23	27	21	25	04	07	26	10	06	11	18	15	16

APPENDIX D

KEYBITS OF LAST FOUR S-BOXES

		S-5	S-6	S-7	S-8
KEY 1	–	30 31 32 33 34 35	36 37 38 39 40 41	42 43 44 45 46 47	48 49 50 51 52 53
KEY 2	–	50 46 43 49 54 37	33 44 30 32 48 47	40 56 51 38 53 55	35 41 57 39 34 36
KEY 3	–	42 36 31 47 38 51	41 39 57 56 37 52	35 46 32 50 33 34	44 55 40 43 45 49
KEY 4	–	48 49 53 52 50 32	55 43 40 46 51 54	44 36 56 42 41 45	39 34 35 31 30 47
KEY 5	–	37 47 33 54 42 56	34 31 35 36 32 38	39 49 46 48 55 30	43 45 44 53 57 52
KEY 6	–	51 52 41 38 48 46	45 53 44 49 56 50	43 47 36 37 34 57	31 30 39 33 40 54
KEY 7	–	32 54 55 50 37 36	30 33 39 47 46 42	31 52 49 51 45 40	53 57 43 41 35 38
KEY 8	–	56 38 34 42 51 49	57 41 43 52 36 48	53 54 47 32 30 35	33 40 31 55 44 50
KEY 9	–	31 30 54 40 39 41	42 47 56 34 33 35	36 45 55 43 50 37	49 48 46 52 51 57
KEY 10	–	53 57 38 35 43 55	48 52 46 45 41 44	49 30 34 31 42 51	47 37 36 54 32 40
KEY 11	–	33 40 50 44 31 34	37 54 36 30 55 39	47 57 45 53 48 32	52 51 49 38 56 35
KEY 12	–	41 35 42 39 53 45	51 38 49 57 34 43	52 40 30 33 37 56	54 32 47 50 46 44
KEY 13	–	55 44 48 43 33 30	32 50 47 40 45 31	54 35 57 41 51 46	38 56 52 42 36 39
KEY 14	–	34 39 37 31 41 57	56 42 52 35 30 53	38 44 40 55 32 36	50 46 54 48 49 43
KEY 15	–	45 43 51 53 55 40	46 48 54 44 57 33	50 39 35 34 56 49	42 36 38 37 47 31
KEY 16	–	38 56 39 36 52 48	53 35 45 51 42 49	57 32 37 54 31 41	40 33 30 44 55 46

APPENDIX E

CONTENTS OF S-BOXES

DIRECT MODE

S-1

	0000	0001	0010	0011	0100	0101	0110	0111
00	1110	0100	1101	0001	0010	1111	1011	1000
01	0000	1111	0111	0100	1110	0010	1101	0001
10	0100	0001	1110	1000	1101	0110	0010	1011
11	1111	1100	1000	0010	0100	1001	0001	0111

	1000	1001	1010	1011	1100	1101	1110	1111
00	0011	1010	0110	1100	0101	1001	0000	0111
01	1010	0110	1100	1011	1001	0101	0011	1000
10	1111	1100	1001	0111	0011	1010	0101	0000
11	0101	1011	0011	1110	1010	0000	0110	1101

S-2

	0000	0001	0010	0011	0100	0101	0110	0111
00	1111	0001	1000	1110	0110	1011	0011	0100
01	0011	1101	0100	0111	1111	0010	1000	1110
10	0000	1110	0111	1011	1010	0100	1101	0001
11	1101	1000	1010	0001	0011	1111	0100	0010

	1000	1001	1010	1011	1100	1101	1110	1111
00	1001	0111	0010	1101	1100	0000	0101	1010
01	1100	0000	0001	1010	0110	1001	1011	0101
10	0101	1000	1100	0110	1001	0011	0010	1111
11	1011	0110	0111	1100	0000	0101	1110	1001

S-3

	0000	0001	0010	0011	0100	0101	0110	0111
00	1010	0000	1001	1110	0110	0011	1111	0101
01	1101	0111	0000	1001	0011	0100	0110	1010
10	1101	0110	0100	1001	1000	1111	0011	0000
11	0001	1010	1101	0000	0110	1001	1000	0111

	1000	1001	1010	1011	1100	1101	1110	1111
00	0001	1101	1100	0111	1011	0100	0010	1000
01	0010	1000	0101	1110	1100	1011	1111	0001
10	1011	0001	0010	1100	0101	1010	1110	0111
11	0100	1111	1110	0011	1011	0101	0010	1100

S-4

	0000	0001	0010	0011	0100	0101	0110	0111
00	0111	1101	1110	0011	0000	0110	1001	1010
01	1101	1000	1011	0101	0110	1111	0000	0011
10	1010	0110	1001	0000	1100	1011	0111	1101
11	0011	1111	0000	0110	1010	0001	1101	1000

	1000	1001	1010	1011	1100	1101	1110	1111
00	0001	0010	1000	0101	1011	1100	0100	1111
01	0100	0111	0010	1100	0001	1010	1110	1001
10	1111	0001	0011	1110	0101	0010	1000	0100
11	1001	0100	0101	1011	1100	0111	0010	1110

S-5

	0000	0001	0010	0011	0100	0101	0110	0111
00	0010	1100	0100	0001	0111	1010	1011	0110
01	1110	1011	0010	1100	0100	0111	1101	0001
10	0100	0010	0001	1011	1010	1101	0111	1000
11	1011	1000	1100	0111	0001	1110	0010	1101

	1000	1001	1010	1011	1100	1101	1110	1111
00	1000	0101	0011	1111	1101	0000	1110	1001
01	0101	0000	1111	1010	0011	1001	1000	0110
10	1111	1001	1100	0101	0110	0011	0000	1110
11	0110	1111	0000	1001	1010	0100	0101	0011

S-6

	0000	0001	0010	0011	0100	0101	0110	0111
00	1100	0001	1010	1111	1001	0010	0110	1000
01	1010	1111	0100	0010	0111	1100	1001	0101
10	1001	1110	1111	0101	0010	1000	1100	0011
11	0100	0011	0010	1100	1001	0101	1111	1010

	1000	1001	1010	1011	1100	1101	1110	1111
00	0000	1101	0011	0100	1110	0111	0101	1011
01	0110	0001	1101	1110	0000	1011	0011	1000
10	0111	0000	0100	1010	0001	1101	1011	0110
11	1011	1110	0001	0111	0110	0000	1000	1101

S—7

	0000	0001	0010	0011	0100	0101	0110	0111
00	0100	1011	0010	1110	1111	0000	1000	1101
01	1101	0000	1011	0111	0100	1001	0001	1010
10	0001	0100	1011	1101	1100	0011	0111	1110
11	0110	1011	1101	1000	0001	0100	1010	0111

	1000	1001	1010	1011	1100	1101	1110	1111
00	0011	1100	1001	0111	0101	1010	0110	0001
01	1110	0011	0101	1100	0010	1111	1000	0110
10	1010	1111	0110	1000	0000	0101	1001	0010
11	1001	0101	0000	1111	1110	0010	0011	1100

S—8

	0000	0001	0010	0011	0100	0101	0110	0111
00	1101	0010	1000	0100	0110	1111	1011	0001
01	0001	1111	1101	1000	1010	0011	0111	0100
10	0111	1011	0100	0001	1001	1100	1110	0010
11	0010	0001	1110	0111	0100	1010	1000	1101

	1000	1001	1010	1011	1100	1101	1110	1111
00	1010	1001	0011	1110	0101	0000	1100	0111
01	1100	0101	0110	1011	0000	1110	1001	0010
10	0000	0110	1010	1101	1111	0011	0101	1000
11	1111	1100	1001	0000	0011	0101	0110	1011

APPENDIX F

CONTENTS OF S-BOXES

REVERSE MODE

S-1

00	1110	0011	0100	1000	0001	1100	1010	1111
01	0000	0111	0101	1110	0011	1101	1001	0010
10	1111	0001	0110	1100	0000	1110	0101	1011
11	1101	0110	0011	1010	0100	1000	1110	0111
	0000	0001	0010	0011	0100	0101	0110	0111

00	0111	1101	1001	0110	1011	0010	0000	0101
01	1111	1100	1000	1011	1010	0110	0100	0001
10	0011	1010	1101	0111	1000	0100	0010	1000
11	0010	0101	1100	1001	0001	1111	1011	0000
	1000	1001	1010	1011	1100	1101	1110	1111

S-2

00	1101	0001	1010	0110	0111	1110	0100	1001
01	1001	1010	0101	0000	0010	1111	1100	0011
10	0000	0111	1110	1101	0101	1000	1011	0010
11	1100	0011	0111	0100	0110	1101	1001	1010
	0000	0001	0010	0011	0100	0101	0110	0111

00	0010	1000	1111	0101	1100	1011	0011	0000
01	0110	1101	1011	1110	1000	0001	0111	0100
10	1001	1100	0100	0011	1010	0110	0001	1111
11	0001	1111	0010	1000	1011	0000	1110	0101
	1000	1001	1010	1011	1100	1101	1110	1111

S-3

00	0001	1000	1110	0101	1101	0111	0100	1011
01	0010	1111	1000	0100	0101	1010	0110	0001
10	0111	1001	1010	0110	0010	1100	0001	1111
11	0011	0000	1110	1011	1000	1101	0100	0111
	0000	0001	0010	0011	0100	0101	0110	0111

00	1111	0010	0000	1100	1010	1001	0011	0110
01	1001	0011	0111	1101	1100	0000	1011	1110
10	0100	0011	1101	1000	1011	0000	1110	0101
11	0110	0101	0001	1100	1111	0010	1010	1001
	1000	1001	1010	1011	1100	1101	1110	1111

S-4

00	0100	1000	1001	0011	1110	1011	0101	0000
01	0110	1100	1010	0111	1000	0011	0100	1001
10	0011	1001	1101	1010	1111	1100	0001	0110
11	0010	0101	1110	0000	1001	1010	0011	1101
	0000	0001	0010	0011	0100	0101	0110	0111

00	1010	0110	0111	1100	1101	0001	0010	1111
01	0001	1111	1101	0010	1011	0000	1110	0101
10	1110	0010	0000	0101	0100	0111	1011	1000
11	0111	1000	0100	1011	1100	0110	1111	0001
	1000	1001	1010	1011	1100	1101	1110	1111

00	1101	0011	0000	1010	0010	1001	0111	0100
01	1001	0111	0010	1100	0100	1000	1111	0101
10	1110	0010	0001	1101	0000	1011	1100	0110
11	1010	0100	0110	1111	1101	1110	1000	0011
	0000	0001	0010	0011	0100	0101	0110	0111

00	1000	1111	0101	0110	0001	1100	1110	1011
01	1110	1101	1011	0001	0011	0110	0000	1010
10	0111	1001	0100	0011	1010	0101	1111	1000
11	0001	1011	1100	0000	0010	0111	0101	1001
	1000	1001	1010	1011	1100	1101	1110	1111

S-6

00	1000	0001	0101	1010	1011	1110	0110	1101
01	1100	1001	0011	1110	0010	0111	1000	0100
10	1001	1100	0100	0111	1010	0011	1111	1000
11	1101	1010	0010	0001	0000	0101	1100	1011
	0000	0001	0010	0011	0100	0101	0110	0111

00	0111	0100	0010	1111	0000	1001	1100	0011
01	1111	0110	0000	1101	0101	1010	1011	0001
10	0101	0000	1011	1110	0110	1101	0001	0010
11	1110	0100	0111	1000	0011	1111	1001	0110
	1000	1001	1010	1011	1100	1101	1110	1111

S-7

00	0101	1111	0010	1000	0000	1100	1110	1011
01	0001	0110	1100	1001	0100	1010	1111	0011
10	1100	0000	1111	0101	0001	1101	1010	0110
11	1010	0100	1101	1110	0101	1001	0000	0111
	0000	0001	0010	0011	0100	0101	0110	0111

00	0110	1010	1101	0001	1001	0111	0011	0100
01	1110	0101	0111	0010	1011	0000	1000	1101
10	1011	1110	1000	0010	0100	0011	0111	1001
11	0011	1000	0110	0001	1111	0010	1100	1011
	1000	1001	1010	1011	1100	1101	1110	1111

S-8

00	1101	0111	0001	1010	0011	1100	0100	1111
01	1100	0000	1111	0101	0111	1001	1010	0110
10	1000	0011	0111	1101	0010	1110	1001	0000
11	1011	0001	0000	1100	0100	1101	1110	0011
	0000	0001	0010	0011	0100	0101	0110	0111

00	0010	1001	1000	0110	1110	0000	1011	0101
01	0011	1110	0100	1011	1000	0010	1101	0001
10	1111	0100	1010	0001	0101	1011	0110	1100
11	0110	1010	0101	1111	1001	0111	0010	1000
	1000	1001	1010	1011	1100	1101	1110	1111

APPENDIX G

ENCIPHERING A 64-BIT BLOCK OF PLABITS USING THE DES

```
10 REM (DES)
20 REM *ENCIPHERING A 64-BIT BLOCK OF PLABITS USING THE 'DES'*
30 KEY OFF
40 CLS
50 DIM A$(64),B$(16),C$(64),D$(16),G$(32)
60 DIM S1(4,16),S2(4,16),S3(4,16),S4(4,16),S5(4,16),S6(4,16)
70 DIM S7(4,16),S8(4,16)
80 DIM Y4$(64)
90 FOR I=0 TO 3
100 FOR J=0 TO 15
110 READ S1(I,J)
120 NEXT
130 NEXT
140 DATA 14,4,13,1,2,15,11,8,3,10,6,12,5,9,0,7
150 DATA 0,15,7,4,14,2,13,1,10,6,12,11,9,5,3,8
160 DATA 4,1,14,8,13,6,2,11,15,12,9,7,3,10,5,0
170 DATA 15,12,8,2,4,9,1,7,5,11,3,14,10,0,6,13
180 FOR I=0 TO 3
190 FOR J=0 TO 15
200 READ S2(I,J)
210 NEXT
220 NEXT
230 DATA 15,1,8,14,6,11,3,4,9,7,2,13,12,0,5,10
240 DATA 3,13,4,7,15,2,8,14,12,0,1,10,6,9,11,5
250 DATA 0,14,7,11,10,4,13,1,5,8,12,6,9,3,2,15
260 DATA 13,8,10,1,3,15,4,2,11,6,7,12,0,5,14,9
270 FOR I=0 TO 3
280 FOR J=0 TO 15
290 READ S3(I,J)
300 NEXT
310 NEXT
320 DATA 10,0,9,14,6,3,15,5,1,13,12,7,11,4,2,8
330 DATA 13,7,0,9,3,4,6,10,2,8,5,14,12,11,15,1
340 DATA 13,6,4,9,8,15,3,0,11,1,2,12,5,10,14,7
350 DATA 1,10,13,0,6,9,8,7,4,15,14,3,11,5,2,12
360 FOR I=0 TO 3
370 FOR J=0 TO 15
380 READ S4(I,J)
390 NEXT
400 NEXT
410 DATA 7,13,14,3,0,6,9,10,1,2,8,5,11,12,4,15
420 DATA 13,8,11,5,6,15,0,3,4,7,2,12,1,10,14,9
430 DATA 10,6,9,0,12,11,7,13,15,1,3,14,5,2,8,4
440 DATA 3,15,0,6,10,1,13,8,9,4,5,11,12,7,2,14
450 INPUT "ENTER NUMBER OF ITERATIONS -- ",A
460 IF A>16 OR A<1 THEN 450
470 FOR I=0 TO 3
480 FOR J=0 TO 15
490 READ S5(I,J)
500 NEXT
510 NEXT
```

```
520 DATA 2,12,4,1,7,10,11,6,8,5,3,15,13,0,14,9
530 DATA 14,11,2,12,4,7,13,1,5,0,15,10,3,9,8,6
540 DATA 4,2,1,11,10,13,7,8,15,9,12,5,6,3,0,14
550 DATA 11,8,12,7,1,14,2,13,6,15,0,9,10,4,5,3
560 FOR I=0 TO 3
570 FOR J=0 TO 15
580 READ S6(I,J)
590 NEXT
600 NEXT
610 DATA 12,1,10,15,9,2,6,8,0,13,3,4,14,7,5,11
620 DATA 10,15,4,2,7,12,9,5,6,1,13,14,0,11,3,8
630 DATA 9,14,15,5,2,8,12,3,7,0,4,10,1,13,11,6
640 DATA 4,3,2,12,9,5,15,10,11,14,1,7,6,0,8,13
650 PRINT:PRINT
660 PRINT "ENTER 'DES' MASTER OR EXTERNAL KEY IN BINARY OR HEXADECIMAL FORM -"
670 PRINT "  -------------------------------------------------------------"
680 PRINT "  ----------------"
690 INPUT "   ",A$
700 IF LEN(A$)=64 THEN 1060
710 IF LEN(A$)=16 THEN 740
720 LOCATE 7,3:PRINT SPACE$(75)
730 LOCATE 7:GOTO 690
740 FOR I=1 TO 16
750 A$(I)=MID$(A$,I,1)
760 IF A$(I)="0" THEN B$(I)="0000":GOTO 930
770 IF A$(I)="1" THEN B$(I)="0001":GOTO 930
780 IF A$(I)="2" THEN B$(I)="0010":GOTO 930
790 IF A$(I)="3" THEN B$(I)="0011":GOTO 930
800 IF A$(I)="4" THEN B$(I)="0100":GOTO 930
810 IF A$(I)="5" THEN B$(I)="0101":GOTO 930
820 IF A$(I)="6" THEN B$(I)="0110":GOTO 930
830 IF A$(I)="7" THEN B$(I)="0111":GOTO 930
840 IF A$(I)="8" THEN B$(I)="1000":GOTO 930
850 IF A$(I)="9" THEN B$(I)="1001":GOTO 930
860 IF A$(I)="A" THEN B$(I)="1010":GOTO 930
870 IF A$(I)="B" THEN B$(I)="1011":GOTO 930
880 IF A$(I)="C" THEN B$(I)="1100":GOTO 930
890 IF A$(I)="D" THEN B$(I)="1101":GOTO 930
900 IF A$(I)="E" THEN B$(I)="1110":GOTO 930
910 IF A$(I)="F" THEN B$(I)="1111":GOTO 930
920 C=1
930 NEXT
940 IF C=0 THEN 1020
950 C=0:PRINT
960 PRINT "   ERROR IN 'HEXADECIMAL' ENTRY -- PRESS ANY KEY TO CONTINUE"
970 X$=INKEY$
980 IF X$="" THEN LOCATE,,0:GOTO 970
990 LOCATE 7,3:PRINT SPACE$(75)
1000 LOCATE 9:PRINT SPACE$(60)
1010 LOCATE 7:GOTO 690
1020 A$=""
1030 FOR I=1 TO 16
1040 A$=A$+B$(I)
1050 NEXT
1060 FOR I=1 TO 64
1070 D1$=MID$(A$,I,1)
1080 IF D1$="0" OR D1$="1" THEN 1120
1090 LOCATE 7,3:PRINT SPACE$(75)
1100 LOCATE 9:PRINT SPACE$(60)
1110 LOCATE 7:GOTO 690
1120 NEXT
1130 FOR I=0 TO 3
1140 FOR J=0 TO 15
1150 READ S7(I,J)
1160 NEXT
```

```
1170 NEXT
1180 DATA 4,11,2,14,15,0,8,13,3,12,9,7,5,10,6,1
1190 DATA 13,0,11,7,4,9,1,10,14,3,5,12,2,15,8,6
1200 DATA 1,4,11,13,12,3,7,14,10,15,6,8,0,5,9,2
1210 DATA 6,11,13,8,1,4,10,7,9,5,0,15,14,2,3,12
1220 FOR I=0 TO 3
1230 FOR J=0 TO 15
1240 READ S8(I,J)
1250 NEXT
1260 NEXT
1270 DATA 13,2,8,4,6,15,11,1,10,9,3,14,5,0,12,7
1280 DATA 1,15,13,8,10,3,7,4,12,5,6,11,0,14,9,2
1290 DATA 7,11,4,1,9,12,14,2,0,6,10,13,15,3,5,8
1300 DATA 2,1,14,7,4,10,8,13,15,12,9,0,3,5,6,11
1310 LPRINT "64-BIT 'DES' MASTER OR EXTERNAL KEY --"
1320 LPRINT
1330 LPRINT "2113355-1025554-0214434-1123334-0012343-2021453-0202435-0110454-"
1340 LPRINT "1031975-1176107-2423401-7632789-7452553-0858846-6836043-9495226-"
1350 LPRINT "----------------------------------------------------------------"
1360 LPRINT A$
1370 LPRINT
1380 LPRINT "        KEY IN HEXADECIMAL FORM = ";
1390 FOR I=1 TO 64
1400 A$(I)=MID$(A$,I,1)
1410 NEXT
1420 FOR K=0 TO 15
1430 T1=0:T2=0:T3=0:T4=0:T5=0
1440 IF A$(4*K+1)="1" THEN T1=8
1450 IF A$(4*K+2)="1" THEN T2=4
1460 IF A$(4*K+3)="1" THEN T3=2
1470 IF A$(4*K+4)="1" THEN T4=1
1480 T5=T4+T3+T2+T1
1490 LPRINT HEX$(T5);
1500 NEXT
1510 LPRINT:LPRINT:LPRINT
1520 PRINT
1530 PRINT "ENTER PLAINTEXT - PLABITS - IN EITHER BINARY OR HEXADECIMAL FORM -"
1540 PRINT "  ---------------------------------------------------------------"
1550 PRINT "  ----------------"
1560 INPUT "   ",C$
1570 IF LEN(C$)=64 THEN 1930
1580 IF LEN(C$)=16 THEN 1610
1590 LOCATE 12,3:PRINT SPACE$(75)
1600 LOCATE 12:GOTO 1560
1610 FOR I=1 TO 16
1620 C$(I)=MID$(C$,I,1)
1630 IF C$(I)="0" THEN D$(I)="0000":GOTO 1800
1640 IF C$(I)="1" THEN D$(I)="0001":GOTO 1800
1650 IF C$(I)="2" THEN D$(I)="0010":GOTO 1800
1660 IF C$(I)="3" THEN D$(I)="0011":GOTO 1800
1670 IF C$(I)="4" THEN D$(I)="0100":GOTO 1800
1680 IF C$(I)="5" THEN D$(I)="0101":GOTO 1800
1690 IF C$(I)="6" THEN D$(I)="0110":GOTO 1800
1700 IF C$(I)="7" THEN D$(I)="0111":GOTO 1800
1710 IF C$(I)="8" THEN D$(I)="1000":GOTO 1800
1720 IF C$(I)="9" THEN D$(I)="1001":GOTO 1800
1730 IF C$(I)="A" THEN D$(I)="1010":GOTO 1800
1740 IF C$(I)="B" THEN D$(I)="1011":GOTO 1800
1750 IF C$(I)="C" THEN D$(I)="1100":GOTO 1800
1760 IF C$(I)="D" THEN D$(I)="1101":GOTO 1800
1770 IF C$(I)="E" THEN D$(I)="1110":GOTO 1800
1780 IF C$(I)="F" THEN D$(I)="1111":GOTO 1800
1790 D=1
1800 NEXT
1810 IF D=0 THEN 1890
1820 D=0:PRINT
```

```
1830 PRINT "  ERROR IN 'HEXADECIMAL' ENTRY -- PRESS ANY KEY TO CONTINUE"
1840 X$=INKEY$
1850 IF X$="" THEN LOCATE,,0:GOTO 1840
1860 LOCATE 12,3:PRINT SPACE$(75)
1870 LOCATE 14:PRINT SPACE$(60)
1880 LOCATE 12:GOTO 1560
1890 C$=""
1900 FOR I=1 TO 16
1910 C$=C$+D$(I)
1920 NEXT
1930 FOR I=1 TO 64
1940 E1$=MID$(C$,I,1)
1950 IF E1$="0" OR E1$="1" THEN 1990
1960 LOCATE 12,3:PRINT SPACE$(75)
1970 LOCATE 14:PRINT SPACE$(60)
1980 LOCATE 12:GOTO 1560
1990 NEXT
2000 LPRINT "64-BIT BLOCK OF PLABITS -- (BITS WHICH FORM M-0 AND M-1)"
2010 LPRINT
2020 LPRINT "14140425263603031415251426033625252514032525253603140414140030315"
2030 LPRINT "79029157801335462480791391572424136846680235460279578035681324910"
2040 LPRINT "-----------------------------------------------------------------"
2050 LPRINT C$
2060 LPRINT
2070 LPRINT "PLABITS IN HEXADECIMAL FORM = ";
2080 FOR I=1 TO 64
2090 C$(I)=MID$(C$,I,1)
2100 NEXT
2110 FOR K=0 TO 15
2120 T1=0:T2=0:T3=0:T4=0:T5=0
2130 IF C$(4*K+1)="1" THEN T1=8
2140 IF C$(4*K+2)="1" THEN T2=4
2150 IF C$(4*K+3)="1" THEN T3=2
2160 IF C$(4*K+4)="1" THEN T4=1
2170 T5=T4+T3+T2+T1
2180 LPRINT HEX$(T5);
2190 NEXT
2200 LPRINT:LPRINT
2210 LPRINT STRING$(79,"-")
2220 LPRINT
2230 LPRINT "     3333      3334      4444      4444      4555      5555      5556      6
666"
2240 LPRINT "     3456      7890      1234      5678      9012      3456      7890      1
234"
2250 LPRINT "     ----      ----      ----      ----      ----      ----      ----      -
---"
2260 E$(1)=C$(60)+C$(62)+C$(14)+C$(16)
2270 E$(2)=C$(28)+C$(40)+C$(50)+C$(54)
2280 E$(3)=C$(6)+C$(4)+C$(24)+C$(18)
2290 E$(4)=C$(56)+C$(38)+C$(52)+C$(58)
2300 E$(5)=C$(2)+C$(20)+C$(64)+C$(42)
2310 E$(6)=C$(34)+C$(32)+C$(44)+C$(46)
2320 E$(7)=C$(8)+C$(36)+C$(22)+C$(10)
2330 E$(8)=C$(26)+C$(48)+C$(12)+C$(30)
2340 LPRINT "     ";
2350 IF Z<3 THEN 2420
2360 FOR I=1 TO 8
2370 LPRINT F3$(I);
2380 IF I=8 THEN 2400
2390 LPRINT "  -  ";
2400 NEXT
2410 GOTO 2570
2420 IF Z=2 THEN 2440
2430 GOTO 2510
2440 FOR I=1 TO 8
```

```
2450 LPRINT F$(I);
2460 E$(I)=F$(I)
2470 IF I=8 THEN 2490
2480 LPRINT "  -  ";
2490 NEXT
2500 LPRINT "   M-"+RIGHT$(STR$(Z-1),1):GOTO 2600
2510 FOR I=1 TO 8
2520 M$(I)=""
2530 LPRINT E$(I);
2540 IF I=8 THEN 2560
2550 LPRINT "  -  ";
2560 NEXT
2570 IF Z>1 AND Z>10 THEN LPRINT "   M-"+RIGHT$(STR$(Z-1),2):GOTO 2600
2580 IF Z>1 AND Z<11 THEN LPRINT "   M-"+RIGHT$(STR$(Z-1),1):GOTO 2600
2590 LPRINT "   M-0"
2600 LPRINT
2610 IF Z=A THEN 2650
```
```
2620 LPRINT "    0000      0000      0111      1111      1112      2222      2222      2
333"
2630 LPRINT "    1234      5678      9012      3456      7890      1234      5678      9
012"
2640 GOTO 2670
2650 LPRINT "    3333      3334      4444      4444      4555      5555      5556      6
666"
2660 LPRINT "    3456      7890      1234      5678      9012      3456      7890      1
234"
2670 LPRINT "    ----      ----      ----      ----      ----      ----      ----      -
---"
```
```
2680 IF Z=1 OR Z=2 THEN 2930
2690 IF Z>2 THEN 2860
2700 F$(1)=C$(59)+C$(61)+C$(13)+C$(15)
2710 F$(2)=C$(27)+C$(39)+C$(49)+C$(53)
2720 F$(3)=C$(5)+C$(3)+C$(23)+C$(17)
2730 F$(4)=C$(55)+C$(37)+C$(51)+C$(57)
2740 F$(5)=C$(1)+C$(19)+C$(63)+C$(41)
2750 F$(6)=C$(33)+C$(31)+C$(43)+C$(45)
2760 F$(7)=C$(7)+C$(35)+C$(21)+C$(9)
2770 F$(8)=C$(25)+C$(47)+C$(11)+C$(29)
2780 LPRINT "    ";
2790 FOR I=1 TO 8
2800 LPRINT F$(I);
2810 IF A=1 THEN S2$(I)=F$(I)
2820 IF I=8 THEN 2840
2830 LPRINT "  -  ";
2840 NEXT
2850 GOTO 3090
2860 FOR I=1 TO 8
2870 FOR J=1 TO 4
2880 IF MID$(W$(I),J,1)=MID$(F3$(I),J,1) THEN F1$(I)=F1$(I)+"0"
2890 IF MID$(W$(I),J,1)<>MID$(F3$(I),J,1) THEN F1$(I)=F1$(I)+"1"
2900 NEXT
2910 NEXT
2920 GOTO 2990
2930 FOR I=1 TO 8
2940 FOR J=1 TO 4
2950 IF MID$(W$(I),J,1)=MID$(E$(I),J,1) THEN F1$(I)=F1$(I)+"0"
2960 IF MID$(W$(I),J,1)<>MID$(E$(I),J,1) THEN F1$(I)=F1$(I)+"1"
2970 NEXT
2980 NEXT
2990 LPRINT " = ";
3000 GOTO 3020
3010 LPRINT "    ";
3020 FOR I=1 TO 8
3030 F3$(I)=F2$(I)
3040 F2$(I)=F1$(I)
3050 LPRINT F1$(I);
```

```
3060 IF I=8 THEN 3080
3070 LPRINT "  -  ";
3080 NEXT
3090 IF Z>8 THEN LPRINT "  M-"+RIGHT$(STR$(Z+1),2)
3100 IF Z<9 THEN LPRINT "  M-"+RIGHT$(STR$(Z+1),1)
3110 LPRINT
3120 IF Z=A THEN 6390
3130 LPRINT STRING$(79,".")
3140 LPRINT
3150 LPRINT "22-1022   20-2121   10-0122   20-0131   13-0021   11-3200   02-1130   01-2
102"
3160 LPRINT "59-6701   11-9287   75-1536   62-5810   02-2844   49-2739   92-9306   66-2
145"
3170 LPRINT "-- ----   -- ----   -- ----   -- ----   -- ----   -- ----   -- ----   -- -
---"
3180 IF Z=0 THEN 3240
3190 FOR I=1 TO 8
3200 G$=G$+F1$(I)
3210 F1$(I)=""
3220 NEXT
3230 GOTO 3270
3240 FOR I=1 TO 8
3250 G$=G$+F$(I)
3260 NEXT
3270 FOR I=1 TO 32
3280 G$(I)=MID$(G$,I,1)
3290 NEXT
3300 H$(1)=G$(25)+G$(29)+"-"+G$(16)+G$(7)+G$(20)+G$(21)
3310 H$(2)=G$(21)+G$(1)+"-"+G$(29)+G$(12)+G$(28)+G$(17)
3320 H$(3)=G$(17)+G$(5)+"-"+G$(1)+G$(15)+G$(23)+G$(26)
3330 H$(4)=G$(26)+G$(2)+"-"+G$(5)+G$(18)+G$(31)+G$(10)
3340 H$(5)=G$(10)+G$(32)+"-"+G$(2)+G$(8)+G$(24)+G$(14)
3350 H$(6)=G$(14)+G$(19)+"-"+G$(32)+G$(27)+G$(3)+G$(9)
3360 H$(7)=G$(9)+G$(22)+"-"+G$(19)+G$(13)+G$(30)+G$(6)
3370 H$(8)=G$(6)+G$(16)+"-"+G$(22)+G$(11)+G$(4)+G$(25)
3380 G$=""
3390 FOR I=1 TO 8
3400 M$(I)=""
3410 LPRINT H$(I);
3420 LPRINT "   ";
3430 NEXT
3440 IF Z>8 THEN LPRINT "M-"+RIGHT$(STR$(Z+1),2)+" EXP":LPRINT
3450 IF Z<9 THEN LPRINT "M-"+RIGHT$(STR$(Z+1),1)+" EXP":LPRINT
3460 IF Z=0 THEN 4060
3470 IF Z=1 THEN 4030
3480 IF Z=2 THEN 4000
3490 IF Z=3 THEN 3970
3500 IF Z=4 THEN 3940
3510 IF Z=5 THEN 3910
3520 IF Z=6 THEN 3880
3530 IF Z=7 THEN 3850
3540 IF Z=8 THEN 3820
3550 IF Z=9 THEN 3790
3560 IF Z=10 THEN 3760
3570 IF Z=11 THEN 3730
3580 IF Z=12 THEN 3700
3590 IF Z=13 THEN 3670
3600 IF Z=14 THEN 3640
3610 LPRINT "21-1010   22-2002   22-2002   10-1111   35-3354   53-4544   53-3534   43-3
454"
3620 LPRINT "47-9839   08-2123   71-5476   06-1856   86-9628   35-5129   72-7411   03-0
456"
3630 GOTO 4080
3640 LPRINT "10-1222   01-1211   11-0020   00-0220   44-5554   44-5453   53-3354   43-3
343"
3650 LPRINT "67-0872   64-8475   21-3805   19-2654   53-1350   68-4473   09-5469   26-8
```

```
771"
3660 GOTO 4080
3670 LPRINT "00-2222  21-0020  11-1102  11-0112  33-3345  54-5335  34-4533  54-5
444"
3680 LPRINT "86-4136  21-5403  57-0497  68-7398  49-7117  62-2503  84-0526  06-4
893"
3690 GOTO 4080
3700 LPRINT "12-0021  21-2201  02-2112  00-0102  54-4433  35-4443  53-5454  35-5
433"
3710 LPRINT "42-4253  67-7890  30-4183  85-6211  54-8330  20-7051  45-7116  86-2
269"
3720 GOTO 4080
3730 LPRINT "12-2011  12-2212  10-0102  12-2110  43-4354  53-4534  54-3335  53-4
544"
3740 LPRINT "16-8792  30-3184  09-4755  47-2562  15-2935  18-9743  20-0376  42-7
064"
3750 GOTO 4080
3760 LPRINT "11-2001  10-2000  21-2221  12-2000  34-5433  35-3353  45-4543  55-4
353"
3770 LPRINT "73-1615  29-5254  48-8079  13-6387  30-0414  74-6059  77-5382  21-9
865"
3780 GOTO 4080
3790 LPRINT "21-0210  11-1022  00-2020  12-1110  55-3345  45-4444  43-3345  43-3
534"
3800 LPRINT "02-2263  58-9778  45-1931  75-3046  37-8535  82-6514  90-4121  77-6
420"
3810 GOTO 4080
3820 LPRINT "01-0201  00-0022  22-0121  21-1212  33-5434  44-5333  34-5453  44-4
555"
3830 LPRINT "95-7680  35-1631  87-2856  09-2412  10-4091  27-6435  65-5307  98-6
217"
3840 GOTO 4080
3850 LPRINT "22-2020  11-2011  11-1200  01-2101  53-3454  54-4534  55-4333  34-3
545"
3860 LPRINT "25-0581  93-4951  42-7634  60-3628  68-4219  71-3268  34-7205  30-1
540"
3870 GOTO 4080
3880 LPRINT "21-0221  01-0101  11-2112  22-2000  35-5533  33-3444  35-4544  55-4
433"
3890 LPRINT "69-9716  12-4837  15-0308  24-5875  24-5076  03-9762  12-9150  37-3
158"
3900 GOTO 4080
3910 LPRINT "10-1200  11-2012  10-0122  20-1102  55-4344  45-4455  44-3335  33-3
345"
3920 LPRINT "31-8328  65-8500  73-9241  64-9467  12-1886  53-4960  37-6747  10-9
304"
3930 GOTO 4080
3940 LPRINT "11-0201  00-2220  21-1100  12-0122  34-3545  33-3333  34-4453  44-4
555"
3950 LPRINT "26-5574  83-1749  00-8542  38-1123  77-3426  41-5628  99-6850  35-4
372"
3960 GOTO 4080
3970 LPRINT "10-2101  11-0201  02-0020  12-1122  44-5553  54-4455  43-5444  33-3
334"
3980 LPRINT "58-7961  40-2348  94-5387  21-6765  89-3202  53-0614  46-6215  94-5
107"
3990 GOTO 4080
4000 LPRINT "01-2021  12-0220  10-2120  10-0211  43-3435  43-5535  34-3533  45-4
444"
4010 LPRINT "34-3127  14-7585  84-7016  52-8039  26-1781  19-7672  56-2034  45-0
359"
4020 GOTO 4080
4030 LPRINT "11-2122  10-0122  02-2202  00-1010  54-4453  34-3344  45-5355  34-5
333"
4040 LPRINT "01-5660  74-6917  58-3422  37-4921  06-3947  34-0287  06-1835  51-7
946"
```

```
4050 GOTO 4080
4060 LPRINT "00-0000   00-0111   11-1111   12-2222   33-3333   33-3344   44-4444   44-5
555"
4070 LPRINT "12-3456   78-9012   34-5678   90-1234   01-2345   67-8901   23-4567   89-0
123"
4080 LPRINT "-- ----   -- ----   -- ----   -- ----   -- ----   -- ----   -- ----   -- -
---"
4090 IF Z=0 THEN 5600
4100 IF Z=1 THEN 5510
4110 IF Z=2 THEN 5420
4120 IF Z=3 THEN 5330
4130 IF Z=4 THEN 5240
4140 IF Z=5 THEN 5150
4150 IF Z=6 THEN 5060
4160 IF Z=7 THEN 4970
4170 IF Z=8 THEN 4880
4180 IF Z=9 THEN 4790
4190 IF Z=10 THEN 4700
4200 IF Z=11 THEN 4610
4210 IF Z=12 THEN 4520
4220 IF Z=13 THEN 4430
4230 IF Z=14 THEN 4340
4240 IF Z=15 THEN 4250
4250 L$(1)=A$(18)+A$(25)+"-"+A$(59)+A$(42)+A$(3)+A$(57)
4260 L$(2)=A$(41)+A$(50)+"-"+A$(36)+A$(10)+A$(17)+A$(27)
4270 L$(3)=A$(11)+A$(1)+"-"+A$(43)+A$(34)+A$(33)+A$(52)
4280 L$(4)=A$(2)+A$(49)+"-"+A$(9)+A$(44)+A$(35)+A$(26)
4290 L$(5)=A$(30)+A$(12)+"-"+A$(5)+A$(47)+A$(62)+A$(45)
4300 L$(6)=A$(55)+A$(37)+"-"+A$(38)+A$(13)+A$(61)+A$(31)
4310 L$(7)=A$(6)+A$(28)+"-"+A$(29)+A$(46)+A$(4)+A$(23)
4320 L$(8)=A$(53)+A$(39)+"-"+A$(22)+A$(21)+A$(7)+A$(63)
4330 GOTO 5680
4340 L$(1)=A$(26)+A$(33)+"-"+A$(2)+A$(50)+A$(11)+A$(36)
4350 L$(2)=A$(49)+A$(58)+"-"+A$(44)+A$(18)+A$(25)+A$(35)
4360 L$(3)=A$(19)+A$(9)+"-"+A$(51)+A$(42)+A$(41)+A$(60)
4370 L$(4)=A$(10)+A$(57)+"-"+A$(17)+A$(52)+A$(43)+A$(34)
4380 L$(5)=A$(38)+A$(20)+"-"+A$(13)+A$(55)+A$(7)+A$(53)
4390 L$(6)=A$(63)+A$(45)+"-"+A$(46)+A$(21)+A$(6)+A$(39)
4400 L$(7)=A$(14)+A$(5)+"-"+A$(37)+A$(54)+A$(12)+A$(31)
4410 L$(8)=A$(61)+A$(47)+"-"+A$(30)+A$(29)+A$(15)+A$(4)
4420 GOTO 5680
4430 L$(1)=A$(42)+A$(49)+"-"+A$(18)+A$(1)+A$(27)+A$(52)
4440 L$(2)=A$(36)+A$(9)+"-"+A$(60)+A$(34)+A$(41)+A$(51)
4450 L$(3)=A$(35)+A$(25)+"-"+A$(2)+A$(58)+A$(57)+A$(11)
4460 L$(4)=A$(26)+A$(44)+"-"+A$(33)+A$(3)+A$(59)+A$(50)
4470 L$(5)=A$(54)+A$(5)+"-"+A$(29)+A$(4)+A$(23)+A$(6)
4480 L$(6)=A$(12)+A$(61)+"-"+A$(62)+A$(37)+A$(22)+A$(55)
4490 L$(7)=A$(30)+A$(21)+"-"+A$(53)+A$(7)+A$(28)+A$(47)
4500 L$(8)=A$(14)+A$(63)+"-"+A$(46)+A$(45)+A$(31)+A$(20)
4510 GOTO 5680
4520 L$(1)=A$(58)+A$(36)+"-"+A$(34)+A$(17)+A$(43)+A$(3)
4530 L$(2)=A$(52)+A$(25)+"-"+A$(11)+A$(50)+A$(57)+A$(2)
4540 L$(3)=A$(51)+A$(41)+"-"+A$(18)+A$(9)+A$(44)+A$(27)
4550 L$(4)=A$(42)+A$(60)+"-"+A$(49)+A$(19)+A$(10)+A$(1)
4560 L$(5)=A$(7)+A$(21)+"-"+A$(45)+A$(20)+A$(39)+A$(22)
4570 L$(6)=A$(28)+A$(14)+"-"+A$(15)+A$(53)+A$(38)+A$(4)
4580 L$(7)=A$(46)+A$(37)+"-"+A$(6)+A$(23)+A$(13)+A$(63)
4590 L$(8)=A$(30)+A$(12)+"-"+A$(62)+A$(61)+A$(47)+A$(5)
4600 GOTO 5680
4610 L$(1)=A$(9)+A$(52)+"-"+A$(50)+A$(33)+A$(59)+A$(19)
4620 L$(2)=A$(3)+A$(41)+"-"+A$(27)+A$(1)+A$(44)+A$(18)
4630 L$(3)=A$(2)+A$(57)+"-"+A$(34)+A$(25)+A$(60)+A$(43)
4640 L$(4)=A$(58)+A$(11)+"-"+A$(36)+A$(35)+A$(26)+A$(17)
4650 L$(5)=A$(23)+A$(37)+"-"+A$(61)+A$(5)+A$(55)+A$(38)
4660 L$(6)=A$(13)+A$(30)+"-"+A$(31)+A$(6)+A$(54)+A$(20)
4670 L$(7)=A$(62)+A$(53)+"-"+A$(22)+A$(39)+A$(29)+A$(12)
```

```
4680 L$(8)=A$(46)+A$(28)+"-"+A$(15)+A$(14)+A$(63)+A$(21)
4690 GOTO 5680
4700 L$(1)=A$(25)+A$(3)+"-"+A$(1)+A$(49)+A$(10)+A$(35)
4710 L$(2)=A$(19)+A$(57)+"-"+A$(43)+A$(17)+A$(60)+A$(34)
4720 L$(3)=A$(18)+A$(44)+"-"+A$(50)+A$(41)+A$(11)+A$(59)
4730 L$(4)=A$(9)+A$(27)+"-"+A$(52)+A$(51)+A$(42)+A$(33)
4740 L$(5)=A$(39)+A$(53)+"-"+A$(14)+A$(21)+A$(4)+A$(54)
4750 L$(6)=A$(29)+A$(46)+"-"+A$(47)+A$(22)+A$(7)+A$(5)
4760 L$(7)=A$(15)+A$(6)+"-"+A$(38)+A$(55)+A$(45)+A$(28)
4770 L$(8)=A$(62)+A$(13)+"-"+A$(31)+A$(30)+A$(12)+A$(37)
4780 GOTO 5680
4790 L$(1)=A$(41)+A$(19)+"-"+A$(17)+A$(36)+A$(26)+A$(51)
4800 L$(2)=A$(35)+A$(44)+"-"+A$(59)+A$(33)+A$(11)+A$(50)
4810 L$(3)=A$(34)+A$(60)+"-"+A$(1)+A$(57)+A$(27)+A$(10)
4820 L$(4)=A$(25)+A$(43)+"-"+A$(3)+A$(2)+A$(58)+A$(49)
4830 L$(5)=A$(55)+A$(6)+"-"+A$(30)+A$(37)+A$(20)+A$(7)
4840 L$(6)=A$(45)+A$(62)+"-"+A$(63)+A$(38)+A$(23)+A$(21)
4850 L$(7)=A$(31)+A$(22)+"-"+A$(54)+A$(4)+A$(61)+A$(13)
4860 L$(8)=A$(15)+A$(29)+"-"+A$(47)+A$(46)+A$(28)+A$(53)
4870 GOTO 5680
4880 L$(1)=A$(57)+A$(35)+"-"+A$(33)+A$(52)+A$(42)+A$(2)
4890 L$(2)=A$(51)+A$(60)+"-"+A$(10)+A$(49)+A$(27)+A$(1)
4900 L$(3)=A$(50)+A$(11)+"-"+A$(17)+A$(44)+A$(43)+A$(26)
4910 L$(4)=A$(41)+A$(59)+"-"+A$(19)+A$(18)+A$(9)+A$(36)
4920 L$(5)=A$(4)+A$(22)+"-"+A$(46)+A$(53)+A$(5)+A$(23)
4930 L$(6)=A$(61)+A$(15)+"-"+A$(12)+A$(54)+A$(39)+A$(37)
4940 L$(7)=A$(47)+A$(38)+"-"+A$(7)+A$(20)+A$(14)+A$(29)
4950 L$(8)=A$(31)+A$(45)+"-"+A$(63)+A$(62)+A$(13)+A$(6)
4960 GOTO 5680
4970 L$(1)=A$(36)+A$(43)+"-"+A$(41)+A$(60)+A$(50)+A$(10)
4980 L$(2)=A$(59)+A$(3)+"-"+A$(18)+A$(57)+A$(35)+A$(9)
4990 L$(3)=A$(58)+A$(19)+"-"+A$(25)+A$(52)+A$(51)+A$(34)
5000 L$(4)=A$(49)+A$(2)+"-"+A$(27)+A$(26)+A$(17)+A$(44)
5010 L$(5)=A$(12)+A$(30)+"-"+A$(54)+A$(61)+A$(13)+A$(31)
5020 L$(6)=A$(6)+A$(23)+"-"+A$(20)+A$(62)+A$(47)+A$(45)
5030 L$(7)=A$(55)+A$(46)+"-"+A$(15)+A$(28)+A$(22)+A$(37)
5040 L$(8)=A$(39)+A$(53)+"-"+A$(4)+A$(7)+A$(21)+A$(14)
5050 GOTO 5680
5060 L$(1)=A$(52)+A$(59)+"-"+A$(57)+A$(11)+A$(1)+A$(26)
5070 L$(2)=A$(10)+A$(19)+"-"+A$(34)+A$(44)+A$(51)+A$(25)
5080 L$(3)=A$(9)+A$(35)+"-"+A$(41)+A$(3)+A$(2)+A$(50)
5090 L$(4)=A$(36)+A$(18)+"-"+A$(43)+A$(42)+A$(33)+A$(60)
5100 L$(5)=A$(28)+A$(46)+"-"+A$(7)+A$(14)+A$(29)+A$(47)
5110 L$(6)=A$(22)+A$(39)+"-"+A$(5)+A$(15)+A$(63)+A$(61)
5120 L$(7)=A$(4)+A$(62)+"-"+A$(31)+A$(13)+A$(38)+A$(53)
5130 L$(8)=A$(55)+A$(6)+"-"+A$(20)+A$(23)+A$(37)+A$(30)
5140 GOTO 5680
5150 L$(1)=A$(3)+A$(10)+"-"+A$(44)+A$(27)+A$(17)+A$(42)
5160 L$(2)=A$(26)+A$(35)+"-"+A$(50)+A$(60)+A$(2)+A$(41)
5170 L$(3)=A$(25)+A$(51)+"-"+A$(57)+A$(19)+A$(18)+A$(1)
5180 L$(4)=A$(52)+A$(34)+"-"+A$(59)+A$(58)+A$(49)+A$(11)
5190 L$(5)=A$(13)+A$(62)+"-"+A$(23)+A$(30)+A$(45)+A$(63)
5200 L$(6)=A$(38)+A$(55)+"-"+A$(21)+A$(31)+A$(12)+A$(14)
5210 L$(7)=A$(20)+A$(15)+"-"+A$(47)+A$(29)+A$(54)+A$(6)
5220 L$(8)=A$(4)+A$(22)+"-"+A$(5)+A$(39)+A$(53)+A$(46)
5230 GOTO 5680
5240 L$(1)=A$(19)+A$(26)+"-"+A$(60)+A$(43)+A$(33)+A$(58)
5250 L$(2)=A$(42)+A$(51)+"-"+A$(1)+A$(11)+A$(18)+A$(57)
5260 L$(3)=A$(41)+A$(2)+"-"+A$(44)+A$(35)+A$(34)+A$(17)
5270 L$(4)=A$(3)+A$(50)+"-"+A$(10)+A$(9)+A$(36)+A$(27)
5280 L$(5)=A$(29)+A$(15)+"-"+A$(39)+A$(46)+A$(61)+A$(12)
5290 L$(6)=A$(54)+A$(4)+"-"+A$(37)+A$(47)+A$(28)+A$(30)
5300 L$(7)=A$(5)+A$(31)+"-"+A$(63)+A$(45)+A$(7)+A$(22)
5310 L$(8)=A$(20)+A$(38)+"-"+A$(21)+A$(55)+A$(6)+A$(62)
5320 GOTO 5680
```

```
5330 L$(1)=A$(35)+A$(42)+"-"+A$(11)+A$(59)+A$(49)+A$(9)
5340 L$(2)=A$(58)+A$(2)+"-"+A$(17)+A$(27)+A$(34)+A$(44)
5350 L$(3)=A$(57)+A$(18)+"-"+A$(60)+A$(51)+A$(50)+A$(33)
5360 L$(4)=A$(19)+A$(1)+"-"+A$(26)+A$(25)+A$(52)+A$(43)
5370 L$(5)=A$(45)+A$(31)+"-"+A$(55)+A$(62)+A$(14)+A$(28)
5380 L$(6)=A$(7)+A$(20)+"-"+A$(53)+A$(63)+A$(13)+A$(46)
5390 L$(7)=A$(21)+A$(47)+"-"+A$(12)+A$(61)+A$(23)+A$(38)
5400 L$(8)=A$(5)+A$(54)+"-"+A$(37)+A$(4)+A$(22)+A$(15)
5410 GOTO 5680
5420 L$(1)=A$(51)+A$(58)+"-"+A$(27)+A$(10)+A$(36)+A$(25)
5430 L$(2)=A$(9)+A$(18)+"-"+A$(33)+A$(43)+A$(50)+A$(60)
5440 L$(3)=A$(44)+A$(34)+"-"+A$(11)+A$(2)+A$(1)+A$(49)
5450 L$(4)=A$(35)+A$(17)+"-"+A$(42)+A$(41)+A$(3)+A$(59)
5460 L$(5)=A$(61)+A$(47)+"-"+A$(4)+A$(15)+A$(30)+A$(13)
5470 L$(6)=A$(23)+A$(5)+"-"+A$(6)+A$(12)+A$(29)+A$(62)
5480 L$(7)=A$(37)+A$(63)+"-"+A$(28)+A$(14)+A$(39)+A$(54)
5490 L$(8)=A$(21)+A$(7)+"-"+A$(53)+A$(20)+A$(38)+A$(31)
5500 GOTO 5680
5510 L$(1)=A$(2)+A$(9)+"-"+A$(43)+A$(26)+A$(52)+A$(41)
5520 L$(2)=A$(25)+A$(34)+"-"+A$(49)+A$(59)+A$(1)+A$(11)
5530 L$(3)=A$(60)+A$(50)+"-"+A$(27)+A$(18)+A$(17)+A$(36)
5540 L$(4)=A$(51)+A$(33)+"-"+A$(58)+A$(57)+A$(19)+A$(10)
5550 L$(5)=A$(14)+A$(63)+"-"+A$(20)+A$(31)+A$(46)+A$(29)
5560 L$(6)=A$(39)+A$(21)+"-"+A$(22)+A$(28)+A$(45)+A$(15)
5570 L$(7)=A$(53)+A$(12)+"-"+A$(13)+A$(30)+A$(55)+A$(7)
5580 L$(8)=A$(37)+A$(23)+"-"+A$(6)+A$(5)+A$(54)+A$(47)
5590 GOTO 5680
5600 L$(1)=A$(10)+A$(17)+"-"+A$(51)+A$(34)+A$(60)+A$(49)
5610 L$(2)=A$(33)+A$(42)+"-"+A$(57)+A$(2)+A$(9)+A$(19)
5620 L$(3)=A$(3)+A$(58)+"-"+A$(35)+A$(26)+A$(25)+A$(44)
5630 L$(4)=A$(59)+A$(41)+"-"+A$(1)+A$(36)+A$(27)+A$(18)
5640 L$(5)=A$(22)+A$(4)+"-"+A$(28)+A$(39)+A$(54)+A$(37)
5650 L$(6)=A$(47)+A$(29)+"-"+A$(30)+A$(5)+A$(53)+A$(23)
5660 L$(7)=A$(61)+A$(20)+"-"+A$(21)+A$(38)+A$(63)+A$(15)
5670 L$(8)=A$(45)+A$(31)+"-"+A$(14)+A$(13)+A$(62)+A$(55)
5680 FOR I=1 TO 8
5690 LPRINT L$(I);
5700 LPRINT " ";
5710 NEXT
5720 LPRINT "KEY"Z+1
5730 LPRINT
5740 FOR I=1 TO 8
5750 FOR J=1 TO 7
5760 IF J=3 THEN M$(I)=M$(I)+"-":GOTO 5790
5770 IF MID$(H$(I),J,1)=MID$(L$(I),J,1) THEN M$(I)=M$(I)+"0"
5780 IF MID$(H$(I),J,1)<>MID$(L$(I),J,1) THEN M$(I)=M$(I)+"1"
5790 NEXT
5800 NEXT
5810 FOR I=1 TO 8
5820 LPRINT M$(I)+"   ";
5830 NEXT
5840 LPRINT "ENTER"
5850 LPRINT
5860 LPRINT "     ";
5870 FOR I=1 TO 8
5880 IF LEFT$(M$(I),2)="00" THEN U=0
5890 IF LEFT$(M$(I),2)="01" THEN U=1
5900 IF LEFT$(M$(I),2)="10" THEN U=2
5910 IF LEFT$(M$(I),2)="11" THEN U=3
5920 IF RIGHT$(M$(I),4)="0000" THEN V=0:GOTO 6080
5930 IF RIGHT$(M$(I),4)="0001" THEN V=1:GOTO 6080
5940 IF RIGHT$(M$(I),4)="0010" THEN V=2:GOTO 6080
5950 IF RIGHT$(M$(I),4)="0011" THEN V=3:GOTO 6080
5960 IF RIGHT$(M$(I),4)="0100" THEN V=4:GOTO 6080
5970 IF RIGHT$(M$(I),4)="0101" THEN V=5:GOTO 6080
5980 IF RIGHT$(M$(I),4)="0110" THEN V=6:GOTO 6080
5990 IF RIGHT$(M$(I),4)="0111" THEN V=7:GOTO 6080
```

```
6000 IF RIGHT$(M$(I),4)="1000" THEN V=8:GOTO 6080
6010 IF RIGHT$(M$(I),4)="1001" THEN V=9:GOTO 6080
6020 IF RIGHT$(M$(I),4)="1010" THEN V=10:GOTO 6080
6030 IF RIGHT$(M$(I),4)="1011" THEN V=11:GOTO 6080
6040 IF RIGHT$(M$(I),4)="1100" THEN V=12:GOTO 6080
6050 IF RIGHT$(M$(I),4)="1101" THEN V=13:GOTO 6080
6060 IF RIGHT$(M$(I),4)="1110" THEN V=14:GOTO 6080
6070 IF RIGHT$(M$(I),4)="1111" THEN V=15
6080 IF I=1 THEN W=S1(U,V):GOTO 6230
6090 IF I=2 THEN W=S2(U,V):GOTO 6230
6100 IF I=3 THEN W=S3(U,V):GOTO 6230
6110 IF I=4 THEN W=S4(U,V):GOTO 6230
6120 IF I=5 THEN W=S5(U,V):GOTO 6230
6130 IF I=6 THEN W=S6(U,V):GOTO 6230
6140 IF I=7 THEN W=S7(U,V):GOTO 6230
6150 IF I=8 THEN W=S8(U,V):GOTO 6230
6160 IF I=8 THEN LPRINT "   EXIT":GOTO 6180
6170 LPRINT "  -  ";
6180 NEXT
6190 Z=Z+1
6200 LPRINT
6210 LPRINT " + ";
6220 GOTO 2350
6230 IF W=0 THEN W$(I)="0000":LPRINT "0000";:GOTO 6160
6240 IF W=1 THEN W$(I)="0001":LPRINT "0001";:GOTO 6160
6250 IF W=2 THEN W$(I)="0010":LPRINT "0010";:GOTO 6160
6260 IF W=3 THEN W$(I)="0011":LPRINT "0011";:GOTO 6160
6270 IF W=4 THEN W$(I)="0100":LPRINT "0100";:GOTO 6160
6280 IF W=5 THEN W$(I)="0101":LPRINT "0101";:GOTO 6160
6290 IF W=6 THEN W$(I)="0110":LPRINT "0110";:GOTO 6160
6300 IF W=7 THEN W$(I)="0111":LPRINT "0111";:GOTO 6160
6310 IF W=8 THEN W$(I)="1000":LPRINT "1000";:GOTO 6160
6320 IF W=9 THEN W$(I)="1001":LPRINT "1001";:GOTO 6160
6330 IF W=10 THEN W$(I)="1010":LPRINT "1010";:GOTO 6160
6340 IF W=11 THEN W$(I)="1011":LPRINT "1011";:GOTO 6160
6350 IF W=12 THEN W$(I)="1100":LPRINT "1100";:GOTO 6160
6360 IF W=13 THEN W$(I)="1101":LPRINT "1101";:GOTO 6160
6370 IF W=14 THEN W$(I)="1110":LPRINT "1110";:GOTO 6160
6380 IF W=15 THEN W$(I)="1111":LPRINT "1111";:GOTO 6160
6390 LPRINT STRING$(79,"-")
6400 LPRINT
6410 A6$=STR$(A)
6420 A7$=STR$(A+1)
6430 IF A>9 THEN A5$=RIGHT$(A6$,2)
6440 IF A<10 THEN A5$=RIGHT$(A6$,1)
6450 IF A+1>9 THEN A4$=RIGHT$(A7$,2)
6460 IF A+1<10 THEN A4$=RIGHT$(A7$,1)
6470 LPRINT "RESULTING 64-BIT BLOCK OF CIBITS -- (FORMED FROM M-"A5$" AND M-"A4$
")"
6480 LPRINT
6490 LPRINT "14140425263603031415251426033625252514032525253603140414403031415"
6500 LPRINT "79029157801335462480791391572424136846680235460279578035241368 91"
6510 LPRINT STRING$(64,"-")
6520 IF A=1 THEN 6850
6530 FOR I=1 TO 8
6540 Y1$=Y1$+F3$(I)
6550 Y2$=Y2$+F1$(I)
6560 NEXT
6570 FOR I=1 TO 32
6580 READ P
6590 Y3$=Y3$+MID$(Y1$,P,1)
6600 Y3$=Y3$+MID$(Y2$,P,1)
6610 NEXT
6620 DATA 17,10,9,25,28,31,3,4,12,18,27,11,29,5,32,22,21,26,14,6,20
6630 DATA 23,24,30,7,15,8,13,16,1,2,19
6640 LPRINT Y3$
```

```
6650 LPRINT
6660 FOR I=1 TO 64
6670 Y4$(I)=MID$(Y3$,I,1)
6680 NEXT
6690 LPRINT " CIBITS IN HEXADECIMAL FORM = ";
6700 PRINT
6710 PRINT "  RESULTING 'CIBITS' IN HEXADECIMAL FORM = ";
6720 FOR I=0 TO 15
6730 T9=0:T8=0:T7=0:T6=0:T5=0
6740 IF Y4$(4*I+1)="1" THEN T5=8
6750 IF Y4$(4*I+2)="1" THEN T6=4
6760 IF Y4$(4*I+3)="1" THEN T7=2
6770 IF Y4$(4*I+4)="1" THEN T8=1
6780 T9=T5+T6+T7+T8
6790 LPRINT HEX$(T9);
6800 PRINT HEX$(T9);
6810 NEXT
6820 LPRINT:LPRINT:LPRINT:LPRINT
6830 PRINT:PRINT
6840 END
6850 FOR I=1 TO 8
6860 Y1$=Y1$+S2$(I)
6870 Y2$=Y2$+F1$(I)
6880 NEXT
6890 GOTO 6570
```

APPENDIX H

EXAMPLE OF A 16-ITERATION ENCIPHERMENT

64-BIT 'DES' MASTER OR EXTERNAL KEY --

2113355-1025554-0214434-1123334-0012343-2021453-0202435-0110454-
1031975-1176107-2423401-7632789-7452553-0858846-6836043-9495226-
----
0000011110100111000100110111000001000101110110100010101000010110

   KEY IN HEXIDECIMAL FORM = 07A7137045DA2A16

64-BIT BLOCK OF PLABITS -- (BITS WHICH FORM M-0 AND M-1)

1414042526360303141525142603362525251403252525360314041414030315
7902915780133546248079139157242413684668023546027957803568132491

0011101111011101000100011001000001001001001101110010100000000010

PLABITS IN HEXIDECIMAL FORM = 3BDD119049372802

```
    3333      3334      4444      4444      4555      5555      5556      6666
    3456      7890      1234      5678      9012      3456      7890      1234
    ----      ----      ----      ----      ----      ----      ----      ----
    0011  -   1100  -   0110  -   0000  -   0100  -   1011  -   1001  -   0110   M-0

    0000      0000      0111      1111      1112      2222      2222      2333
    1234      5678      9012      3456      7890      1234      5678      9012
    ----      ----      ----      ----      ----      ----      ----      ----
    0010  -   0001  -   1100  -   0110  -   0010  -   0010  -   1001  -   1100   M-1
```

. . . .

```
  22-1022   20-2121   10-0122   20-0131   13-0021   11-3200   02-1130   01-2102
  59-6701   11-9287   75-1536   62-5810   02-2844   49-2739   92-9306   66-2145
  -- ----   -- ----   -- ----   -- ----   -- ----   -- ----   -- ----   -- ----
  11-0000   00-1010   00-0110   00-0001   10-0101   11-0011   10-1010   00-0001   M-1 EXP

  00-0000   00-0111   11-1111   12-2222   33-3333   33-3344   44-4444   44-5555
  12-3456   78-9012   34-5678   90-1234   01-2345   67-8901   23-4567   89-0123
  -- ----   -- ----   -- ----   -- ----   -- ----   -- ----   -- ----   -- ----
  00-1110   01-0010   00-0101   01-0010   00-1000   10-0011   01-0111   10-1011   KEY 1

  11-1110   01-1000   00-0011   01-0011   10-1101   01-0000   11-1101   10-1010   ENTER

    0110  -   1100  -   1110  -   0101  -   0011  -   1010  -   0010  -   1010   EXIT

  + 0011  -   1100  -   0110  -   0000  -   0100  -   1011  -   1001  -   0110   M-0

    0000      0000      0111      1111      1112      2222      2222      2333
    1234      5678      9012      3456      7890      1234      5678      9012
    ----      ----      ----      ----      ----      ----      ----      ----
  = 0101  -   0000  -   1000  -   0101  -   0111  -   0001  -   1011  -   1100   M-2
```

. . . .

```
22-1022   20-2121   10-0122   20-0131   13-0021   11-3200   02-1130   01-2102
59-6701   11-9287   75-1536   62-5810   02-2844   49-2739   92-9306   66-2145
-- ----    -- ----    -- ----    -- ----    -- ----    -- ----    -- ----    -- ----
11-1010   00-1010   00-0000   01-0100   00-1011   11-0101   10-1010   01-0011   M-2 EXP

11-2122   10-0122   02-2202   00-1010   54-4453   34-3344   45-5355   34-5333
01-5660   74-6917   58-3422   37-4921   06-3947   34-0287   06-1835   51-7946
-- ----    -- ----    -- ----    -- ----    -- ----    -- ----    -- ----    -- ----
01-0101   01-0001   10-1000   10-0000   11-1000   00-0111   10-0011   01-1001   KEY 2

10-1111   01-1011   10-1000   11-0100   11-0011   11-0010   00-1001   00-1010   ENTER

   0000  -  1010  -  1011  -  1010  -  0111  -  0010  -  1100  -  0011   EXIT

 + 0010  -  0001  -  1100  -  0110  -  0010  -  0010  -  1001  -  1100   M-1

   0000      0000      0111      1111      1112      2222      2222      2333
   1234      5678      9012      3456      7890      1234      5678      9012
   ----      ----      ----      ----      ----      ----      ----      ----
 = 0010  -  1011  -  0111  -  1100  -  0101  -  0000  -  0101  -  1111   M-3

............................................................................

22-1022   20-2121   10-0122   20-0131   13-0021   11-3200   02-1130   01-2102
59-6701   11-9287   75-1536   62-5810   02-2844   49-2739   92-9306   66-2145
-- ----    -- ----    -- ----    -- ----    -- ----    -- ----    -- ----    -- ----
01-0110   00-1110   01-0001   10-1111   11-0101   10-1010   00-0110   00-0100   M-3 EXP

01-2021   12-0220   10-2120   10-0211   43-3435   43-5535   34-3533   45-4444
34-3127   14-7585   84-7016   52-8039   26-1781   19-7672   56-2034   45-0359
-- ----    -- ----    -- ----    -- ----    -- ----    -- ----    -- ----    -- ----
10-1000   10-0001   11-1000   00-1100   01-0100   10-1001   01-1100   01-1110   KEY 3

11-1110   10-1111   10-1001   10-0011   10-0001   00-0011   01-1010   01-1010   ENTER

   0110  -  1111  -  0001  -  0000  -  0010  -  1111  -  0101  -  0110   EXIT

 + 0101  -  0000  -  1000  -  0101  -  0111  -  0001  -  1011  -  1100   M-2

   0000      0000      0111      1111      1112      2222      2222      2333
   1234      5678      9012      3456      7890      1234      5678      9012
   ----      ----      ----      ----      ----      ----      ----      ----
 = 0011  -  1111  -  1001  -  0101  -  0101  -  1110  -  1110  -  1010   M-4

............................................................................

22-1022   20-2121   10-0122   20-0131   13-0021   11-3200   02-1130   01-2102
59-6701   11-9287   75-1536   62-5810   02-2844   49-2739   92-9306   66-2145
-- ----    -- ----    -- ----    -- ----    -- ----    -- ----    -- ----    -- ----
11-1111   10-1100   01-0011   10-1110   00-0101   10-0111   11-0001   11-1011   M-4 EXP

10-2101   11-0201   02-0020   12-1122   44-5553   54-4455   43-5444   33-3334
58-7961   40-2348   94-5387   21-6765   89-3202   53-0614   46-6215   94-5107
-- ----    -- ----    -- ----    -- ----    -- ----    -- ----    -- ----    -- ----
01-1001   00-0111   00-1100   00-1000   10-1111   11-1100   01-0011   00-0001   KEY 4

10-0110   10-1011   01-1111   10-0110   10-1010   01-1011   10-0010   11-1010   ENTER

   0010  -  0110  -  0001  -  0111  -  1100  -  1110  -  1011  -  1001   EXIT

 + 0010  -  1011  -  0111  -  1100  -  0101  -  0000  -  0101  -  1111   M-3
```

```
     0000        0000        0111        1111        1112        2222        2222        2333
     1234        5678        9012        3456        7890        1234        5678        9012
     ----        ----        ----        ----        ----        ----        ----        ----
  = 0000  -    1101  -    0110  -    1011  -    1001  -    1110  -    1110  -    0110   M-5

..........................................................................................

22-1022     20-2121     10-0122     20-0131     13-0021     11-3200     02-1130     01-2102
59-6701     11-9287     75-1536     62-5810     02-2844     49-2739     92-9306     66-2145
-- ----     -- ----     -- ----     -- ----     -- ----     -- ----     -- ----     -- ----
10-1011     10-0001     11-0111     10-1011     10-0100     00-0100     01-0111     11-1101   M-5 EXP

11-0201     00-2220     21-1100     12-0122     34-3545     33-3333     34-4453     44-4555
26-5574     83-1749     00-8542     38-1123     77-3426     41-5628     99-6850     35-4372
-- ----     -- ----     -- ----     -- ----     -- ----     -- ----     -- ----     -- ----
01-1000     11-0100     10-1010     00-0101     01-0000     00-0110     00-1110     11-0111   KEY 5

11-0011     01-0101     01-1101     10-1110     11-0100     00-0010     01-1001     00-1010   ENTER

  0010  -    0010  -    1011  -    1000  -    0001  -    1010  -    0011  -    0011   EXIT

+ 0011  -    1111  -    1001  -    0101  -    0101  -    1110  -    1110  -    1010   M-4

     0000        0000        0111        1111        1112        2222        2222        2333
     1234        5678        9012        3456        7890        1234        5678        9012
     ----        ----        ----        ----        ----        ----        ----        ----
  = 0001  -    1101  -    0010  -    1101  -    0100  -    0100  -    1101  -    1001   M-6

..........................................................................................

22-1022     20-2121     10-0122     20-0131     13-0021     11-3200     02-1130     01-2102
59-6701     11-9287     75-1536     62-5810     02-2844     49-2739     92-9306     66-2145
-- ----     -- ----     -- ----     -- ----     -- ----     -- ----     -- ----     -- ----
11-1000     00-1010     01-0001     10-1100     01-0101     10-1000     01-0101     11-1111   M-6 EXP

10-1200     11-2012     10-0122     20-1102     55-4344     45-4455     44-3335     33-3345
31-8328     65-8500     73-9241     64-9467     12-1886     53-4960     37-6747     10-9304
-- ----     -- ----     -- ----     -- ----     -- ----     -- ----     -- ----     -- ----
00-1101     10-0101     01-0000     01-0001     01-1011     11-0001     11-1001     00-0010   KEY 6

11-0101     10-1111     00-0001     11-1101     00-1110     01-1001     10-1100     11-1101   ENTER

  1001  -    1111  -    0000  -    0111  -    1110  -    0001  -    0000  -    0101   EXIT

+ 0000  -    1101  -    0110  -    1011  -    1001  -    1110  -    1110  -    0110   M-5

     0000        0000        0111        1111        1112        2222        2222        2333
     1234        5678        9012        3456        7890        1234        5678        9012
     ----        ----        ----        ----        ----        ----        ----        ----
  = 1001  -    0010  -    0110  -    1100  -    0111  -    1111  -    1110  -    0011   M-7

..........................................................................................

22-1022     20-2121     10-0122     20-0131     13-0021     11-3200     02-1130     01-2102
59-6701     11-9287     75-1536     62-5810     02-2844     49-2739     92-9306     66-2145
-- ----     -- ----     -- ----     -- ----     -- ----     -- ----     -- ----     -- ----
10-0111     11-0000     00-1011     10-0111     11-0011     11-1100     01-1100     00-1111   M-7 EXP

21-0221     01-0101     11-2112     22-2000     35-5533     33-3444     35-4544     55-4433
69-9716     12-4837     15-0308     24-5875     24-5076     03-9762     12-9150     37-3158
-- ----     -- ----     -- ----     -- ----     -- ----     -- ----     -- ----     -- ----
00-0101     00-1110     10-1000     00-0101     10-1101     00-0110     01-0011     11-1100   KEY 7
```

```
 10-0010   11-1110   10-0011   10-0010   01-1110   11-1010   00-1111   11-0011   ENTER

    1110 -    1110 -    1001 -    1001 -    1000 -    0001 -    0001 -    0111   EXIT

  + 0001 -    1101 -    0010 -    1101 -    0100 -    0100 -    1101 -    1001   M-6

    0000      0000      0111      1111      1112      2222      2222      2333
    1234      5678      9012      3456      7890      1234      5678      9012
    ----      ----      ----      ----      ----      ----      ----      ----
  = 1111 -    0011 -    1011 -    0100 -    1100 -    0101 -    1100 -    1110   M-8

.............................................................................

 22-1022   20-2121   10-0122   20-0131   13-0021   11-3200   02-1130   01-2102
 59-6701   11-9287   75-1536   62-5810   02-2844   49-2739   92-9306   66-2145
 -- ----   -- ----   -- ----   -- ----   -- ----   -- ----   -- ----   -- ----
 11-0100   01-1101   10-1001   11-0110   00-1111   10-0011   11-0010   00-1111   M-8 EXP

 22-2020   11-2011   11-1200   01-2101   53-3454   54-4534   55-4333   34-3545
 25-0581   93-4951   42-7634   60-3628   68-4219   71-3268   34-7205   30-1540
 -- ----   -- ----   -- ----   -- ----   -- ----   -- ----   -- ----   -- ----
 00-1100   00-0001   00-0011   00-1101   00-0000   11-1111   10-1100   01-0101   KEY 8

 11-1000   01-1100   10-1010   11-1011   00-1111   01-1100   01-1110   01-1010   ENTER

    0101 -    0110 -    0010 -    1011 -    1001 -    0000 -    1000 -    0110   EXIT

  + 1001 -    0010 -    0110 -    1100 -    0111 -    1111 -    1110 -    0011   M-7

    0000      0000      0111      1111      1112      2222      2222      2333
    1234      5678      9012      3456      7890      1234      5678      9012
    ----      ----      ----      ----      ----      ----      ----      ----
  = 1100 -    0100 -    0100 -    0111 -    1110 -    1111 -    0110 -    0101   M-9

.............................................................................

 22-1022   20-2121   10-0122   20-0131   13-0021   11-3200   02-1130   01-2102
 59-6701   11-9287   75-1536   62-5810   02-2844   49-2739   92-9306   66-2145
 -- ----   -- ----   -- ----   -- ----   -- ----   -- ----   -- ----   -- ----
 00-1001   11-0001   10-1111   11-0101   11-1011   11-1100   01-1011   11-1000   M-9 EXP

 01-0201   00-0022   22-0121   21-1212   33-5434   44-5333   34-5453   44-4555
 95-7680   35-1631   87-2856   09-2412   10-4091   27-6435   65-5307   98-6217
 -- ----   -- ----   -- ----   -- ----   -- ----   -- ----   -- ----   -- ----
 00-0010   11-0010   01-0101   10-0010   00-0101   01-0000   11-1110   01-1101   KEY 9

 00-1011   00-0011   11-1010   01-0111   11-1110   10-1100   10-0101   10-0101   ENTER

    1100 -    1110 -    1110 -    0011 -    0101 -    0001 -    0011 -    1100   EXIT

  + 1111 -    0011 -    1011 -    0100 -    1100 -    0101 -    1100 -    1110   M-8

    0000      0000      0111      1111      1112      2222      2222      2333
    1234      5678      9012      3456      7890      1234      5678      9012
    ----      ----      ----      ----      ----      ----      ----      ----
  = 0011 -    1101 -    0101 -    0111 -    1001 -    0100 -    1111 -    0010   M-10

.............................................................................

 22-1022   20-2121   10-0122   20-0131   13-0021   11-3200   02-1130   01-2102
 59-6701   11-9287   75-1536   62-5810   02-2844   49-2739   92-9306   66-2145
 -- ----   -- ----   -- ----   -- ----   -- ----   -- ----   -- ----   -- ----
 10-1010   00-0111   11-0101   10-1011   10-0101   10-0110   01-0001   11-1011   M-10 EXP
```

```
21-0210   11-1022   00-2020   12-1110   55-3345   45-4444   43-3345   43-3534
02-2263   58-9778   45-1931   75-3046   37-8535   82-6514   90-4121   77-6420
--  ----  --  ----  --  ----  --  ----  --  ----  --  ----  --  ----  --  ----
10-0011   01-0010   11-0010   00-0000   11-0011   11-1110   00-0000   10-1011   KEY 10

00-1001   01-0101   00-0111   10-1011   01-0110   01-1000   01-0001   01-0000   ENTER

   1010  -  0010  -  0101  -  1110  -  1101  -  0110  -  0000  -  0001   EXIT

+  1100  -  0100  -  0100  -  0111  -  1110  -  1111  -  0110  -  0101   M-9

   0000     0000     0111     1111     1112     2222     2222     2333
   1234     5678     9012     3456     7890     1234     5678     9012
   ----     ----     ----     ----     ----     ----     ----     ----
=  0110  -  0110  -  0001  -  1001  -  0011  -  1001  -  0110  -  0100   M-11

. . . . . . . . . . . . . . . . . . . . . . . . . . . . . . . . . . . . . . . .

22-1022   20-2121   10-0122   20-0131   13-0021   11-3200   02-1130   01-2102
59-6701   11-9287   75-1536   62-5810   02-2844   49-2739   92-9306   66-2145
--  ----  --  ----  --  ----  --  ----  --  ----  --  ----  --  ----  --  ----
00-1111   10-0100   00-0001   11-0000   00-1010   01-0110   00-1111   11-0000   M-11 EXP

11-2001   10-2000   21-2221   12-2000   34-5433   35-3353   45-4543   55-4353
73-1615   29-5254   48-8079   13-6387   30-0414   74-6059   77-5382   21-9865
--  ----  --  ----  --  ----  --  ----  --  ----  --  ----  --  ----  --  ----
00-0000   00-0011   01-0110   11-0110   01-1000   00-1010   11-1111   10-0000   KEY 11

00-1111   10-0111   01-0111   00-0110   01-0010   01-1100   11-0000   01-0000   ENTER

   0111  -  0001  -  1010  -  1001  -  0010  -  0000  -  0110  -  0001   EXIT

+  0011  -  1101  -  0101  -  0111  -  1001  -  0100  -  1111  -  0010   M-10

   0000     0000     0111     1111     1112     2222     2222     2333
   1234     5678     9012     3456     7890     1234     5678     9012
   ----     ----     ----     ----     ----     ----     ----     ----
=  0100  -  1100  -  1111  -  1110  -  1011  -  0100  -  1001  -  0011   M-12

. . . . . . . . . . . . . . . . . . . . . . . . . . . . . . . . . . . . . . . .

22-1022   20-2121   10-0122   20-0131   13-0021   11-3200   02-1130   01-2102
59-6701   11-9287   75-1536   62-5810   02-2844   49-2739   92-9306   66-2145
--  ----  --  ----  --  ----  --  ----  --  ----  --  ----  --  ----  --  ----
10-0010   00-0111   11-0100   01-1011   11-1001   11-1001   11-1101   10-1101   M-12 EXP

12-2011   12-2212   10-0102   12-2110   43-4354   53-4534   54-3335   53-4544
16-8792   30-3184   09-4755   47-2562   15-2935   18-9743   20-0376   42-7064
--  ----  --  ----  --  ----  --  ----  --  ----  --  ----  --  ----  --  ----
10-0000   01-1010   00-1010   01-0010   10-0011   00-0101   11-0000   01-1110   KEY 12

00-0010   01-1101   11-1110   00-1001   01-1010   11-1100   00-1101   11-0011   ENTER

   1101  -  1001  -  0010  -  0010  -  1111  -  0110  -  1010  -  0111   EXIT

+  0110  -  0110  -  0001  -  1001  -  0011  -  1001  -  0110  -  0100   M-11

   0000     0000     0111     1111     1112     2222     2222     2333
   1234     5678     9012     3456     7890     1234     5678     9012
   ----     ----     ----     ----     ----     ----     ----     ----
=  1011  -  1111  -  0011  -  1011  -  1100  -  1111  -  1100  -  0011   M-13
```

```
. . . . . . . . . . . . . . . . . . . . . . . . . . . . . . . . . . . . . . . . .

22-1022   20-2121   10-0122   20-0131   13-0021   11-3200   02-1130   01-2102
59-6701   11-9287   75-1536   62-5810   02-2844   49-2739   92-9306   66-2145
-- ----   -- ----   -- ----   -- ----   -- ----   -- ----   -- ----   -- ----
10-1101   11-0101   11-1111   10-1110   01-0110   00-1010   01-0101   11-1111   M-13 EXP


12-0021   21-2201   02-2112   00-0102   54-4433   35-4443   53-5454   35-5433
42-4253   67-7890   30-4183   85-6211   54-8330   20-7051   45-7116   86-2269
-- ----   -- ----   -- ----   -- ----   -- ----   -- ----   -- ----   -- ----
00-1000   00-1000   11-0111   11-0000   10-1100   11-1110   00-1101   00-1010   KEY 13

10-0101   11-1101   00-1000   01-1110   11-1010   11-0100   01-1000   11-0101   ENTER

  0110  -  0101  -  0001  -  1110  -  0000  -  1001  -  1110  -  1010   EXIT

+ 0100  -  1100  -  1111  -  1110  -  1011  -  0100  -  1001  -  0011   M-12

  0000      0000      0111      1111      1112      2222      2222      2333
  1234      5678      9012      3456      7890      1234      5678      9012
  ----      ----      ----      ----      ----      ----      ----      ----
= 0010  -  1001  -  1110  -  0000  -  1011  -  1101  -  0111  -  1001   M-14


. . . . . . . . . . . . . . . . . . . . . . . . . . . . . . . . . . . . . . . . .

22-1022   20-2121   10-0122   20-0131   13-0021   11-3200   02-1130   01-2102
59-6701   11-9287   75-1536   62-5810   02-2844   49-2739   92-9306   66-2145
-- ----   -- ----   -- ----   -- ----   -- ----   -- ----   -- ----   -- ----
01-0011   10-1011   11-0001   10-1001   11-0110   01-1111   11-1000   00-1100   M-14 EXP


00-2222   21-0020   11-1102   11-0112   33-3345   54-5335   34-4533   54-5444
86-4136   21-5403   57-0497   68-7398   49-7117   62-2503   84-0526   06-4893
-- ----   -- ----   -- ----   -- ----   -- ----   -- ----   -- ----   -- ----
10-0010   01-1111   00-0001   11-0000   00-0011   00-1001   00-1111   11-0101   KEY 14

11-0001   11-0100   11-0000   01-1001   11-0101   01-0110   11-0111   11-1001   ENTER

  1100  -  0011  -  0001  -  0111  -  1110  -  1001  -  0111  -  1100   EXIT

+ 1011  -  1111  -  0011  -  1011  -  1100  -  1111  -  1100  -  0011   M-13

  0000      0000      0111      1111      1112      2222      2222      2333
  1234      5678      9012      3456      7890      1234      5678      9012
  ----      ----      ----      ----      ----      ----      ----      ----
= 0111  -  1100  -  0010  -  1100  -  0010  -  0110  -  1011  -  1111   M-15


. . . . . . . . . . . . . . . . . . . . . . . . . . . . . . . . . . . . . . . . .

22-1022   20-2121   10-0122   20-0131   13-0021   11-3200   02-1130   01-2102
59-6701   11-9287   75-1536   62-5810   02-2844   49-2739   92-9306   66-2145
-- ----   -- ----   -- ----   -- ----   -- ----   -- ----   -- ----   -- ----
11-0000   00-1010   01-0010   01-1010   01-1001   11-1110   01-1111   10-1111   M-15 EXP


10-1222   01-1211   11-0020   00-0220   44-5554   44-5453   53-3354   43-3343
67-0872   64-8475   21-3805   19-2654   53-1350   68-4473   09-5469   26-8771
-- ----   -- ----   -- ----   -- ----   -- ----   -- ----   -- ----   -- ----
10-0010   00-1000   01-1111   00-0001   11-0111   11-0010   10-0000   01-0010   KEY 15

01-0010   00-0010   00-1101   01-1011   10-1110   00-1100   11-1111   11-1101   ENTER

  0111  -  1000  -  0100  -  1100  -  0000  -  1110  -  1100  -  0101   EXIT
```

```
 + 0010  -  1001  -  1110  -  0000  -  1011  -  1101  -  0111  -  1001  M-14

   0000       0000      0111      1111      1112      2222      2222      2333
   1234       5678      9012      3456      7890      1234      5678      9012
   ----       ----      ----      ----      ----      ----      ----      ----
 = 0101  -  0001  -  1010  -  1100  -  1011  -  0011  -  1011  -  1100  M-16

.....................................................................................

22-1022    20-2121   10-0122   20-0131   13-0021   11-3200   02-1130   01-2102
59-6701    11-9287   75-1536   62-5810   02-2844   49-2739   92-9306   66-2145
-- ----    -- ----   -- ----   -- ----   -- ----   -- ----   -- ----   -- ----
11-0010    00-1011   10-0010   01-0000   00-1111   11-0101   10-1110   00-0111  M-16 EXP

21-1010    22-2002   22-2002   10-1111   35-3354   53-4544   53-3534   43-3454
47-9839    08-2123   71-5476   06-1856   86-9628   35-5129   72-7411   03-0456
-- ----    -- ----   -- ----   -- ----   -- ----   -- ----   -- ----   -- ----
00-0100    10-0001   10-0100   00-1101   00-0111   10-1000   11-0001   10-0011  KEY 16

11-0110    10-1010   00-0110   01-1101   00-1000   01-1101   01-1111   10-0100  ENTER

   0001  -  1100  -  1111  -  1010  -  1000  -  1011  -  0110  -  1001  EXIT

 + 0111  -  1100  -  0010  -  1100  -  0010  -  0110  -  1011  -  1111  M-15

   3333       3334      4444      4444      4555      5555      5556      6666
   3456       7890      1234      5678      9012      3456      7890      1234
   ----       ----      ----      ----      ----      ----      ----      ----
 = 0110  -  0000  -  1101  -  0110  -  1010  -  1101  -  1101  -  0110  M-17

-------------------------------------------------------------------------------

RESULTING 64-BIT BLOCK OF CIBITS -- (FORMED FROM M-16 AND M-17)

1414042526360303141525142603362525251403252525360314041403031415
7902915780133546248079139157242413684668023546027957803524136891
----------------------------------------------------------------
1101111111010110010010101000000101011100101011110001101000001111

CIBITS IN HEXIDECIMAL FORM = DFD64A815CAF1A0F
```

APPENDIX I

SEARCHING FOR KEYBITS IN THE THREE-ITERATION PROBLEM

```
10 REM (SPEC-1)
20 REM *SEARCHING FOR KEYBITS IN CHAPTER V*
30 KEY OFF
40 CLS
50 DIM S$(4,16),E1$(40),P9$(64),R9$(16)
60 DIM T8(64)
70 FOR I=0 TO 3
80 FOR J=0 TO 15
90 READ S$(I,J)
100 NEXT
110 NEXT
120 DATA 1100,0001,1010,1111,1001,0010,0110,1000
130 DATA 0000,1101,0011,0100,1110,0111,0101,1011
140 DATA 1010,1111,0100,0010,0111,1100,1001,0101
150 DATA 0110,0001,1101,1110,0000,1011,0011,1000
160 DATA 1001,1110,1111,0101,0010,1000,1100,0011
170 DATA 0111,0000,0100,1010,0001,1101,1011,0110
180 DATA 0100,0011,0010,1100,1001,0101,1111,1010
190 DATA 1011,1110,0001,0111,0110,0000,1000,1101
200 PRINT
210 IF A9=4 THEN CLS:PRINT:PRINT "COUPLET NO. 3":GOTO 240
220 IF A9=2 THEN CLS:PRINT:PRINT "COUPLET NO. 2":GOTO 240
230 PRINT "COUPLET NO. 1"
240 PRINT:PRINT
250 PRINT "ENTER PLAINTEXT IN HEXADECIMAL FORM -"
260 PRINT "       ----------------"
270 INPUT "      ",P9$
280 IF A9=0 THEN CA$=P9$
290 IF A9=2 THEN CB$=P9$
300 IF A9=4 THEN CC$=P9$
310 FOR I=1 TO 16
320 P9$(I)=MID$(P9$,I,1)
330 IF P9$(I)="0" THEN R9$(I)="0000":GOTO 490
340 IF P9$(I)="1" THEN R9$(I)="0001":GOTO 490
350 IF P9$(I)="2" THEN R9$(I)="0010":GOTO 490
360 IF P9$(I)="3" THEN R9$(I)="0011":GOTO 490
370 IF P9$(I)="4" THEN R9$(I)="0100":GOTO 490
380 IF P9$(I)="5" THEN R9$(I)="0101":GOTO 490
390 IF P9$(I)="6" THEN R9$(I)="0110":GOTO 490
400 IF P9$(I)="7" THEN R9$(I)="0111":GOTO 490
410 IF P9$(I)="8" THEN R9$(I)="1000":GOTO 490
420 IF P9$(I)="9" THEN R9$(I)="1001":GOTO 490
430 IF P9$(I)="A" THEN R9$(I)="1010":GOTO 490
440 IF P9$(I)="B" THEN R9$(I)="1011":GOTO 490
450 IF P9$(I)="C" THEN R9$(I)="1100":GOTO 490
460 IF P9$(I)="D" THEN R9$(I)="1101":GOTO 490
470 IF P9$(I)="E" THEN R9$(I)="1110":GOTO 490
480 IF P9$(I)="F" THEN R9$(I)="1111"
490 NEXT
500 T9$=""
```

```
510  FOR I=1 TO 16
520  T9$=T9$+R9$(I)
530  NEXT
540  FOR I=1 TO 64
550  T8(I)=VAL(MID$(T9$,I,1))
560  NEXT
570  IF A9=5 THEN 910
580  IF A9=4 THEN 870
590  IF A9=3 THEN 830
600  IF A9=2 THEN 790
610  IF A9=1 THEN 750
620  M(1)=T8(37):M(2)=T8(63):M(3)=T8(29):M(4)=T8(21):M(5)=T8(13)
630  M(6)=T8(5)
640  M1(1)=T8(34):M1(2)=T8(32):M1(3)=T8(44):M1(4)=T8(46)
650  PRINT:PRINT
660  PRINT "ENTER CIPHERTEXT IN HEXADECIMAL FORM -"
670  PRINT "      ----------------"
680  INPUT "      ",P9$
690  IF A9=0 THEN CD$=P9$
700  IF A9=3 THEN CE$=P9$
710  IF A9=5 THEN CF$=P9$
720  IF A9=5 THEN 310
730  IF A9=3 THEN 310
740  A9=1:GOTO 310
750  M2(1)=T8(37):M2(2)=T8(63):M2(3)=T8(29):M2(4)=T8(21)
760  M2(5)=T8(13):M2(6)=T8(5)
770  M3(1)=T8(34):M3(2)=T8(32):M3(3)=T8(44):M3(4)=T8(46)
780  A9=2:GOTO 200
790  N(1)=T8(37):N(2)=T8(63):N(3)=T8(29):N(4)=T8(21)
800  N(5)=T8(13):N(6)=T8(5)
810  N1(1)=T8(34):N1(2)=T8(32):N1(3)=T8(44):N1(4)=T8(46)
820  A9=3:GOTO 650
830  N2(1)=T8(37):N2(2)=T8(63):N2(3)=T8(29):N2(4)=T8(21)
840  N2(5)=T8(13):N2(6)=T8(5)
850  N3(1)=T8(34):N3(2)=T8(32):N3(3)=T8(44):N3(4)=T8(46)
860  A9=4:GOTO 210
870  O(1)=T8(37):O(2)=T8(63):O(3)=T8(29):O(4)=T8(21)
880  O(5)=T8(13):O(6)=T8(5)
890  O3(1)=T8(34):O3(2)=T8(32):O3(3)=T8(44):O3(4)=T8(46)
900  A9=5:GOTO 650
910  O2(1)=T8(37):O2(2)=T8(63):O2(3)=T8(29):O2(4)=T8(21)
920  O2(5)=T8(13):O2(6)=T8(5)
930  O4(1)=T8(34):O4(2)=T8(32):O4(3)=T8(44):O4(4)=T8(46)
940  CLS
950  LPRINT:LPRINT
960  LPRINT "COUPLET NO. 1 --    PLAINTEXT = "CA$
970  LPRINT "                   CIPHERTEXT = "CD$
980  LPRINT
990  LPRINT "COUPLET NO. 2 --    PLAINTEXT = "CB$
1000 LPRINT "                   CIPHERTEXT = "CE$
1010 LPRINT
1020 LPRINT "COUPLET NO. 3 --    PLAINTEXT = "CC$
1030 LPRINT "                   CIPHERTEXT = "CF$
1040 LPRINT:LPRINT
1050 LPRINT "                          COUPLET NO. 1"
1060 LPRINT
1070 LPRINT "          3   3 - 3   3   4   4     4   3 - 5   5   3   5"
1080 LPRINT " M-2      6   7 - 8   9   0   1     1   9 - 7   6   7   2"
1090 LPRINT "----      ------------------     ------------------"
1100 FOR I=1 TO 9
1110 A(I)=0
1120 NEXT
1130 Y$=""
1140 Y1$=""
1150 X=X+1
1160 PRINT X;
```

```
1170 FOR I=1 TO 6
1180 IF A(I)=M(I) THEN W(I)=0 ELSE W(I)=1
1190 NEXT
1200 B(1)=A(6):B(2)=A(4):B(3)=A(7):B(4)=A(8):B(5)=A(2):B(6)=A(9)
1210 FOR I=1 TO 6
1220 IF B(I)=M2(I) THEN W1(I)=0 ELSE W1(I)=1
1230 NEXT
1240 U1=W1(1)+W1(1)+W1(2)
1250 V1=8*W1(3)+4*W1(4)+2*W1(5)+W1(6)
1260 Z1$=S$(U1,V1)
1270 U=W(1)+W(1)+W(2)
1280 V=8*W(3)+4*W(4)+2*W(5)+W(6)
1290 Z$=S$(U,V)
1300 FOR I=1 TO 4
1310 Z(I)=VAL(MID$(Z$,I,1))
1320 IF M1(I)=Z(I) THEN Y$(I)="0"
1330 IF M1(I)<>Z(I) THEN Y$(I)="1"
1340 Z1(I)=VAL(MID$(Z1$,I,1))
1350 IF M3(I)=Z1(I) THEN Y1$(I)="0"
1360 IF M3(I)<>Z1(I) THEN Y1$(I)="1"
1370 NEXT
1380 FOR I=1 TO 4
1390 Y$=Y$+Y$(I)
1400 Y1$=Y1$+Y1$(I)
1410 NEXT
1420 IF Y$=Y1$ THEN GOTO 1930
1430 A(9)=A(9)+1
1440 IF A(9)=2 THEN A(9)=0:A(8)=A(8)+1
1450 IF A(8)=2 THEN A(8)=0:A(7)=A(7)+1
1460 IF A(7)=2 THEN A(7)=0:A(6)=A(6)+1
1470 IF A(6)=2 THEN A(6)=0:A(5)=A(5)+1
1480 IF A(5)=2 THEN A(5)=0:A(4)=A(4)+1
1490 IF A(4)=2 THEN A(4)=0:A(3)=A(3)+1
1500 IF A(3)=2 THEN A(3)=0:A(2)=A(2)+1
1510 IF A(2)=2 THEN A(2)=0:A(1)=A(1)+1
1520 IF A(1)=2 THEN 1540
1530 GOTO 1130
1540 LPRINT:LPRINT
1550 LPRINT "                         COUPLET NO. 2"
1560 LPRINT
1570 LPRINT "          3   3 - 3   3   4   4      4   3 - 5   5   3   5"
1580 LPRINT " M-2      6   7 - 8   9   0   1      1   9 - 7   6   7   2"
1590 LPRINT "----      ------------------      ------------------"
1600 FOR J=1 TO R9
1610 LPRINT E1$(J)"      ";
1620 FOR I=1 TO 6
1630 IF I=2 THEN LPRINT E2(J,I)"-";:GOTO 1650
1640 LPRINT E2(J,I);
1650 NEXT
1660 LPRINT "     ";
1670 FOR I=1 TO 6
1680 IF I=2 THEN LPRINT E3(J,I)"-";:GOTO 1700
1690 LPRINT E3(J,I);
1700 NEXT
1710 LPRINT
1720 NEXT
1730 LPRINT:LPRINT
1740 LPRINT "                         COUPLET NO. 3"
1750 LPRINT
1760 LPRINT "          3   3 - 3   3   4   4      4   3 - 5   5   3   5"
1770 LPRINT " M-2      6   7 - 8   9   0   1      1   9 - 7   6   7   2"
1780 LPRINT "----      ------------------      ------------------"
1790 FOR J=1 TO Q1
1800 LPRINT Q2$(J)"      ";
```

```
1810 FOR I=1 TO 6
1820 IF I=2 THEN LPRINT Q3(J,I)"-";:GOTO 1840
1830 LPRINT Q3(J,I);
1840 NEXT
1850 LPRINT "    ";
1860 FOR I=1 TO 6
1870 IF I=2 THEN LPRINT Q4(J,I)"-";:GOTO 1890
1880 LPRINT Q4(J,I);
1890 NEXT
1900 LPRINT
1910 NEXT
1920 END
1930 LPRINT Y$"    ";
1940 FOR I=1 TO 6
1950 IF I=2 THEN LPRINT A(I)"-";:GOTO 1970
1960 LPRINT A(I);
1970 NEXT
1980 LPRINT "    ";
1990 FOR I=1 TO 6
2000 IF I=2 THEN LPRINT B(I)"-";:GOTO 2020
2010 LPRINT B(I);
2020 NEXT
2030 LPRINT
2040 FOR I=1 TO 6
2050 IF N(I)=A(I) THEN G(I)=0 ELSE G(I)=1
2060 IF N2(I)=B(I) THEN H(I)=0 ELSE H(I)=1
2070 NEXT
2080 U2=G(1)+G(1)+G(2)
2090 V2=8*G(3)+4*G(4)+2*G(5)+G(6)
2100 U3=H(1)+H(1)+H(2)
2110 V3=8*H(3)+4*H(4)+2*H(5)+H(6)
2120 Z4$=S$(U2,V2)
2130 Z5$=S$(U3,V3)
2140 FOR I=1 TO 4
2150 R(I)=VAL(MID$(Z4$,I,1))
2160 IF N1(I)=R(I) THEN T$(I)="0"
2170 IF N1(I)<>R(I) THEN T$(I)="1"
2180 R1(I)=VAL(MID$(Z5$,I,1))
2190 IF N3(I)=R1(I) THEN T1$(I)="0"
2200 IF N3(I)<>R1(I) THEN T1$(I)="1"
2210 NEXT
2220 Y2$=""
2230 Y3$=""
2240 FOR I=1 TO 4
2250 Y2$=Y2$+T$(I)
2260 Y3$=Y3$+T1$(I)
2270 NEXT
2280 IF Y2$=Y3$ THEN 2300
2290 GOTO 1430
2300 FOR I=1 TO 6
2310 IF A(I)=O(I) THEN W7(I)=0 ELSE W7(I)=1
2320 NEXT
2330 FOR I=1 TO 6
2340 IF B(I)=O2(I) THEN W8(I)=0 ELSE W8(I)=1
2350 NEXT
2360 U7=W7(1)+W7(1)+W7(2)
2370 V8=8*W7(3)+4*W7(4)+2*W7(5)+W7(6)
2380 Z7$=S$(U7,V8)
2390 U6=W8(1)+W8(1)+W8(2)
2400 V7=8*W8(3)+4*W8(4)+2*W8(5)+W8(6)
2410 Z8$=S$(U6,V7)
2420 FOR I=1 TO 4
2430 Z7(I)=VAL(MID$(Z7$,I,1))
2440 Z8(I)=VAL(MID$(Z8$,I,1))
2450 NEXT
```

```
2460 FOR I=1 TO 4
2470 IF Z7(I)=O3(I) THEN F6$(I)="0"
2480 IF Z7(I)<>O3(I) THEN F6$(I)="1"
2490 IF Z8(I)=O4(I) THEN F7$(I)="0"
2500 IF Z8(I)<>O4(I) THEN F7$(I)="1"
2510 NEXT
2520 P6$=""
2530 P7$=""
2540 FOR I=1 TO 4
2550 P6$=P6$+F6$(I)
2560 P7$=P7$+F7$(I)
2570 NEXT
2580 IF P6$=P7$ THEN 2660
2590 R9=R9+1
2600 E1$(R9)=Y2$
2610 FOR I=1 TO 6
2620 E2(R9,I)=A(I)
2630 E3(R9,I)=B(I)
2640 NEXT
2650 GOTO 1430
2660 Q1=Q1+1
2670 Q2$(Q1)=P6$
2680 FOR I=1 TO 6
2690 Q3(Q1,I)=A(I)
2700 Q4(Q1,I)=B(I)
2710 NEXT
2720 GOTO 2590
```

APPENDIX J

ANALYZING THE S-BOXES

```
10 REM (S-BOXES)
20 REM *ANALYZING THE S-BOXES*
30 DIM A(63),A$(63),B(32),B$(32,5)
40 DIM D(32,5),C$(32)
50 DIM R$(720)
60 FOR I=0 TO 63
70 READ A(I)
80 X$=STR$(A(I)+10000)
90 A$(I)=RIGHT$(X$,4)
100 NEXT
110 DATA 1110,0100,1101,0001,0010,1111,1011,1000
120 DATA 0011,1010,0110,1100,0101,1001,0000,0111
130 DATA 0000,1111,0111,0100,1110,0010,1101,0001
140 DATA 1010,0110,1100,1011,1001,0101,0011,1000
150 DATA 0100,0001,1110,1000,1101,0110,0010,1011
160 DATA 1111,1100,1001,0111,0011,1010,0101,0000
170 DATA 1111,1100,1000,0010,0100,1001,0001,0111
180 DATA 0101,1011,0011,1110,1010,0000,0110,1101
190 GOTO 1250
200 RESTORE 210
210 DATA 1111,0001,1000,1110,0110,1011,0011,0100
220 DATA 1001,0111,0010,1101,1100,0000,0101,1010
230 DATA 0011,1101,0100,0111,1111,0010,1000,1110
240 DATA 1100,0000,0001,1010,0110,1001,1011,0101
250 DATA 0000,1110,0111,1011,1010,0100,1101,0001
260 DATA 0101,1000,1100,0110,1001,0011,0010,1111
270 DATA 1101,1000,1010,0001,0011,1111,0100,0010
280 DATA 1011,0110,0111,1100,0000,0101,1110,1001
290 FOR I=0 TO 63
300 READ A(I)
310 X$=STR$(A(I)+10000)
320 A$(I)=RIGHT$(X$,4)
330 NEXT
340 GOTO 1470
350 RESTORE 360
360 DATA 1010,0000,1001,1110,0110,0011,1111,0101
370 DATA 0001,1101,1100,0111,1011,0100,0010,1000
380 DATA 1101,0111,0000,1001,0011,0100,0110,1010
390 DATA 0010,1000,0101,1110,1100,1011,1111,0001
400 DATA 1101,0110,0100,1001,1000,1111,0011,0000
410 DATA 1011,0001,0010,1100,0101,1010,1110,0111
420 DATA 0001,1010,1101,0000,0110,1001,1000,0111
430 DATA 0100,1111,1110,0011,1011,0101,0010,1100
440 FOR I=0 TO 63
450 READ A(I)
460 X$=STR$(A(I)+10000)
470 A$(I)=RIGHT$(X$,4)
480 NEXT
490 GOTO 1470
500 RESTORE 510
510 DATA 0111,1101,1110,0011,0000,0110,1001,1010
520 DATA 0001,0010,1000,0101,1011,1100,0100,1111
530 DATA 1101,1000,1011,0101,0110,1111,0000,0011
540 DATA 0100,0111,0010,1100,0001,1010,1110,1001
550 DATA 1010,0110,1001,0000,1100,1011,0111,1101
560 DATA 1111,0001,0011,1110,0101,0010,1000,0100
570 DATA 0011,1111,0000,0110,1010,0001,1101,1000
580 DATA 1001,0100,0101,1011,1100,0111,0010,1110
```

```
590 FOR I=0 TO 63
600 READ A(I)
610 X$=STR$(A(I)+10000)
620 A$(I)=RIGHT$(X$,4)
630 NEXT
640 GOTO 1470
650 RESTORE 660
660 DATA 0010,1100,0100,0001,0111,1010,1011,0110
670 DATA 1000,0101,0011,1111,1101,0000,1110,1001
680 DATA 1110,1011,0010,1100,0100,0111,1101,0001
690 DATA 0101,0000,1111,1010,0011,1001,1000,0110
700 DATA 0100,0010,0001,1011,1010,1101,0111,1000
710 DATA 1111,1001,1100,0101,0110,0011,0000,1110
720 DATA 1011,1000,1100,0111,0001,1110,0010,1101
730 DATA 0110,1111,0000,1001,1010,0100,0101,0011
740 FOR I=0 TO 63
750 READ A(I)
760 X$=STR$(A(I)+10000)
770 A$(I)=RIGHT$(X$,4)
780 NEXT
790 GOTO 1470
800 RESTORE 810
810 DATA 1100,0001,1010,1111,1001,0010,0110,1000
820 DATA 0000,1101,0011,0100,1110,0111,0101,1011
830 DATA 1010,1111,0100,0010,0111,1100,1001,0101
840 DATA 0110,0001,1101,1110,0000,1011,0011,1000
850 DATA 1001,1110,1111,0101,0010,1000,1100,0011
860 DATA 0111,0000,0100,1010,0001,1101,1011,0110
870 DATA 0100,0011,0010,1100,1001,0101,1111,1010
880 DATA 1011,1110,0001,0111,0110,0000,1000,1101
890 FOR I=0 TO 63
900 READ A(I)
910 X$=STR$(A(I)+10000)
920 A$(I)=RIGHT$(X$,4)
930 NEXT
940 GOTO 1470
950 RESTORE 960
960 DATA 0100,1011,0010,1110,1111,0000,1000,1101
970 DATA 0011,1100,1001,0111,0101,1010,0110,0001
980 DATA 1101,0000,1011,0111,0100,1001,0001,1010
990 DATA 1110,0011,0101,1100,0010,1111,1000,0110
1000 DATA 0001,0100,1011,1101,1100,0011,0111,1110
1010 DATA 1010,1111,0110,1000,0000,0101,1001,0010
1020 DATA 0110,1011,1101,1000,0001,0100,1010,0111
1030 DATA 1001,0101,0000,1111,1110,0010,0011,1100
1040 FOR I=0 TO 63
1050 READ A(I)
1060 X$=STR$(A(I)+10000)
1070 A$(I)=RIGHT$(X$,4)
1080 NEXT
1090 GOTO 1470
1100 RESTORE 1110
1110 DATA 1101,0010,1000,0100,0110,1111,1011,0001
1120 DATA 1010,1001,0011,1110,0101,0000,1100,0111
1130 DATA 0001,1111,1101,1000,1010,0011,0111,0100
1140 DATA 1100,0101,0110,1011,0000,1110,1001,0010
1150 DATA 0111,1011,0100,0001,1001,1100,1110,0010
1160 DATA 0000,0110,1010,1101,1111,0011,0101,1000
1170 DATA 0010,0001,1110,0111,0100,1010,1000,1101
1180 DATA 1111,1100,1001,0000,0011,0101,0110,1011
```

```
1190 FOR I=0 TO 63
1200 READ A(I)
1210 X$=STR$(A(I)+10000)
1220 A$(I)=RIGHT$(X$,4)
1230 NEXT
1240 GOTO 1470
1250 RESTORE 1260
1260 DATA 00000,00001,00010,00011,00100,00101,00110,00111
1270 DATA 01000,01001,01010,01011,01100,01101,01110,01111
1280 DATA 10000,10001,10010,10011,10100,10101,10110,10111
1290 DATA 11000,11001,11010,11011,11100,11101,11110,11111
1300 FOR I=1 TO 32
1310 READ X
1320 X$=STR$(X+100000!)
1330 C$(I)=RIGHT$(X$,5)
1340 NEXT
1350 FOR I=1 TO 32
1360 FOR J=1 TO 5
1370 X$=MID$(C$(I),J,1)
1380 D(I,J)=VAL(X$)
1390 NEXT
1400 NEXT
1410 FOR I=1 TO 6
1420 READ R
1430 R$(I)=RIGHT$(STR$(R),6)
1440 NEXT
1450 DATA 612345,162345,126345,123645,123465,123456
1460 R1(1)=32:R1(2)=16:R1(3)=8:R1(4)=4:R1(5)=2:R1(6)=1
1470 D9=D9+1
1480 IF D9>6 THEN D9=0:U1=U1+1:GOTO 2110
1490 FOR I=1 TO 6
1500 X$=MID$(R$(D9),I,1)
1510 R(I)=VAL(X$)
1520 NEXT
1530 FOR I=1 TO 6
1540 S(R(I))=R1(I)
1550 NEXT
1560 LPRINT
1570 U1$=STR$(U1+1)
1580 U2$=RIGHT$(U1$,1)
1590 LPRINT " S-"U2$" BOX"
1600 LPRINT
1610 IF D9=1 THEN LPRINT " (32) 16 - 8  4  2  1":GOTO 1670
1620 IF D9=2 THEN LPRINT " 32 (16) - 8  4  2  1":GOTO 1670
1630 IF D9=3 THEN LPRINT " 32 16 - (8) 4  2  1":GOTO 1670
1640 IF D9=4 THEN LPRINT " 32 16 - 8 (4) 2  1":GOTO 1670
1650 IF D9=5 THEN LPRINT " 32 16 - 8  4 (2) 1":GOTO 1670
1660 LPRINT " 32 16 - 8  4  2 (1)"
1670 LPRINT
1680 L=0
1690 L=L+1
1700 IF L>32 THEN 1920
1710 E=D(L,1)*S(1)+D(L,2)*S(2)+D(L,3)*S(3)+D(L,4)*S(4)+D(L,5)*S(5)
1720 F=E+S(6)
1730 G$=A$(E)
1740 FOR I=1 TO 4
1750 Y$=MID$(G$,I,1)
1760 IF Y$="0" THEN G8(I)=G8(I)+1
1770 NEXT
```

```
1780 H$=A$(F)
1790 FOR I=1 TO 4
1800 Z$=MID$(H$,I,1)
1810 IF Z$="0" THEN G9(I)=G9(I)+1
1820 NEXT
1830 IF F<10 THEN LPRINT "  E"= "G$"       "F"= "H$"     ---     ";:GOTO 1860
1840 IF E<10 THEN LPRINT "  E"= "G$"     "F"= "H$"     ---     ";:GOTO 1860
1850 LPRINT E"= "G$"     "F"= "H$"     ---     ";
1860 FOR J=1 TO 4
1870 IF MID$(G$,J,1)=MID$(H$,J,1) THEN LPRINT "0";:K(J)=K(J)+1
1880 IF MID$(G$,J,1)<>MID$(H$,J,1) THEN LPRINT "1";
1890 NEXT
1900 LPRINT
1910 GOTO 1690
1920 LPRINT
1930 IF K(1)<10 THEN LPRINT "     1 ="G8(1)"       1 ="G9(1)"       1 = ";
1940 IF K(1)<10 THEN LPRINT K(1):GOTO 1960
1950 LPRINT "     1 ="G8(1)"       1 ="G9(1)"       1 ="K(1)
1960 IF K(2)<10 THEN LPRINT "     2 ="G8(2)"       2 ="G9(2)"       2 = ";
1970 IF K(2)<10 THEN LPRINT K(2):GOTO 1990
1980 LPRINT "     2 ="G8(2)"       2 ="G9(2)"       2 ="K(2)
1990 IF K(3)<10 THEN LPRINT "     3 ="G8(3)"       3 ="G9(3)"       3 = ";
2000 IF K(3)<10 THEN LPRINT K(3):GOTO 2020
2010 LPRINT "     3 ="G8(3)"       3 ="G9(3)"       3 ="K(3)
2020 IF K(4)<10 THEN LPRINT "     4 ="G8(4)"       4 ="G9(4)"       4 = ";
2030 IF K(4)<10 THEN LPRINT K(4):GOTO 2050
2040 LPRINT "     4 ="G8(4)"       4 ="G9(4)"       4 ="K(4)
2050 G8(1)=0:G8(2)=0:G8(3)=0:G8(4)=0
2060 G9(1)=0:G9(2)=0:G9(3)=0:G9(4)=0
2070 K(1)=0:K(2)=0:K(3)=0:K(4)=0
2080 LPRINT:LPRINT:LPRINT
2090 GOTO 1470
2100 END
2110 IF U1=1 THEN 200
2120 IF U1=2 THEN 350
2130 IF U1=3 THEN 500
2140 IF U1=4 THEN 650
2150 IF U1=5 THEN 800
2160 IF U1=6 THEN 950
2170 IF U1=7 THEN 1100
2180 END
```

APPENDIX K

SEARCHING FOR A "TRAPDOOR" IN THE S-4 BOX

S-4 BOX

(32) 16 - 8   4   2   1

0 = 0111	32 = 1010	---	1101
1 = 1101	33 = 0110	---	1011
2 = 1110	34 = 1001	---	0111
3 = 0011	35 = 0000	---	0011
4 = 0000	36 = 1100	---	1100
5 = 0110	37 = 1011	---	1101
6 = 1001	38 = 0111	---	1110
7 = 1010	39 = 1101	---	0111
8 = 0001	40 = 1111	---	1110
9 = 0010	41 = 0001	---	0011
10 = 1000	42 = 0011	---	1011
11 = 0101	43 = 1110	---	1011
12 = 1011	44 = 0101	---	1110
13 = 1100	45 = 0010	---	1110
14 = 0100	46 = 1000	---	1100
15 = 1111	47 = 0100	---	1011
16 = 1101	48 = 0011	---	1110
17 = 1000	49 = 1111	---	0111
18 = 1011	50 = 0000	---	1011
19 = 0101	51 = 0110	---	0011
20 = 0110	52 = 1010	---	1100
21 = 1111	53 = 0001	---	1110
22 = 0000	54 = 1101	---	1101
23 = 0011	55 = 1000	---	1011
24 = 0100	56 = 1001	---	1101
25 = 0111	57 = 0100	---	0011
26 = 0010	58 = 0101	---	0111
27 = 1100	59 = 1011	---	0111
28 = 0001	60 = 1100	---	1101
29 = 1010	61 = 0111	---	1101
30 = 1110	62 = 0010	---	1100
31 = 1001	63 = 1110	---	0111

1 = 16	1 = 16	1 = 10
2 = 16	2 = 16	2 = 10
3 = 16	3 = 16	3 = 10
4 = 16	4 = 16	4 = 10

S-4 BOX

32 (16) - 8   4   2   1

```
 0 = 0111      16 = 1101      ---      1010
 1 = 1101      17 = 1000      ---      0101
 2 = 1110      18 = 1011      ---      0101
 3 = 0011      19 = 0101      ---      0110
 4 = 0000      20 = 0110      ---      0110
 5 = 0110      21 = 1111      ---      1001
 6 = 1001      22 = 0000      ---      1001
 7 = 1010      23 = 0011      ---      1001
 8 = 0001      24 = 0100      ---      0101
 9 = 0010      25 = 0111      ---      0101
10 = 1000      26 = 0010      ---      1010
11 = 0101      27 = 1100      ---      1001
12 = 1011      28 = 0001      ---      1010
13 = 1100      29 = 1010      ---      0110
14 = 0100      30 = 1110      ---      1010
15 = 1111      31 = 1001      ---      0110
32 = 1010      48 = 0011      ---      1001
33 = 0110      49 = 1111      ---      1001
34 = 1001      50 = 0000      ---      1001
35 = 0000      51 = 0110      ---      0110
36 = 1100      52 = 1010      ---      0110
37 = 1011      53 = 0001      ---      1010
38 = 0111      54 = 1101      ---      1010
39 = 1101      55 = 1000      ---      0101
40 = 1111      56 = 1001      ---      0110
41 = 0001      57 = 0100      ---      0101
42 = 0011      58 = 0101      ---      0110
43 = 1110      59 = 1011      ---      0101
44 = 0101      60 = 1100      ---      1001
45 = 0010      61 = 0111      ---      0101
46 = 1000      62 = 0010      ---      1010
47 = 0100      63 = 1110      ---      1010
```

```
    1 = 16         1 = 16         1 = 16
    2 = 16         2 = 16         2 = 16
    3 = 16         3 = 16         3 = 16
    4 = 16         4 = 16         4 = 16
```

S-4 BOX

32 16 - (8) 4 2 1

0 = 0111	8 = 0001	---	0110
1 = 1101	9 = 0010	---	1111
2 = 1110	10 = 1000	---	0110
3 = 0011	11 = 0101	---	0110
4 = 0000	12 = 1011	---	1011
5 = 0110	13 = 1100	---	1010
6 = 1001	14 = 0100	---	1101
7 = 1010	15 = 1111	---	0101
16 = 1101	24 = 0100	---	1001
17 = 1000	25 = 0111	---	1111
18 = 1011	26 = 0010	---	1001
19 = 0101	27 = 1100	---	1001
20 = 0110	28 = 0001	---	0111
21 = 1111	29 = 1010	---	0101
22 = 0000	30 = 1110	---	1110
23 = 0011	31 = 1001	---	1010
32 = 1010	40 = 1111	---	0101
33 = 0110	41 = 0001	---	0111
34 = 1001	42 = 0011	---	1010
35 = 0000	43 = 1110	---	1110
36 = 1100	44 = 0101	---	1001
37 = 1011	45 = 0010	---	1001
38 = 0111	46 = 1000	---	1111
39 = 1101	47 = 0100	---	1001
48 = 0011	56 = 1001	---	1010
49 = 1111	57 = 0100	---	1011
50 = 0000	58 = 0101	---	0101
51 = 0110	59 = 1011	---	1101
52 = 1010	60 = 1100	---	0110
53 = 0001	61 = 0111	---	0110
54 = 1101	62 = 0010	---	1111
55 = 1000	63 = 1110	---	0110

1 = 15	1 = 17	1 = 12
2 = 17	2 = 15	2 = 12
3 = 15	3 = 17	3 = 12
4 = 15	4 = 17	4 = 12

S-4 BOX

32 16 - 8 (4) 2   1

0 = 0111	4 = 0000	---	0111
1 = 1101	5 = 0110	---	1011
2 = 1110	6 = 1001	---	0111
3 = 0011	7 = 1010	---	1001
8 = 0001	12 = 1011	---	1010
9 = 0010	13 = 1100	---	1110
10 = 1000	14 = 0100	---	1100
11 = 0101	15 = 1111	---	1010
16 = 1101	20 = 0110	---	1011
17 = 1000	21 = 1111	---	0111
18 = 1011	22 = 0000	---	1011
19 = 0101	23 = 0011	---	0110
24 = 0100	28 = 0001	---	0101
25 = 0111	29 = 1010	---	1101
26 = 0010	30 = 1110	---	1100
27 = 1100	31 = 1001	---	0101
32 = 1010	36 = 1100	---	0110
33 = 0110	37 = 1011	---	1101
34 = 1001	38 = 0111	---	1110
35 = 0000	39 = 1101	---	1101
40 = 1111	44 = 0101	---	1010
41 = 0001	45 = 0010	---	0011
42 = 0011	46 = 1000	---	1011
43 = 1110	47 = 0100	---	1010
48 = 0011	52 = 1010	---	1001
49 = 1111	53 = 0001	---	1110
50 = 0000	54 = 1101	---	1101
51 = 0110	55 = 1000	---	1110
56 = 1001	60 = 1100	---	0101
57 = 0100	61 = 0111	---	0011
58 = 0101	62 = 0010	---	0111
59 = 1011	63 = 1110	---	0101

1 = 18	1 = 14	1 = 12
2 = 16	2 = 16	2 = 12
3 = 16	3 = 16	3 = 12
4 = 14	4 = 18	4 = 12

S-4 BOX

32 16 - 8   4 (2) 1

0 = 0111	2 = 1110	---	1001
1 = 1101	3 = 0011	---	1110
4 = 0000	6 = 1001	---	1001
5 = 0110	7 = 1010	---	1100
8 = 0001	10 = 1000	---	1001
9 = 0010	11 = 0101	---	0111
12 = 1011	14 = 0100	---	1111
13 = 1100	15 = 1111	---	0011
16 = 1101	18 = 1011	---	0110
17 = 1000	19 = 0101	---	1101
20 = 0110	22 = 0000	---	0110
21 = 1111	23 = 0011	---	1100
24 = 0100	26 = 0010	---	0110
25 = 0111	27 = 1100	---	1011
28 = 0001	30 = 1110	---	1111
29 = 1010	31 = 1001	---	0011
32 = 1010	34 = 1001	---	0011
33 = 0110	35 = 0000	---	0110
36 = 1100	38 = 0111	---	1011
37 = 1011	39 = 1101	---	0110
40 = 1111	42 = 0011	---	1100
41 = 0001	43 = 1110	---	1111
44 = 0101	46 = 1000	---	1101
45 = 0010	47 = 0100	---	0110
48 = 0011	50 = 0000	---	0011
49 = 1111	51 = 0110	---	1001
52 = 1010	54 = 1101	---	0111
53 = 0001	55 = 1000	---	1001
56 = 1001	58 = 0101	---	1100
57 = 0100	59 = 1011	---	1111
60 = 1100	62 = 0010	---	1110
61 = 0111	63 = 1110	---	1001

1 = 17	1 = 15	1 = 12
2 = 15	2 = 17	2 = 12
3 = 15	3 = 17	3 = 12
4 = 15	4 = 17	4 = 12

S-4 BOX

32 16 - 8 4 2 (1)

0 = 0111	1 = 1101	---	1010
2 = 1110	3 = 0011	---	1101
4 = 0000	5 = 0110	---	0110
6 = 1001	7 = 1010	---	0011
8 = 0001	9 = 0010	---	0011
10 = 1000	11 = 0101	---	1101
12 = 1011	13 = 1100	---	0111
14 = 0100	15 = 1111	---	1011
16 = 1101	17 = 1000	---	0101
18 = 1011	19 = 0101	---	1110
20 = 0110	21 = 1111	---	1001
22 = 0000	23 = 0011	---	0011
24 = 0100	25 = 0111	---	0011
26 = 0010	27 = 1100	---	1110
28 = 0001	29 = 1010	---	1011
30 = 1110	31 = 1001	---	0111
32 = 1010	33 = 0110	---	1100
34 = 1001	35 = 0000	---	1001
36 = 1100	37 = 1011	---	0111
38 = 0111	39 = 1101	---	1010
40 = 1111	41 = 0001	---	1110
42 = 0011	43 = 1110	---	1101
44 = 0101	45 = 0010	---	0111
46 = 1000	47 = 0100	---	1100
48 = 0011	49 = 1111	---	1100
50 = 0000	51 = 0110	---	0110
52 = 1010	53 = 0001	---	1011
54 = 1101	55 = 1000	---	0101
56 = 1001	57 = 0100	---	1101
58 = 0101	59 = 1011	---	1110
60 = 1100	61 = 0111	---	1011
62 = 0010	63 = 1110	---	1100

1 = 16	1 = 16	1 = 12
2 = 18	2 = 14	2 = 12
3 = 18	3 = 14	3 = 12
4 = 16	4 = 16	4 = 12